America's Demographic Tapestry

America's Demographic Tapestry

Baseline for the New Millennium

*Edited by James W. Hughes
and Joseph J. Seneca*

R *Rutgers University Press*

New Brunswick, New Jersey, and London

Library of Congress Cataloging-in-Publication Data

America's demographic tapestry : baseline for the new millennium /
    edited by James W. Hughes and Joseph J. Seneca.
        p.   cm.
    Includes bibliographical references and index.
    ISBN 0-8135-2646-9 (cloth : alk. paper). — ISBN 0-8135-2647-7
(pbk. : alk. paper)
        1. United States—Population.   2. United States—Population
policy.   3. Population forecasting—United States.   I. Hughes,
James W.   II. Seneca, Joseph J., 1943– .
HB3505.A683 1999
304.6'0973—dc21

                                                                98-44986
                                                                CIP

British Cataloging-in-Publication data for this book is available from the British
Library

Manufactured in the United States of America

Contents

Acknowledgments

This book is an outgrowth of a year-long public policy forum held at the Edward J. Bloustein School of Planning and Public Policy at Rutgers, the State University of New Jersey, during the 1996–1997 academic year. With generous financial support from the Johnson & Johnson Corporation, the forum "America's Changing Demographic Tapestry: Public Policy Challenges" was truly unique in its scope and depth. Twelve of the world's leading demographic experts were brought to Rutgers to explore the public policy implications emanating from demographic change in America and the world. Their superb public presentations formed the bases for the essays that they have contributed to this collection. Their insights and analyses comprise the virtues of this volume.

This project would not have been possible without the initial support of Johnson & Johnson, and it would not have been completed without the exceptional administrative oversight of Thea Berkhout, associate dean of the Bloustein School, and Marla Nelson, research associate at the Bloustein School. They also oversaw all of the events encompassed by the year-long Tapestry Forum. Marlie Wasserman and Marilyn Campbell, of the Rutgers University Press, guided the overall publication effort to completion. We owe them our most sincere thanks.

J.W.H
J.J.S

America's Demographic Tapestry

James W. Hughes and Joseph J. Seneca

Introduction

The Demographic Trajectory and Public Policy

America seems beset by the need to respond to immediate exigencies and short-term crises, but beneath the surface of many momentary issues are powerful evolutionary forces whose long-term public policy effects promise to be much more significant. One of the most important of these forces is the profound demographic change taking place in America, which will have extraordinary social and economic consequences and far-reaching public policy implications. In this book we have compiled a group of essays that profiles the contours of this demographic change and identifies select public policy challenges that arise from it. Our purpose in this introduction is to present a general demographic and policy framework for the contributions that follow.

Age Diversity

The broadest category of forces centers around historic age-structure variations, or *age diversity*. As fundamentals of duration, these variations are not likely to be altered by any unforeseen event. This set of current and future demographic contours is the consequence of historic twentieth-century fluctuations in fertility and birth patterns. The resulting slowdowns and surges in population growth since the 1920s have yielded five broad generations of varying sizes, each of which underpins significant changes in American society. Sequentially, these generations have assumed the conventional labels of the Depression-era birth dearth, the post–World War II baby boom, the great baby bust, the baby-boom echo, and the baby-bust echo. Thus, during the past seventy-five years, America's population cohorts have fluctuated significantly

1

in size due to fertility rate swings; demographically, we have gone from bust to boom to bust to boomlet to bustlet. There have been significant public policy impacts on society and the economy due simply to these size variations.

Many of the dynamics of society are so complex that simple description, much less prediction, becomes difficult. Nonetheless, we can be relatively assured of how America's future age diversity will look. Most, although not all, of the determining elements are already in place. For example, every future householder (18 years of age and older) who will demand housing in the year 2016 has already been born. Basically, the projection considers an aging process modified by expectations of immigration. Thus, the broad contours of the country's future demographic landscape can be foreseen with a reasonable degree of certainty.

The Aging of the Elderly

In the United States during the twentieth century, the elderly (or seniors)—those 65 years of age and over—have grown at above-average population rates. Between the century's beginning and end, the number of elderly has increased approximately elevenfold, the number of nonelderly only threefold. As a result, America's senior population alone presently outnumbers the total population of Canada. But as the 1990s end, the total number of elderly are growing at far slower rates than they have in the past. The 65- to 74–year-old sector—the young elderly—will remain static in numbers into the first decade of the next century because of the limited size of the Depression-era birth dearth, the current source of new elderly recruits. This slow growth alone has a number of implications. For example, pressures on the Social Security system are far less severe now than they will be, since the overall elderly pool is now expanding only minimally. But this demographic window of opportunity will gradually close as the new century fully unfolds.

Because of increased longevity due to medical and economic advances, the number of middle-aged elderly—75 to 84 years of age—is growing at far faster rates than that of the general population, while the numbers of "elderly" elderly—those 85 years of age and over—are growing at explosive rates. As a result, the average age of the elderly is rising, with increasing concentrations of the senior population in the age sectors that need personal assistance with everyday living. This will continue until the beginning of the second decade of the twenty-first century, when the baby boom generation begins to reach age 65. At that time, the ranks of the young elderly will then explode, with significant implications for public programs such as Social Security and Medicare.

Issues of intergenerational equity have already arisen. The economic situation of many seniors has improved dramatically during the past quarter-century, while the number of children in poverty has soared. Nonetheless, the specter of growing elderly dependence has baby boomers concerned about the burdens of support placed upon them.

The Maturing and Middle Aging of America

A maturing of America is *the* demographic transformation of the late twentieth and early twenty-first centuries, simply due to the huge size of the population moving into middle age. The underlying force is the maturation of the baby boom, that oversized population cohort born during the explosive birth period between 1946 and 1964. The baby boom is still the largest generation in U.S. history—77 million strong. Throughout each phase of its life cycle since the 1950s, the baby boom has dominated America and, since the 1960s, has shaped the nation's political life. It was originally the Hula-Hoop generation in the 1950s, overwhelming the nation's educational infrastructure. It then became the Woodstock generation in the 1960s, inundating our colleges and universities. It eventually swamped our labor and housing markets in the 1970s and then formed the yuppie brigades of the 1980s. Mature professionals supplanted yuppies, and the generation as a whole began reproducing itself in earnest, spawning the baby boom echo. Thus, the fabled youth society—in terms of demographic reality and vision—succumbed to its inevitable evolution into middle age.

So in the 1990s this generation has been advancing en masse into its middle years, busily raising families, entering peak earning and income years, and trading up in the housing market. The signature event of this maturation took place on January 1, 1996, when the first baby boomer turned 50 years old. During the subsequent eighteen years, another U.S. baby boomer will turn 50 every seven and one-half seconds. An increasingly common obligation for this cohort is simultaneously to support parents and children.

But the middle-age society will gradually be supplanted by the post–middle-age society. Early in the twenty-first century, the need to both support aged relatives (who will be living longer because of medical advances) and grown children who are living away from home looms as a potential financial nightmare for baby boomers.

As America moves into the second decade of the twenty-first century, the baby boom will finally transition into retirement. Starting in 2011—when the first members of this generation turn 65 years old—there will then be an eighteen-year-long surge in the number of elderly. The post–middle-age society will finally become the retired society. This expectation has raised the specter of a depleted Social Security system by the late 2020s.

The Evolution of Shrinkage

The baby boom flood began to ebb as America exited the 1950s, and births began to plummet as the 1960s matured. The result was the baby bust generation, an undersized population cohort produced during the low-birth era from 1965 through 1976. This cohort of contraction takes the form of a moving indentation on America's age structure charts, mirroring (approximately forty years behind) the moving age structure dent of the Depression-era birth dearth.

Directly following the baby boom, which has always overwhelmed every societal institution it confronted during its life-cycle ride, the baby bust has underwhelmed each of these same institutions during its maturation. For example, the baby boom–spawned school bond issues of the 1950s were ultimately supplanted by the baby bust–induced school-closing issues two decades later. As the 1980s advanced, the longer-term impact of a reduced-scale generation influenced conventional economic wisdom. The potential of future labor shortages, based on the widely shared experience of plummeting school enrollments, entered the nation's consciousness. This frame of demographic reference certainly helped shape the formulation of immigration policy, providing one of the rationales and motivations for increased immigration quotas. As a result, the nation avoided the full consequences of demographic shrinkage in the 1990s but also set in motion additional demographic dimensions of ethnic and cultural diversity.

By the end of the 1990s, the baby bust will fully mature into the 25– to 34–year-old sector of the population, and young adults, despite immigration, will become more scarce. Consequently, throughout most of the 1990s, entry-level housing demand has been in retreat, an event of significant importance to the nation's housing industry. Ultimately, the baby bust will define a smaller middle-age population early in the next century and will provide the relatively smaller base of support for the larger cohort of baby boom retirees.

The Advancing Growth Echo

Ever since the 1960s, demographers have widely anticipated a baby boom echo, an expectation based solely on the massive size of the baby boom generation maturing into its prime child-bearing years. The coming of the echo was virtually assured; it could only be avoided by a fertility rate free-falling to unprecedentedly low levels—a generation refusing to reproduce itself—which did not happen.

The echo began to unfold in 1977 as the baby boomers belatedly began to pair, nest, reproduce, and parent. What started as a boomlet exploded into a very real secondary baby boom as the 1980s matured. The original baby boom was fueled by a sharp ratcheting-up of America's fertility rates. In contrast, the baby boom echo was driven primarily by the huge increase in the number of women of child-bearing age along with an up-tick in fertility (bolstered by the higher fertility rates of new immigrants) from the baby bust lows. This up-tick caused a potent baby boom echo. Consequently, 1990, the peak of the echo, was the seventh-highest birth year on record, higher than all but six of the original baby boom years! The number of births then started to decline, with 1994 currently considered the terminal year of the echo. This is convenient since the echo has the same eighteen-year duration as the original baby boom, although at final account it was somewhat smaller in scale.

The baby boom echo is presently reflected in the sharp growth in the 5– to 14–year-old sector of the nation's population. The number of teenagers, after a long period of decline, will exhibit strong increases into the next century. School enrollments are again growing, necessitating once more the expansion of the nation's educational infrastructure. At about the time that this impact is fully absorbed, growth will then start shifting into the young adult population— that is, 20 to 30 years of age. Early in the next century, there will be a spurt in labor force growth, and entry-level housing demand will increase.

The Nascent Shrinkage

Just as the baby boomers having their children gave rise to a second-ary baby boom generation, so, too, will the baby bust ultimately produce an echo of itself. The annual number of births in the United States declined throughout the first half of the 1990s as the entire baby boom generation passed 30 years of age by 1994. As the decade matures, the number of women in their peak child-bearing ages is trending downward as the baby bust moves into its late 20s and early 30s. The higher fertility of new immigrants of baby bust age appears to be reducing the scale of population shrinkage from the levels origi-nally anticipated. Nonetheless, a secondary baby bust is currently marking the termination of the baby boom echo. Just as that echo is replicating the earlier impact of its parents, the baby bust echo will mirror the impact of its parents.

These five basic dimensions of age-structure diversity, generally correspond-ing to five loosely defined broad generations, establish key contours of America's current and future demography. While they have a reasonable de-gree of certainty, the nation's future age structure will be modified primarily by the scale and composition of immigration. For example, immigration has amplified the long-anticipated baby boom echo while mitigating the full effects of population shrinkage emanating from a maturing baby bust.

Drawing policy implications from the effects of these age-structure varia-tions is not as simple as describing and defining them. Outside the boundaries of age, these are not totally homogeneous generations. For example, the baby boom has never been a monolithic whole, although it sometimes is considered to be a highly uniform group. The generation has exhibited heterogeneous values as befits a group that was born over an eighteen-year span and that has had widely different life-cycle experiences. While the sheer size of the baby boom in and of itself has had major public policy effects on education, labor markets, and housing, the heterogeneity of this generation adds significant complexity to the public policy domain.

Moreover, the parallelism of linked generations is also modified by similar factors. For example, the size of the baby boom echo is replicating the school-expansion impact of the original baby boom. Nevertheless, the educational task facing America is now far more complex. The education of the original baby boom took place in an era reflecting a higher degree of shared cultural values, needs, and expectations. This is no longer the case. Racial and ethnic diversity has added many more complications.

Racial and Ethnic Diversity: Minoritization

A second broad dimension of diversity relates to racial and ethnic composition. The population of the United States has become increasingly varied in its racial and ethnic character. In essence, America now reflects the impact of fundamental shifts in immigration policy that were enacted into federal legislation in 1965. This legislation reduced immigration from Europe (by overturning national origin quotas) and dramatically increased it from nations that had previously been excluded from the United States (by instituting a more open system that emphasizes migrant family unification). Thus, *minoritization*—the increased diversity of America's population—was the result of deliberate public policy choices. Moreover, as the nation progressed through the 1970s and 1980s, the overall scale of immigration was increased. As a result, the total foreign-born population of the United States, and its share of the population, more than doubled between 1970 and 1995. At the end of the century, approximately one in ten Americans will be foreign born. Already, questions about the benefits and burdens that immigrants place on society have entered the national dialogue.

Immigration, which accounts for one-third of our current population growth, directly yields greater racial and ethnic diversity and greater cultural diversity. Hispanics now account for the largest share of America's population growth, while Asians and Pacific Islanders have the highest rates of growth. The end result is that non-Hispanic whites hold a steadily declining share of the nation's total population.

These broad racial-ethnic compositional shifts define another contour of

America's future demography. Even if America's immigration policy were to be significantly modified, the racial-ethnic changes emanating from the immigration that has already taken place since 1965 have become firmly embedded in America's population profile. Suffice it to say that the integrative capacity of society—and the economy—will continue to be tested.

Household Segmentation and Life-style Diversity

Not all future demographic forces are encapsulated by the preceding "certainties." Also significant but subject to far more uncertainty is the way in which the nation's population arranges itself into specific household configurations and the life-style choices associated with these arrangements. America has just passed through the "great household revolution," which coincided with the coming of age of the baby boom. After 1960 life-style and socioeconomic changes drove a seemingly furious process of household segmentation/fragmentation/diversification across the nation. The major pattern has been the surging growth of single-parent families, one-person households, and unmarried couples. A second major household pattern is the slow growth rate of traditional married-couple families. Most dramatic has been the increase in one-person households. At the beginning of the twentieth century, only one out of twenty households in America comprised a lone individual. At the end of the century, one out of four households will consist of a person living alone. This large group of singles has become a much more diverse demographic segment, with the largest subgroup formed by elderly women.

The decline in the demographic share of married couples has also been pronounced. In 1960, approximately three-quarters of all households were married couples. By the mid-1990s, their share was approaching 50 percent. Significantly, married couples with children under the age of 18—a category representing the classic image of the America family—now account for barely one out of four households, the same share as one-person households!

The modular American demography of the early postwar era has thus disappeared and the once homogeneous mass middle economic market has shattered. Segmentation, product differentiation, and niche marketing now define America's commercial economy. The same phenomenon of differentiation and market niches increasingly pervades the public policy world as well.

As a consequence of household and life-style diversity, movement through the traditional family life-cycle stages has become more complex. The old traditional pattern of marriage followed by pre–child rearing, child rearing, and post–child rearing phases of family life has been supplanted by new life-course options. These options include delayed household formation, delayed marriage, delayed child bearing, high divorce rates, household fragmentation, household reformation, and perhaps household refragmentation, all of which have redefined the complex affiliations underlying the "new" American family. Adding further complication are new work and education patterns attached to a changing economy. Overall, life-course diversity reflects fundamental changes in the way in which Americans form and reform families, thereby challenging the traditional assumptions and practices on which societal institutions rest.

The broad pattern of household, life-style, and life-course diversity is even more accentuated for minority America. Among whites the ratio of married couples to spouse-absent families is approximately five to one, but among black households the number of married couples is approximately equal to the number of spouse-absent families. In general, the nation's black and Hispanic household structures are far more heavily diversified than those of whites, with significant economic and social consequences.

Socioeconomic Segmentation

Economic change and the intersection of demographics and the economy define further complexity and uncertainty. Broad fundamental changes in the economy have been influenced by demographics and in turn have defined a number of demographic issues. In particular, life-style, household, and age shifts have distinct economic consequences for many Americans. In turn, broad economic shifts influence demographic well-being and socioeconomic variation. Thus, it is appropriate to review the general economic contours of the post–World War II era in the United States. Many of the public policy issues surrounding demographics have been played out in the changing economy of the last half-century and are reflected in income patterns.

Shifting American Economic Contours

The post–World War II years defined an era of unquestioned American hegemony; the United States stood preeminent and unchallenged in the world economy. As a result, the standard of living in the United States doubled in the space of a single generation, as witnessed by the nation's median family income, which increased by more than 100 percent in real terms between 1950 and 1973. Thus, the 1950s and 1960s—*the* baby boom decades—were characterized by sustained long-term real income gains surmounting short-term business cycle setbacks. But this era of ever-rising living standards came to a close with the first energy crisis in the early 1970s.

The post-Vietnam years saw income peaks succumb to economic cycles and long-term stagnation. The great American income-growth machine stalled for more than two decades. There were income gains during the economic expansions between 1973 and 1991, but business cycle setbacks often caused significant income losses. The end results were real household and family income levels in the first half of the 1990s that were not appreciably different from those of two decades earlier. The escalator of ever-rising living standards seemed to come to a halt.

Income stagnation was largely, but not solely, due to broad economic changes. Productivity increases, after soaring in the postwar years, began to stagnate after 1973. A sharp rise in international competition, external shocks leading to threshold changes in energy costs, lagging investment, and the rise of a service-based economy all contributed to an era in which America's international competitiveness was questioned and its economic self-confidence challenged. Japan and West Germany, symbols of new world economic leadership, appeared to leave America gasping in their wake. Baby boomers, raised in the greatest period of affluence in the nation's history, began to wonder why, when they started to reach middle age, their income did not seem to match their parents'.

But demographics, global as well as domestic, also played a role in America's changing economy. Rapid population growth in developing nations yielded labor surpluses that tended to exert downward pressure on wages. Low-wage countries were a magnet to parts of the American industrial economy that were wage- and cost-sensitive as well as footloose. Thus, some U.S. workers became subject to direct competition from burgeoning labor forces abroad. Job migration to the industrializing low-wage countries produced sufficient dislocations to the American economy to affect incomes. Technological transfer, rapid and relatively easy, aided this pattern.

Real income stagnation continued into the early postrecession years of the 1990s, even though the economic picture again shifted. While fears proliferated during the 1970s and 1980s, the American economy was actually undergoing a major long-term transformation that would result in its complete reshaping and redefinition. This transformation was defined by the sustained growth of postindustrial, information-based, knowledge-dependent, service-producing activities, all in the context of a manufacturing sector that eventually became much more efficient and productive. Through the 1990s, observers increasingly noticed that this transformation was powered by the dynamics of economic globalization, the quickening of innovation and its diffusion, the rise to dominance of information technology, and deregulation. This led to what could be called the "great paradox": the world's juggernaut economy was actually America's, not Germany's or Japan's. The United States was increasingly viewed as the global growth model. American society and culture, including demographic diversity as well as business environment, financial systems, and geography, fit globalization far better than did Europe or Japan. The paradox was that, by the mid-1990s, this transformation had not yet translated into a rise in living standards for the broad middle class. The benefits of the economic transformation seemed to accrue to a less-than-wide band of recipients.

The exact reasons for this paradox remain unclear. One explanation suggests that the wrenching transition from the industrial era to the information age has placed a premium on knowledge and high levels of education—that is, the skill bias of technological change. Those lacking higher-order educational competencies were being left behind. Thus, in contrast to the industrial era, which created a vast middle class, the information age appeared to be creating social polarization, with the winners and losers segmented by knowledge and skill levels. This polarization has particularly worked to the general economic disadvantage of those American groups that lag in educational attainment.

By the second half of the 1990s, however, wage and income advancement had begun to inch upward, and consumer confidence began to reach record levels. The new economy has been redefining all dimensions of the American dream of current and future living standards, of the potential for upward mobility, and of the fiscal capacities to support the institutions and programs necessary to cope with some of the demographically driven issues raised in this volume. It is shaping the character of baby boom aging and the fiscal realities of its retirement.

Income and Demographic Change

Income, a barometer of America's ability to deliver the "good life," is determined not only by the effects of a changing economy but also by the very demographic forces described earlier. For example, age structure diversity can play a major role. The ascendancy of the baby boom into adulthood led to record growth of the nation's work force in the 1970s and early 1980s, a phenomenon reinforced by the rapid rise of women's labor force participation rates (which in turn was partly due to increasing life-style diversity). The resulting labor "surplus" had the effect of constraining entry-level wages and, subsequently, incomes. Moreover, the sheer size of the baby boom placed record proportions of the labor force in the age brackets in which incomes are lowest. Thus, growth in overall real household and family incomes began to moderate significantly from the rapid pace of the decades immediately following World War II. The latter had been due not only to remarkable economic growth but also to labor force shortages tied to the Depression-era birth dearth, which led to upward pressures on wages.

Thus, an age-related household income cycle came into play. As individuals mature, so do their incomes, with young households and families generally having lower incomes than older ones. Household incomes then rise to a peak at advanced middle age. Thereafter, incomes start to fall as retirement age is reached. This age-related income cycle is a major demographic phenomenon.

The conventional wisdom of the mid-1980s was that the maturing and middle aging of the massive baby boom generation into its peak earning and income years would yield an era of demographically driven affluence during the 1990s. Nevertheless, recession and the powerful changes of the new economy intervened. Globalization and drastic corporate restructuring quickly short-circuited trendline expectations. Thus, while demographics did its job in the first half of the 1990s and delivered the huge baby boom into its peak income years, the economy failed to cooperate.

It is conceivable, however, that the demographics of affluence may actually be happening as the century comes to a close. The new information-age economy may yield the sustained inflation-free growth that would in turn yield real broad-based income gains to support the relentless march of the baby boom up the age-related income ladder.

Similarly, there are income variations linked to household type, another key demographic variable. Married couples stand on the top of the household income ladder, single-parent configurations at the bottom. The surging growth of single-parent configurations during the past two decades has certainly contributed to lagging household and family income statistics and to a rise in child poverty. Moreover, it is not surprising that concentrations of child poverty are far higher for many of America's minority groups based on the relative youthfulness of their households and their more diverse household structures—that is, more single-parent families in the mix of household configurations.

The intersection of demographics, economic change, and income has numerous and significant implications for society. One bottom-line conclusion is that economic diversity further complicates cultural diversity. For example, the educational arena not only confronts broad growth pressures and surging absolute student numbers but also faces a student pool drawn from unprecedented household and economic diversity. In particular, parental quantity (one versus two) varies enormously as do household-linked financial resources. Thus, far more household fragmentation and economic variation characterizes the living arrangements of children today compared to the original baby boom. Mix in cultural diversity, and an unprecedented era of complexity emerges for America's educational system.

Geographic Variation

While demographic change is evident in every geographic corner of America, it is not taking place uniformly across the country. One reason is that this change is simply a consequence of varying spatial economic and population growth rates. The overarching pattern is one of enduring suburban and sunbelt domination of growth.

The post–World War II nesting generation defined the era of tract-house suburbia—and the mass democratization of suburbia. The baby boom was the first generation largely born, reared, and educated in suburbia. Thus, the great educational expansion of the 1950s and 1960s primarily had a suburban locus. Subsequently, the baby boom largely preferred to live and work in suburbia. A baby boom moving into adulthood led to the emergence of second-generation suburbia characterized by a much broader and more diverse set of housing types and economic activities. The great development waves of the 1980s— the office-building boom and the "over-retail-storing" of America—were overwhelmingly a suburban and metropolitan-edge phenomenon and reflected baby boom life- and work-style preferences.

By the 1990s, residential development responding to a middle-aged, child-rearing baby boom trading up in the housing market pushed the suburban envelope into exurban green fields. This third-generation suburban residential development is tied to the baby boom echo and is producing the second great school building era of the second half of the twentieth century. Many of the most affected jurisdictions had minimal educational infrastructure to begin with. The end results are a number of demographic issues amplified in high-growth suburbia while remaining muted in slower-growth geographic settings.

But not completely. Soaring school enrollments are also prevalent in many older urban and suburban areas whose overall population levels are not expanding significantly. Much of this increase is due to immigration from abroad and the higher fertility of new immigrants. The demand on educational infrastructure here is also significant because part of the older infrastructure was jettisoned during the baby bust era and much of the remainder is obsolete.

The variation is also significant at larger spatial scales. The northeast and midwest have long been settings of slow population growth, with the northeast also beset by a sustained net out-migration of population. In contrast, the south, and more recently the Rocky Mountain states of the west, have dominated growth and been important migration destinations. Moreover, the growth of the south has been bolstered in the 1990s by the increasing movement of blacks to the region, reversing the half-century exodus. Much of the movement has been to the south's economically strong rural and urban areas. As a result, the region has been capturing a majority of the nation's black population growth.

Future demographic projections paint the same picture: the south and the west will continue to dominate population growth. The U.S. Census Bureau also projects the greatest growth and concentrations of elderly in these areas.

Moreover, the older regions of the country, such as the northeast, will tend to have lower proportions of youth in the future, while areas of heavy in-migration, such as the west, will have higher proportions. Such tendencies will exaggerate or reduce some of the consequences of age diversity depending on a region's overall growth.

Racial and ethnic diversity also exhibits patterns of geographic diversity. Immigration from abroad concentrates in selected gateway regions, while it is very modest in others. While no area or region does not reflect some degree of racial and ethnic diversity, the concentrations of immigrants in states such as California, New York, Texas, Florida, New Jersey, and Illinois—the destina-tions of more than three-quarters of all immigrants in the 1980s—greatly intensify all of the issues attached to racial and ethnic diversity. This is par-ticularly the case if there is white and black flight from the new immigrant concentrations.

Organization and Contributions

This new demographic reality is reshaping America and its public policy agenda. The patterns and concerns we have delineated suggest some of the dimensions of the policy world of tomorrow. But the contributors to this volume provide much deeper probes into the dynamics to come. Their per-spectives have been organized into the following six sections:

The Baselines of Demographic Change and the Broad Policy Framework

The first section sets the stage by providing an overview of the major demographic trends in America. It then furnishes an introductory discussion of the policy framework and key policy issues.

In "America's Changing Demographic Tapestry," Martha Farnsworth Riche and Judith Waldrop examine the patterns formed by America's demographic trends. Their basic premise is that identifying and tracking demographic trends is vital for informed decision making at all levels of government. Five key de-mographic trends are isolated: increasing cultural diversity, age diversity, life-style diversity, socioeconomic diversity, and life-course diversity, all of which yield a vast segmentation of the nation's needs. From these baselines, cultural challenges are discussed, generational issues presented, and the consequences for children and seniors reviewed. The basic conclusion is that public policy is being forced to target ever smaller and more complex niches, that policy-makers need to know their audience at increasingly personal levels, and that in-creased flexibility is needed to target policy responses to changing constituencies.

In "Family Policies and Demographic Realities," Peter A. Morrison targets two family issues that emanate from household fragmentation, life-course shifts, and other demographic upheavals. The first problem is unique among industrialized countries: the high level of poverty of American children, which derives largely from family structures that predispose it. The second is the need to care for seniors of unprecedented advancing longevity whose family members have limited practical means for providing such support. The basic conclusion is that traditional principles that once guided policy often do not mesh with today's complex family situations. Future policies aimed at reinforcing universal principles of family responsibility must accommodate the actual diversity and complexities of families and must recognize what families alone do best—care for their own members—and retain that function within families, whatever their form.

Global Demographics: Ramifications

The second section steps back from the immediacies of America and looks at the worldwide demographic situation. America's demographic profiles, while positioned at the high-growth edge of the industrialized nations, pale in the shadow of the massive population and labor-force expansion of the developing world. The global demographic framework has significant ramifications not only for America's demography but for its economy as well.

In "The Global Population Outlook," Charles F. Westoff provides an overview of the world's population growth prospects. No matter how fast fertility declines, world demographic momentum ensures that the planet is in for a great deal of future growth. Despite massive world population growth during the past several decades, the situation has generated only limited public concern. Moreover, large aggregate growth masks significant variations across countries and regions. Much of the developed world will grow much slower than the United States, with fertility extremely low in many countries of Europe. In contrast, fertility rates are very high in many sub-Saharan countries of Africa. In particular, while immigration has the attention of considerable public policy discussion in the United States, its origins—a surging world population—are rarely referenced.

Jane S. De Lung, in "Population Growth: The Complicating Element," advances the broad implications of the global population parameters established by Westoff. Rapid population growth in the developing world produces a surplus of labor and intense pressures for job generation. Labor surpluses also tend to exert downward pressures on wages. This affects the status of the United States in the global economy since certain jobs and sectors of the economy have a tendency to migrate to low-wage, labor-surplus countries. Moreover, the desire to escape from labor-surplus situations is a prime impetus for immigration to the United States, either legal or illegal. In addition, the environmental consequences of rapid global population growth in conjunction with advancing industrialization has significant implications for America.

People on the Move: Immigration and Migration

Immigration to the United States has raised a number of public policy issues. Key among them are the labor market consequences of an increased supply of labor, the scale of illegal immigration, and the fiscal impact on states and municipalities of new immigrants.

In "The Challenge of Illegal Immigration," Thomas J. Espenshade examines the demographic dimensions of undocumented immigration to the United States, the determinants and consequences of these migration streams, public attitudes toward the phenomenon, efforts to control unauthorized immigration, and appropriate policy responses. With the global scale of the population seeking to gain access to economic opportunity and quality of life in the United States at record levels and with employers seeking to hold down costs in a competitive global economy, the increasing immigration pressures are not surprising. Illegal immigration has always confronted the country with significant policy challenges, but its dimension and scale in the 1990s is unprecedented.

In "Immigration and Demographic Balkanization: Toward One America or Two?" William H. Frey explores a new demographic divide in the nation's geography spawned by immigration and immigration change: a separation of those regions of the country that serve as immigration gateways from other areas of the country in which the new immigration has negligible impact on demographic change. As a result of the concentration of new immigrants in the gateway regions, and with the potential displacement of less-skilled and poorer native-born residents, these regions are becoming increasingly younger, multi-ethnic, and culturally diverse, portending a new demographic divide. This divide is of unprecedented geographic scope, potentially replicating at a regional and an intermetropolitan scale the bifurcation that has been long evident at the intrametropolitan (urban-suburban) level. A continuation of this trend will have many social and economic consequences and poses public policy questions at least as difficult as those framing the classic central city–suburb concern.

Demographics, Income, and Economic Mobility

Advancing upward mobility is part of the nation's public policy foundation and is integral to the basic American dream of social and economic advancement. This section examines the broad theme of upward mobility in terms of the changing living standards of Americans as gauged by income and the long-term immigrant experience of advancement, measured by spatial mobility, poverty shifts, and homeownership. The intersection of demographic and economic change has altered historic American income trajectories and has led to vexing questions, particularly for the baby boom generation. Determining the reality of upward mobility of immigrants is a key element in the ongoing public policy debate of the scale and composition of immigration to the United States.

In "How Big Is the Income Dilemma?" Frank Levy attempts to untangle the basic question of whether America really suffers from stagnant incomes by analyzing the path of living standards as average husband-wife families have experienced them over the past fifteen years. While this income change has been at the center of public policy debate in the 1990s, the search for clearcut analytical solutions has proved elusive. The weapons in the nation's statistical arsenal that measure income and real income change all have some limitation in determining the economic well-being of households, families, and individuals, and this has contributed to the unsettled debate. These shortfalls are extensively documented before the income analyses are undertaken. The analyses are then set against public attitudes toward living standards, which suggest a slow improvement in the standard of living depending on education level. The bottom line is not a dramatic resolution of the enduring income question: the nation is moving through a period of slow general growth and fast economic restructuring. While the position of many families' income is improving slowly, the position of others is holding or falling behind.

Dowell Myers, in "Upward Mobility in Space and Time: Lessons from Immigration," focuses on one of the nation's most significant gateway regions, southern California, where immigrants have congregated. He demographically analyzes over time multiple immigrant cohorts, defined by arrival period and birth period, to ascertain their true rate of upward mobility. Indicators of upward mobility are immigrants' movement out of the central city over time (a path taken by predecessor ethnic groups); escape from poverty and economic dependence as measured by poverty rates; and movement into homeownership, the central enduring ingredient of the American dream. The overall conclusion is that this is a very complex situation—a conclusion that is common in most contributions to this volume—but that the immigrant experience in southern California has been one of positive and reassuring progress across all three measures of upward mobility. Nonetheless, among the policy dilemmas that remain are the conflicts between policies for places versus policies for people.

The Great American Family Dilemma

The household revolution in the United States has yielded a reduced incidence of married-couple families in the household profile and a corresponding increase in fatherless families, a shift at its most extreme for parts of minority America. The concurrent shifts in the economy have driven increases in female labor force participation, which in turn have contributed to income variations across family types, and have demanded more time from parents in all family configurations. The result of these changes is a series of policy questions about the raising of children in America.

In "Balancing Act: If You've Got the Money, Honey, I've Got the Time," Daphne Spain sees these economic and family changes as creating historically new demands on women that affect the entire family's disposable time as certainly as their disposable income. Historically, husbands made the money and wives made the time for family life. Now there is a persistently gendered distribution of housework and child care, which, when taken in the context of the economic imperatives of working motherhood, has led to a gradual erosion of family time. In other words, both women and men may now have the money, but nobody has the time, particularly in single-parent families. Establishing public policies that address the time concerns of families as they currently exist are seen as much more productive than policy changes that would attempt to reverse the trend toward single-parent families. A series of policies at the federal, state, and local levels are sketched out.

David Popenoe, in "American Family Decline: Public Policy Considerations," confronts the issue of family decline (that is, the weakening of the family as a social institution) leading to the deterioration of child well-being. In particular, growing child poverty is viewed as largely a consequence of the retreat of fathers from the lives of their children and the rise of single-parent families. After reviewing the debate about whether or not the family has declined—and whether negative child outcomes can be directly linked to family change—Popenoe shifts focus to policies that would lower the rates of divorce and out-of-wedlock births, thereby increasing the percentage of children being raised by two-parent families. Suggested parameters for governmental family policies are based on two simple propositions: children are our future, and the family is the most important institution for child well-being. Eight basic pro-marriage and pro-family policies are presented.

America in Transition

Diversity and the maturing baby boom, two of the enduring demographic parameters we have already discussed, will continually challenge public policy in America well into the next century. The search for successful policy solutions to accommodate racial and ethnic change has proven elusive during the past generation. Most likely it will still be on our agenda as the new century matures. Similarly, the impact of the baby boom since its inception has always been a staple public policy concern. The key manifestation in the next century will be the fiscal consequences of a baby boom in retirement.

In "Separate and Not Equal: America's Diversity Crisis," Edward Blakely confronts the following basic questions: Can a primarily western European nation evolve into a nation whose demographic stock will increasingly be from all over the world? Can social and economic parity, a fundamental tenet of the social philosophy of the United States, be achieved when the historic majority trends toward a new minority? What will be the structure of public policy when race ascends to a far more prominent and different role? Because race shapes social life more than any other issue, Blakely takes a close look at the dimensions that form the core of the racial policy debate. Directions for a national diversity policy are discussed, and goals with respect to such a policy are examined.

In "Baby Boom Retirement Crisis: Myth or Reality?" Richard C. Leone challenges the assumptions that the baby boom in retirement will place undue burdens on the working population of twenty-first–century America and that the standard of living of retired boomers will be bound to unravel. Leone believes that fears of the future are out of proportion and that future demographic changes in the United States will be well short of catastrophic. Instead, our demographic destiny is seen as a mild challenge. Public policies will ultimately be crafted that strike a balance among the competing demands of Americans of all ages.

Part I

The Baselines of Demographic Change and the Broad Policy Framework

Chapter 1

Martha Farnsworth Riche and Judith Waldrop

America's Changing Demographic Tapestry

American society is like a modern tapestry. The weave may be traditional, but the colors and patterns seem somehow outlandish compared to familiar designs. To appreciate the artistry, we need to understand how design supports function.

America's demographic trends form an intricate pattern. Whites are still the majority of Americans—and will be for many years to come—but other groups are growing rapidly. The country is growing older, but there is also a substantial youth population that cannot be ignored. Every trend seems to produce a countertrend. We cannot talk about the increase in the wealthy without recognizing the persistence of poverty. We cannot talk about changing families now without understanding how the family has developed within the context of our history.

A complex array of competing factors makes it difficult to understand how the interplay of new trends is influencing our nation's needs. But identifying and tracking demographic trends are vital for informed decision making at all levels of government and in every business or nonprofit organization. The following five demographic trends are important to the American tapestry: increasing cultural diversity, age diversity, life-style diversity, socioeconomic diversity, and life-course diversity.

Cultural Diversity

One trend that stands out because it is easy to observe and frequently controversial is the growing cultural and ethnic diversity of our population, especially in our coastal areas, along our southern border, and in our big cities.

The foreign-born population more than doubled between 1970 and 1995, rising from about 10 million to 23 million. Net immigration was far above the Census Bureau's expectations. The bureau anticipated adding 10 million people through immigration, but the real number was closer to 15 million. The foreign-born population leaped from 4.8 percent of the U.S. total to nearly 9 percent.[1]

Although the government does not have an official definition for minorities, the Census Bureau distinguishes four major racial groups in its population surveys and censuses: white; African American or black; Asian and Pacific Islander; and American Indian, Eskimo, and Aleut. A fifth group, Hispanics, is an ethnic group and includes people of all races.

In 1995, almost 263 million people were living in the United States, an increase of 6 percent over the 1990 census count. Almost three-quarters of these residents, or 194 million people, were white and not of Hispanic origin. This non-Hispanic white group increased slowly, however, growing only 3 percent over the first half of the decade. All of the other racial and ethnic groups increased much faster than the total population of the United States.[2]

The most rapidly growing population group is Asian and Pacific Islanders, up 25 percent since 1990. Nevertheless, this group is still a small share of all people living in the United States, numbering fewer than 10 million in 1995. During the first half of the decade, large-scale immigration accounted for much of the rapid growth among Asians and Pacific Islanders as well as among Hispanics.[3]

The large Hispanic-origin population is growing rapidly. In 1995, there were 27 million people of Hispanic origin living in the United States, an increase of 21 percent over 1990. The black population, with 33 million people, is still larger, but it grew only 9 percent over the first half of the decade.[4] In addition, Census Bureau projections indicate that Hispanics will replace blacks as the nation's largest majority early in the next century.[5]

The American Indian, Eskimo, and Aleut group is smallest, but it, too, is growing more rapidly than the population as a whole. Between 1990 and 1995, a 9 percent increase brought this group up to more than 2 million people.[6]

Almost half of all Americans were aged 34 or younger in 1995. But the median age or halfway point for non-Hispanic whites was older—nearly 37—and the four other major racial and ethnic populations were all younger than Americans in general. In 1995, the median age was about 30 for the Asian and Pacific Islander population, and half of African Americans were aged 29 or younger. The youngest racial and ethnic groups were American Indians, Eskimos, and Aleuts and Hispanics, with median ages of 27 and 26 respectively.

Only 24 percent of non-Hispanic whites were under age 18, compared with 36 percent of all Hispanics.[7]

Cultural Challenges

The comparative youth of minority groups has been particularly significant in our school systems. In 1970, one in five students in primary and secondary schools was a minority; now the ratio is one in three.[8] While we often think of school systems in Los Angeles and New York as dealing with children from many cultures, the phenomenon is spreading to different parts of the country. For instance, the school systems in the Atlanta metropolitan area must educate children who together speak eighty different languages in their homes.[9]

The impact of cultural diversity is not evenly distributed across the nation. For example, 53 percent of blacks lived in the south in 1990, while only 34 percent of the total population lived in the south. The other major minority groups are most likely to be found in the west. Although only 21 percent of all Americans lived in the west in 1990, fully 45 percent of people of Hispanic origin did. Almost half (48 percent) of American Indians, Eskimos, and Aleuts were westerners, and the west is home to 56 percent of Asians and Pacific Islanders.[10] While the non-Hispanic white population will remain a majority nationwide, by 2010 it will be a minority in the District of Columbia and three states: California, New Mexico, and Hawaii.[11]

Changing cultural and ethnic concentrations and growing language diversity present new challenges for communications and service delivery problems. There is more room for misunderstanding and conflict. People from different cultures often have different needs and expectations, and sometimes they have different ideas about what is right and wrong. People from other cultures, for example, may not feel comfortable if someone from outside their families (a police officer, a teacher, or a health care provider) touches them, especially if that person is of the opposite sex. Some immigrants won't speak to authority figures unless they are asked. Others avoid eye contact because it is considered aggressive behavior, not because they are being evasive. Hand gestures are frequently misunderstood.[12] If authorities in the workplace, hospitals, police work, or schools are unaware of differences like these, problems can arise.

Much of the change that has occurred could not have been anticipated twenty-five years ago. Who would have guessed that in 1995 blacks would make up less than 50 percent of the minority population? Who would have guessed that in 1995 more Hispanics than non-Hispanic whites would be added to the U.S. population each year?

Even so, this discussion oversimplifies the evolving racial and ethnic patterns. Each group is composed of people from many nationalities with different cultural perspectives. New immigrants add more diversity to each group. This change is highly visible in our school systems, in the media, and even in the street signs we see in our hometowns.

Age Diversity

American media often give the impression that youth dominates the nation, but our population is actually growing older. The number of births over the last twenty-five years was below the Census Bureau's expectations, as was the number of deaths.[13]

Between 1970 and 1995, the median age rose from 28 to more than 34. The elderly population, those people over 65, grew 67 percent. The oldest group, those over age 85, grew by more than 150 percent.[14]

Again, this change is not taking place uniformly across the country. Although the elderly population is expected to increase in all states over the next thirty years, it is growing especially fast in the south and west. Already the south and west contain 54 percent of the elderly, the reverse of the situation twenty-five years ago.[15]

The largest number of elderly will continue to live in the states that have the largest numbers today: California and Florida. Nevertheless, the number of elderly will grow fastest in Alaska, Utah, Idaho, Colorado, Nevada, Wyoming, and Washington. Within these states, the number of persons 65 years and older is expected to double.[16]

In 1995, Florida had the largest proportion of elderly of any state: 19 percent. The state with the smallest share was Alaska, with 5 percent. This ranking will remain constant for at least the next thirty years, according to Census Bureau projections. In 2025, however, more than a quarter of the population in Florida will be aged 65 or older, and 10 percent of people in Alaska will be that old. In 1995, only four states had an elderly population of at least 15 percent. But in 2025, 15 percent of the population in all states, except Alaska and California, will be that old.[17]

Generational Issues

In contrast to the elderly population, the population under age 18 is expected to shrink in all regions of the United States between 1995 and 2025. It will decline most in the midwest and the south—by 3 percentage points. The smallest declines, 1 percentage point, will be in the west and the northeast. The Census Bureau anticipates that births will outnumber deaths two to one in the west. This trend and high immigration rates will sustain the area's youthful population.[18]

As a result, in 2025, approximately 27 percent of the west's population will be age 18 or younger, and about 24 percent of the population in the northeast and the midwest will be that young. By a narrow margin, the south will have the lowest percent of people 18 or under—just 23 percent.[19]

Not too long ago, the rebellious baby boom generation challenged parents' leadership, values, and traditions. As this group ages, it will be numerically stronger than any elderly generation in the history of this nation. By 2010, people aged 45 and older will become the majority of voters. These trends raise important questions. For example, will there be more emphasis on the needs of the older population, such as Medicaid, Social Security, and research on aging? Will the supply of resources for young people, such as schools and recreational facilities, face serious challenges?

Life-style Diversity

Twenty-five years ago, the typical American family was comprised of a married couple with children cared for by their stay-at-home mother. But this pattern has changed too—in part because people live longer, in part because changes in our economy have created more choices.

Married couples still head the majority of America's households, but only half of these homes have children in them.[20] And the majority of America's mothers work outside the home. Single-parent households, most frequently headed by mothers, have risen rapidly.[21] Although out-of-wedlock births were once hidden, now they are widespread and highly visible. And today one out of every four households is a person living alone.

How people choose to live their lives and with whom they choose to live have significant implications for service and product delivery. Increasing numbers of one-parent families place greater demands on school systems to provide social programs. After-school care is a major issue. Unsupervised children are a challenge for both schools and police. Legal and financial issues arise concerning unmarried partners and children of cohabiting and absentee parents.

Between 1970 and 1995, the share of households maintained by married couples with children fell from 40 percent to 26 percent as the result of numerous factors.[22] Divorce has become commonplace in families with or without children, although the rate of divorce has declined in recent years. People who never marry or never have children at all represent a small but growing segment of the population. Others choose to have children without being married.

More recently, the children of the aging baby boomers have begun to leave the nest. Increasing longevity means that many older couples continue to enjoy life together long after the children leave.

Between 1970 and 1995, the proportion within the population aged 18 and older who are divorced increased from 3 percent to 9 percent, while the proportion of children living with only one parent rose from 12 percent to 27 percent.[23] In the late 1970s and 1980s, half of all first marriages ended in divorce. Although there have been more than 1 million divorces each year since 1975, the actual rate of divorce has declined since the mid-1980s. Some of this decline is the result of the aging population. Older couples are less likely to divorce than younger ones are.

Since the 1970s, more than 1 million children per year have been involved in divorces. Although the total number of divorces has risen over the past two decades, the number of births per woman has dropped. Therefore, the average number of children per divorce decree has fallen from 1.22 children in 1970 to 0.90 in 1990. In 1990, more than half of divorces involved children under 18, according to vital statistics data.[24]

The Consequences for Children

The economic changes that families experience after the father leaves the household were tracked in the 1980s by the Census Bureau's Survey of Income and Program Participation. To compensate for the loss of the father as an income provider, the percent of mothers working full time increased to 41 percent from a predivorce level of 33 percent. Even so, monthly family income decreased by almost 40 percent, and the proportion of families in poverty increased. Before the father left, 19 percent of children in these families were in poverty; soon after his departure, this share nearly doubled.[25]

In 1992, 10 million women in the United States were the custodial parents of 17 million children under 21 years of age. Of these mothers, 49 percent were supposed to receive child support payments in 1991, but only about half of these women got all of what they were due. The remainder was split about evenly between those receiving partial payments and those receiving no money at all from the absent father.[26]

In 1991, the average amount of child support actually received was only about $3,000 and comprised just 17 percent of the custodial mother's income. More than 35 percent of custodial mothers lived in poverty. Nevertheless, the poverty rate for those receiving child support was 23 percent compared to fully 43 percent for women with no child support award.[27]

Children of divorced parents frequently experience new child care arrangements. Because of the loss of the father's income, children of divorced mothers depend more on the relatively less expensive assistance of grandmothers and other family members to care for them after school and when the mother is working.[28] Evidence from a recent Census Bureau survey also suggests that children of single mothers are more likely to be left alone after school than are children of married parents.[29]

Although it is still customary for the mother to have custody of the children after a divorce, a growing proportion of children of divorced parents are living with their fathers. Between 1970 and 1995, the proportion of children of divorced parents living with their father rose from just 7 percent to fully 16 percent, according to Census Bureau surveys.[30] A 1992 survey showed that the average income of all custodial father households is approximately double that of households headed by a custodial mother.[31] Between 1970 and 1995, the proportion of children under 18 years old living with only one parent rose from 12 percent to 27 percent.[32] Divorce is one explanation; another is the increase in out-of-wedlock child bearing. In 1970, just one in ten births was attributable to an unwed mother. By 1994, that ratio had increased to one in three, according to vital statistics information collected by the National Center for Health Statistics.[33]

In 1995, 15 percent of the population—41 million people—were without health insurance for the entire year. The share of children under age 18 without insurance was 14 percent, leaving 10 million uninsured. These estimates were statistically unchanged from the previous year.[34]

Children under 18 continue to represent a very large segment of the poor. Even though they were only a little more than one-fourth of the total population in 1995, they were 40 percent of the poor. Today, one in every five children lives in poverty.[35]

The children of poverty are clustered in certain racial and ethnic groups and are concentrated in certain regions. Although 61 percent of all poor children are white, the poverty rate of whites is the lowest among all major racial and ethnic groups: 16 percent. About 42 percent of black children and 40 percent of Hispanic children were poor in 1995.[36]

With a poverty rate of 24 percent, the south is home to the largest share of America's poor children. Fully 39 percent of all of the nation's poor children live in the south. The west has the next highest poverty rate for children, 22 percent, followed by the northeast with 19 percent and the midwest with 17 percent.[37]

About 30 percent of married women with children under age 6 at home were in the labor force in 1970. Today almost 64 percent are.[38] Perhaps because so many mothers are in the work force, children start school earlier. Over the past twenty-five years, nursery school attendance has quadrupled, from about

1 million to more than 4 million. More than 60 percent of 3– to 5–year-olds were in preschool in 1994.[39]

Older Life-styles

The changing life-styles of children is not the only household trend placing greater demands on American resources. Between 1970 and 1995, the proportion of households that contained only one person rose from 17 percent to 25 percent. This trend has many causes; one often overlooked is the increasing share of the population in older ages. Thanks to advances in health knowledge and care, more people are living beyond the family-raising years.[40] Single-person households can be targets for crime, especially when the occupants are elderly. In addition, health service delivery for the elderly living alone is an especially challenging problem.

For all persons aged 15 and over, the percentage of those living alone has increased from 7 percent in 1970 to 12 percent in 1995. Because the likelihood of living alone sharply increases with age, some of this change is the result of the overall aging of the population. Fewer than 5 percent of young adults aged 15 to 24 years old lived alone in 1995. But about 10 to 15 percent of those aged 45 to 64 years old did.[41]

Between 1970 and 1995, more people were living alone in every age group. Most of the change occurred between 1970 and 1980; since 1980, this increase has slowed. The increase in numbers of those living alone has been especially dramatic among people under 55 years of age. The share of this group in single-person households has doubled over the twenty-five-year period. The likelihood of living alone, however, has also increased sharply among the oldest Americans. For those aged 75 and older, the share increased from 30 percent to 42 percent.[42]

A higher proportion of elderly women live alone than do elderly men. In 1970, 32 percent of women aged 65 to 74 lived alone compared with only 11 percent of men. Although the proportion of elderly women living alone remained at about the same level in 1995, the share of men increased to 14 percent. Among people aged 75 and over, 37 percent of women and 19 percent of men lived alone in 1970. These percentages rose to 53 and 23 percent, respectively, by 1995.[43]

In all, almost 10 million persons aged 65 years and older were maintaining a household alone in 1995, and three-quarters of these householders were women.[44] Even so, this growing number of single-person households suggests increasing independence among the elderly and less dependence on their children and other relatives. While the poverty rate among persons under age 18 increased from 14 percent to 21 percent between 1969 and 1994, the rate for elderly adults declined dramatically, from 25 percent to 11 percent.[45]

Socioeconomic Diversity

It is no wonder that the life-style changes of the past twenty-five years have had a major impact on household income. Between 1968 and 1994, the share of aggregate income received by the top quintile of households rose from 43 to 49 percent.[46] A number of studies, however, suggest that between 1994 and 1995 the long-term trend toward increasing economic inequality is stabilizing.

A strong link between education and income places poorly educated people at an extreme disadvantage. While the highly educated have made some gains, the long-term trend has meant that those who are less educated have slipped even further behind. In 1995, the mean earnings of men working year round, full time, with at least a college degree were almost $61,000 compared with just $31,000 for those with a high-school diploma. Those who did not complete their high-school degree earned only about $24,000. The real earnings of male college-degree holders grew by 15 percent since 1975, while high school graduates lost 7 percent. The earnings of men without a diploma plummeted 23 percent.[47]

Overall, poverty declined for families in the United States from 1994 to 1995. The share of white families in poverty dropped from 9 percent in 1994 to 8.5 percent in 1995. Black and Hispanic families, however, experienced no significant change in poverty status. In 1995, the poverty rate was about 26 percent for black families and 27 percent for Hispanic families.[48]

Educational attainment is the best predictor of earnings. Despite gains in educational attainment, blacks, American Indians, and Hispanics are still the least likely to have completed high school. Non-Hispanic whites are the most likely to have completed high school, but Asians are the most likely to have completed college.[49]

Working Men and Women

Over the past twenty-five years, college enrollment has increased more for women than men, and that trend has been partially responsible for women's growing success in the workplace.[50] For every dollar that men working year round, full time earned in 1969, women working year round, full time earned only 59 cents. Although still far from equal, the gap has narrowed. By 1994, women's earning had increased to 72 cents for every dollar that men earned.[51]

Between 1969 and 1994, the median earnings of women working year round, full time increased almost 17 percent, from about $19,300 to $22,500 in 1995 dollars. Nevertheless, the narrowing gap between men's and women's earnings cannot be explained solely by increasing gains for women. Over the twenty-five-year period, the real earnings of men working year round, full time declined by about 4 percent, dropping from about $32,700 to $31,500.[52]

Since 1950, labor force participation rates for men and women have moved in opposite directions. While the labor force participation rates for women have risen dramatically, those of men have declined. In 1950, 30 percent of working-age women participated in the labor force; by 1990, this rate nearly had doubled to 57 percent. This increase among women more than offset the decline in labor force participation rates among men from 82 percent in 1950 to 74 percent in 1990.[53]

Not only are women more likely to be in the labor force than they were twenty-five years ago, but they are also spending more time at work. The percentage of women working year round, full time has increased from 41 percent in 1970 to about 53 percent in 1993. This is the result of more women who are working year round rather than more who are working full time each week. The percent of women working full time was relatively stable over the same period.[54]

While women remain concentrated in occupations different from those of men, they have moved into occupations that have been expanding rapidly. The proportion of women in managerial occupations more than doubled between 1974 and 1994, while the percent of women employed as operators, fabricators, and laborers declined substantially over the period.[55]

Much of the change in income distribution has been forced by the increasing advantage of higher education as well as the multiplicative effect of marriage so that now many wives have incomes too. Households with the highest earnings are two-earner households in which both earners have high levels of educational attainment.

Life-course Diversity

Increasing diversity is changing who Americans are and how they live, and it is also complicating their passage into different life stages. New mothers are older than they were twenty-five years ago, college students can be of any age, and retirees are looking younger every day. Today's Americans do not necessarily follow the sequential life path of graduation, job, marriage, family, and retirement.

Birth rates fell sharply in the early 1970s after women gained control over their fertility. Since then, fertility rates have increased for women in their 30s. Older women, frequently with more financial resources than their younger counterparts have, are likely to have trouble becoming pregnant, resulting in an industry that has grown up around their desire to conceive.

In the past twenty-five years, college enrollment has doubled, but the increased number of students is partially the result of growing numbers of students aged twenty-five and older.[56] Older students do not have the same needs as people just out of high school. They do not need the residence hall rooms, but they may need night classes or child care. They bring to the classroom different life experiences, resources, and needs.

In addition, the number of persons working at home (including farmers) increased 27 percent between 1970 and 1990, from 2.7 million to 3.4 million. The twenty-year trend, however, masks two different ten-year changes. Between 1970 and 1980, workers at home declined by 19 percent. Between 1980 and 1990, they increased by 56 percent.[57] In recent years, the ability to work at home has been facilitated by industries designed to serve these workers, including home office equipment (from fax machines to computers) and specialty services (from overnight delivery to all-night print shops).

Demographic diversity has an impact on several levels of American life. Even government must target smaller niches. It is no longer possible to be guided by sweeping assumptions about the American family or the American workplace. Policymakers need to know their audiences at an increasingly personal level.

Both government and business need the flexibility to adapt to changing constituencies. The need to constantly monitor change through censuses and surveys is increasing. Our review of Census Bureau surveys and data reveals America's top five trends—diversity, diversity, diversity, diversity, and more diversity.

Notes

1. U.S. Bureau of the Census, "How We're Changing," *Current Population Report* (Special Studies Series), P23–193: 2.
2. U.S. Bureau of the Census, "U.S. Population Estimates by Age, Race, and Sex, 1990 to 1995," PPL-41 (February 14, 1997): 13, 25.
3. Ibid., 27.
4. Ibid., 12, 22.
5. Jennifer Cheeseman Day, "Population Projections of the United States by Age, Sex, Race, and Hispanic Origin: 1995 to 2025," *Current Population Reports,* P25–1130 (February 1996): 50.
6. U.S. Bureau of the Census, "U.S. Population Estimates by Age, Race, and Sex, 1990 to 1995," PPL-41 (February 14, 1997): 13, 25.
7. Ibid., 13.

8. Rosalind R. Bruno and Andrea Curry, "School Enrollment—Social and Economic Characteristics of Students: October 1994," *Current Population Reports,* P20–487 (September 1996): x.

9. Linda C. Shrenko, *The Status of Students of Limited English Proficiency in Georgia Public Schools, 1994–1995* (Atlanta: Georgia Department of Education, State Superintendent, 1996).

10. "Summary of Population and Housing Characteristics," *1990 Census of Population and Housing,* Series CPH1–1 (Washington D.C.: U.S. Bureau of the Census, March 1992), tab. 2.

11. Day, "Population Projections of the United States," 66–67.

12. Judith Waldrop, "The Newest Southerners," *American Demographics* 15 (1993): 3843.

13. Martha F. Riche, "Population and America's Future," paper presented for the Population Resource Center, Washington, D.C.,October 27, 1995.

14. U.S. Bureau of the Census, *Statistical Abstract of the United States: 1995* (Washington, D.C.: U.S. Bureau of the Census, 1996), tab. 13, pp. 14–15; U.S. Bureau of the Census, "U.S. Population Estimates by Age, Race, and Sex, 1990 to 1995," PPL-41 (February 14, 1997): 12.

15. Day, "Population Projections of the United States," 74.

16. Ibid., 22.

17. U.S. Bureau of the Census, "Warmer, older, more diverse: State by state population changes to 2025," *Census Brief* 961 (December 1996): 15.

18. Day, "Population Projections of the United States," 55.

19. Ibid., 78.

20. Ken Bryson, "Household and Family Characteristics: March 1995," *Current Population Reports,* P20–488 (October 1996): 1.

21. Ibid.

22. Ibid.

23. Arlene F. Saluter, "Marital Status and Living Arrangements: March 1995," *Current Population Reports,* PPL-52 (December 1996): A1, A6.

24. S. E. Clark, "Advance Report of Final Divorce Statistics, 1989 and 1990," *Vital Statistics of the United States* 43, no. 8 (1995): tab. 3.

25. Suzanne Bianchi and Edith McArthur, "Family Distribution and Economic Hardship: The Short-Term Picture for Children," *Current Population Reports,* P70–23 (1991): 8.

26. Lydia Schoon-Rogers and Gordon Lester, "Child Support for Custodial Mothers and Fathers: 1991," *Current Population Reports,* P60–187 (August 1995): tab. 1, p. 14.

27. Ibid.

28. Lynne M. Casper, "Who's Minding Our Preschoolers?" *Current Population Reports,* P70–53 (March 1996): 4.

29. Lynne M. Casper, Mary Hawkins, and Martin O'Connell, "Who's Minding the Kids? Child Care Arrangements: Fall 1991," *Current Population Reports,* P70–36 (1994): 12.

30. Saluter, "Marital Status and Living Arrangements: March 1995," tab. A11.

31. Lydia Schoon-Rogers and Gordon Lester, unpublished data from U.S. Bureau of the Census, "Child Support Supplement of the Current Population Survey" (April 1992): tab. 1.

32. Saluter, "Marital Status and Living Arrangements: March 1995," A6.

33. National Center for Health Statistics, *Marriage and Divorce,* annual issues.
34. U.S. Bureau of the Census, "U.S. Current Population Survey Data" (as listed on the Internet).
35. Eleanor Baugher and Leatha Lamison-White, "Poverty in the United States: 1995," *Current Population Reports,* P60–194 (September 1996): tab. A.
36. Ibid., tab. 2.
37. Ibid.
38. U.S. Bureau of the Census, *Statistical Abstract of the United States: 1996* (Washington, D.C.: U.S. Bureau of the Census, 1996), tab. 626.
39. U.S. Bureau of the Census, *1970 Census of Population,* vol. 1, part 1; P20–491, tab. 1.
40. Martha Farnsworth Riche, "From Pyramids to Pillars: The New Demographic Realities," paper delivered at the Technical Meeting on Population Aging, UNFPA, Brussels, October 1998.
41. Arlene F. Saluter, "Marital Status and Living Arrangements, March 1994," *Current Population Reports,* P20–484 (February 1996): tab. A8; Arlene F. Saluter, "Marital Status and Living Arrangements, March 1995 (Update)," *Current Population Reports,* P20–491 (December 1996): tab. A.
42. Ibid.
43. Ibid.
44. Saluter, "Marital Status and Living Arrangements: March 1995," iii.
45. Baugher and Lamison-White, "Poverty in the United States: 1995," tab. B3.
46. Daniel H. Weinberg, "A Brief Look at Postwar U.S. Income Inequity," *Current Population Reports,* P60–191 (June 1996): 2.
47. U.S. Bureau of the Census, Internet Time Series, tabs. P10, P10A.
48. Baugher and Lamison-White, "Poverty in the United States: 1995," tab. C3.
49. U.S. Bureau of the Census, *1990 Census of Population Social and Economic Characteristics: United States,* CP21 (Washington D.C.: U.S. Bureau of the Census, 1990), tab. 42, p. 42.
50. U.S. Bureau of the Census, *Statistical Abstract of the United States: 1996,* tab. 240.
51. U.S. Bureau of the Census, "Current Population Survey," Internet Time Series, tab. P14.
52. Ibid., tab. P13.
53. U.S. Bureau of the Census, "Population Profile of the United States: 1995," *Current Population Reports,* P23–189 (1995): 39.
54. U.S. Department of Labor, Bureau of Labor Statistics, "Women in the Workforce: An Overview," Report 892 (July 1995): 56.
55. Ibid., 7.
56. Bruno and Curry, "School Enrollment," tab. A6.
57. Unpublished 1990 census data.

Chapter 2

Peter A. Morrison

Family Policies and Demographic Realities

Demographic upheaval has been likened to an earthquake or revolution, but it most resembles a glacier: change materializes gradually and on a massive scale, accompanied by massive need. A glacierlike demographic upheaval now casts a long, cold shadow across American families. In the aftermath of federal welfare reform, it challenges social policy to reinforce universally held principles of family responsibility within the complex affiliations that define present-day families.

Political concern with family issues gained prominence in the 1996 presidential campaign, and they remain a continuing focus of the Clinton administration. Public opinion is aroused: Americans have grown deeply concerned about what has happened to families. A recent Gallup poll listed the following two problems among the top four deemed critical for the nation:

- Children being born to single parents (deemed critical to 43 percent of the public)
- Divorces involving parents with young children (deemed critical to 37 percent)[1]

The barometer of public opinion is squarely on target. The United States is a rich nation with poor children—a unique problem among advanced industrialized countries—and the poverty of American children derives largely from predisposing family structures.[2]

Demographic upheaval also casts a shadow of need across tomorrow's elderly. Seniors with unprecedented longevity advance in years, while family members with the emotional will to care for them find they have no practical means of doing so. Typically, adult daughters and sons already hold full-time jobs.

Against this demographic backdrop, what are the limits and realistic future possibilities of family policies? How can public policies be crafted to anchor responsibility within families in which the will traditionally exists? Experience shows that traditional principles in the abstract do not always mesh with the complex realities to which legislation gets applied.

In the mid-1980s, for example, Wisconsin enacted a law on grandparents' liability, a commonsense approach to the problem of teenage child bearing. The law made parents financially responsible for infants born to their unmarried teenage children, thus giving parents a major stake in their children's sex education. The first Wisconsin couple to be held liable for a teenage daughter's baby, however, turned out to be divorced. The question left unanswered was which grandparent has the duty of support. Moreover, what if the divorced mother had remarried, and years later her unmarried daughter made her a grandmother? Would the state of Wisconsin bill the biological grandfather or the stepgrandfather or both?

In addition, laws that no longer fit demographic realities may destroy family ties. For example, some states have required children of Medicaid recipients to help pay for their parents' nursing home care. Consider a widow with minor children—a family whose father has perished in a car accident. Suppose she remarries, gaining a new husband who later develops a costly health condition. If he adopts her children, are those children legally obligated to pay some of his medical expenses when they become adults?

Another example is from southern California, where undocumented immigrants form families and bear children. Their children are born as U.S. citizens but remain inadvertent members of binational families. These offspring of a noncitizen mother or father (or both) remain entitled to social services in the communities in which they live. Under tightened immigration laws, though, their parents could effectively lose that entitlement. Here the unanswered question is who remains on the family scene to assure that the citizen child gets fed, clothed, and sent to school each day.

As these illustrations suggest, the realities of present-day families confound efforts to define and enforce simplistic notions of family responsibility. Traditional principles that once guided policy often do not mesh with today's complex family situations.[3]

Demographic Perspectives on Childhood

Let us examine these situations more closely with an eye to the first of two central concerns: children's well-being. A host of demographic research shows the extent to which changes in family structure have reshaped the period of childhood. Whether it takes a village or simply a family to raise a child, neither institution actually operates as idealized on behalf of children. Many families are ill-equipped, and villages understaffed, to take up the slack. (A glance inside any big-city public library late in the afternoon reveals de facto day care in operation.)

The gap between what is expected from families and what is feasible will surely widen. In today's family, adults usually hold jobs (sometimes more than one). Close to 65 percent of married couples are families in which both spouses are employed, up from 43 percent a generation ago. The majority of new mothers resume employment within a year of giving birth compared to a minority of their earlier counterparts. For children, the home front remains a patchwork of tenuous arrangements, inspiring much rhetoric (and some progress) toward making the workplace more family friendly through arrangements such as family leave and flexible work schedules.

In many families, women alone—mothers, grandmothers, older sisters, aunts—disproportionately shoulder responsibility for children, socializing them and supporting them economically. Yet many children live in poverty, which is often traced to family structure. Increasingly, children live with one parent (overwhelmingly the mother) who is often submerged in transient or chronic poverty. What has long been a reality among black families is becoming more the reality among every group.

Astonishingly, poverty is more common in the United States among children (just over 20 percent) than the elderly (just over 10 percent).[4] Even when their parents work, many children are poverty-stricken. One of every three impoverished children lives in a family classified as "working poor"—that is, in which parents' earnings are inadequate to keep their children above the poverty line.

The most powerful factors behind child poverty (echoing the public opinion data I have mentioned) are marital disruption and, increasingly, single child bearing. One of every three infants today is born to a woman who is unmarried at the time; in 1960, the proportion was one in twenty. Among children born to married couples, half will see their parents divorce during childhood. Both factors together largely account for the continuing rise in the proportion of families headed by only one parent, demonstrably the strongest determinant of poverty in childhood.

The future, it is said, creeps in on tiny feet. A nation that allows poverty to undermine children's health and cut short their education incurs lasting economic costs. The quality of this nation's work force and its future competitiveness in the world economy depend on the future productivity of its young people. A rich nation that tolerates poor children in its midst surely wastes the means to enrich itself further.

Demographic Perspectives on Old Age

A second concern for family policy is how well-equipped Americans are to care for their elderly. That question is now on many minds as people of all ages and political persuasions contemplate how to arrange the care that elderly family members will need. Today, 13 percent of Americans are aged 65 or older; by 2030, about 20 percent will be—an entire nation, on average, with the feel of Florida today.

Undoubtedly, families retain the will to care for their elderly members. Can policies be crafted to help them find a way? At one time, adult daughters cared for elderly parents at home. Today, those daughters (and any spouses) are in the work force, leaving little time for traditional home responsibilities. Of women now in their 20s, four-fifths will likely hold jobs when their mothers receive their first Social Security checks.

Moreover, nuclear families now are smaller but structurally more complex in kinship. Tomorrow's elderly will have fewer living biological children and more stepchildren to depend on. Next century, there will be fewer adult children around to serve as caregivers, and labor force participation trends imply that such care will prove impractical for most. Although their life expectancy will be longer, elderly persons will find themselves short on family support where it counts most in old age: at home. The demographic transformations that have fostered commercialization of child care—two incomes and no one home during the day—will fuel commercialization of elder care.

Population aging, therefore, will affect the lives of both the elderly and their family members. Rising longevity in old age means that more people in their 60s and early 70s (the young elderly) themselves will have very old surviving parents. These two-generation geriatric families will need care, but how much care and orchestrated by whom? Social Security taxes may rise, and more of the federal budget surely will flow to the elderly. Nevertheless, Social Security and other federal entitlement programs distribute local dollars, not local care.

Although the aging of population will not begin to crest for another thirteen years, the effects are being felt already in many communities. Suburbs that housed newly settled young families in the 1950s are now communities in which many of those same family members have grown old. Demographers refer to these as "naturally occurring retirement communities" (NORCs)—existing neighborhoods in which many older adults stay on after young people have left. National family policies that are focused on aging, then, will need to address situations unfolding locally, refining existing approaches and testing out new ones.

Certain issues will remain shrouded in demographic uncertainty. One unknown is how much more life expectancy may rise.[5] In 1960, an average 65–year-old could expect to live 14.4 more years, a gain of 2.5 years since 1900. By 1990, the number had risen another 2.9 years, to a life expectancy of 17.3 more years—82.3 years in all. The gain over those thirty years, then, exceeds the entire gain made in the first six decades of the century. By 1996, life expectancy at age 65 had reached 17.4 years.[6]

Among the many factors affecting this trend are access to medical care, new health care technology, life-style changes, and a widespread concern with physical fitness. Adults are smoking less and exercising more and thus are probably gaining lasting benefits. Medical research also continues to find better ways to control diseases associated with aging, such as cardiovascular disease and stroke.

A further unknown is how far the traditional support structures within families can stretch. These are the units likely to remain central to long-term care of elderly people in the community.

Traditional structures of American families have changed. Future legislation aimed at reinforcing universal principles of family responsibility must accommodate the actual diversity and complexity of families. For a nation that emphasizes "family values," the demographic realities of families pose unprecedented challenges:

- About half of today's young children will become distanced from the economic support and care of one of their biological parents at some point during their youth. Family policy must firmly connect the fathering of children with supporting them economically.
- Fewer adults will be available to provide care directly for ailing parents. Although families retain the desire, they will lack a practical way to do so. Keeping long-term care anchored firmly within families means giving their members access to a range of supportive services such as adult day care, housekeeping assistance, and meals-on-wheels.
- The family structures through which social legislation operates will be complex and varied. Nontraditional structures will be more common, traditional ones less permanent. Many children will be part of a blended family containing stepchildren, half-siblings, and stepparents. As adults, a dutiful mixture of responsibility and pragmatism will shape their sense of family obligation.

Forward-looking policies must recognize what families alone do best—care for their own members—and retain that function within families, whatever their form. That will be the continuing challenge for a rich nation with poor children who are growing older each year.

Notes

1. Reported in *Gallup Poll Monthly* (May 1996): 49.
2. Lee Rainwater and Timothy M. Smeeding, *Doing Poorly: The Real Income of American Children in a Comparative Perspective,* LIS working paper, no. 127 (Syracuse, N.Y.: Syracuse University, Center for Policy Research, July 1995); Timothy M. Smeeding and B. B. Torrey, "Poor Children in Rich Countries," *Science* 242 (November 1988): 873–77.
3. For an informative overview of this point, see Larry L. Bumpass and William S. Aquilino, *A Social Map of Midlife: Family and Work Over the Middle Life Course* (Madison: University of Wisconsin, Center for Demography and Ecology, March 1995).
4. Annie E. Casey Foundation, 1997 KIDS COUNT data sheet (Baltimore); Federal Interagency Forum on Child and Family Statistics, *America's Children: Key National Indicators of Well-Being* (Washington, D.C.: Interagency Forum on Child and Family Statistics, 1997).
5. On this issue, see Samuel H. Preston, *American Longevity: Past, Present, and Future,* policy brief, no. 7 (Syracuse, N.Y.: Syracuse University, Center for Policy Research, Maxwell School, 1996); Neil G. Bennett and S. Jay Olshansky, "Forecasting US Age Structure and the Future of Social Security: The Impact of Adjustments to Official Mortality Schedules," *Population and Development Review* 22, no. 4 (1996): 703–27.
6. National Center for Health Statistics; Metropolitan Life Insurance Company; U.S. Bureau of the Census.

Part II
Global Demographics
Ramifications

Chapter 3

Charles F. Westoff

The Global Population Outlook

Although the annual rate of population growth has now declined to 1.4 percent, the world's numbers are growing at nearly 800 million per decade. This means adding a population matching India's in the space of a little more than ten years. In 1998 the total number of people on earth reached 5.9 billion, up from 2.5 billion in 1950. How high will it go, and when will it stop?

When I first learned in elementary school about the size of the world's population, the number was 2 billion. When I first encountered the subject at the university, Malthus was in disrepute, and problems of growth seemed to point toward the threat of population decline in Europe. The large reductions in death rates in developing countries were just beginning, and the full specter of the population explosion had not yet materialized. Indeed, the world's enormous population growth represents a triumph over the forces of mortality, certainly a universal goal. A recent analysis of population growth in the United States estimated that if the mortality rates of 1900 had remained constant during the twentieth century while immigration and fertility rates followed their actual paths, the population today would be only half of what it actually is. Historically mortality has declined much more slowly in the developed world than it has in recent decades in the third world. It is, of course, easier and quicker to reduce mortality than to reduce the high levels of fertility that were demographically necessary during all of earlier history to avoid human extinction. The cultural and institutional supports of early marriage and high fertility are much more resistant to change than are the introduction and acceptance of life-saving technologies.

World Population Growth Prospects

The world is in store for a great deal of future growth regardless of how fast fertility falls. The demographic momentum would add an additional 40 to 50 percent to the current total even if the fertility rate were to drop tomorrow and remain at replacement—that is, at the level that would replace new generations with their same number. This momentum, not unlike trying to brake a moving vehicle, is a legacy of the high fertility of the recent past: there are so many children in the population who are potential parents that, even at lower rates of reproduction, their progeny will swell the total numbers. Under the immediate replacement fertility assumption, the population would reach a total of about 8 billion before it became stationary. That level may be the minimum expectation; however, it actually seems quite unrealistic since the current fertility level is about 40 percent higher than replacement.

It is also instructive to look at the opposite extreme: the population that would result from a continuation of the current rate of fertility. It only makes sense to limit such a projection in time. By the year 2050, the population would reach nearly 15 billion and, of course, would still be growing rapidly. Again, the picture is unrealistic because contraception is spreading and fertility is declining in various parts of the world. This exercise is revealing, however, mainly because it indicates how insupportable the continuation of current levels is even for a short time.

The time it will take for fertility to fall to replacement or lower will mainly determine how much larger the future population will be beyond the level implied by the demographic momentum. Death rates could rise because of AIDS, but current analyses suggest a limited demographic effect except in certain countries. Also, the momentum factor can be reduced somewhat by increasing the average age of child bearing, which would lengthen the measurement of a generation.

The United Nations' population projections, revised in 1998, present conventional ranges of high, medium, and low based on different fertility assumptions and different mortality scenarios. The lowest world total projected is a population of 7.3 billion by the year 2050, which is even lower than the population projected with the immediate and continuing assumption of replacement fertility. One contributing factor here is that in the immediate replacement scenario, the populations currently with below-replacement fertility (such as China, Japan, and most of Europe) are raised to the replacement level. The fertility trajectory in the low variant is extremely optimistic, showing a decline from the present world TFR (the typical number of children a women will bear during her lifetime) of 3 births per woman to 2.1 (the replacement level) by 2010 and continuing to decline to 1.6 some twenty-five years later. The high variant features a decline of fertility to a TFR of 2.6 over the next forty years and indicates a total population of 10.7 billion by 2050. The medium variant projects world fertility to fall to replacement by 2035 and shows a population by 2050 of 8.9 billion.

In short, we are confronted with a range in the middle of the twenty-first century from about 7 to 11 billion with an intermediate value of 8.9 billion as the most likely. These estimates for 2050 are by no means the ultimate levels. The population in 2050 under the high variant would still be increasing at an annual rate of 0.9 percent, the medium at 0.3 percent, and the low at -0.2 percent.

International Differences

World population projections obviously mask enormous variations across countries and regions (see Figure 3.1). Fertility rates are extremely low in many European countries and are very high in many sub-Saharan African countries.

Developed Countries

The TFR for Europe as a whole in 1997 was estimated at only 1.4, considerably below replacement. The birth rate is the same as the death rate. The rate of growth has turned negative in at least ten European countries where the populations are aging rapidly. In Japan, the TFR has fallen to 1.4, and there is some discussion in government circles about providing economic incentives for higher fertility. In the former East Germany, the TFR recently dropped to 0.8 births per woman, which is probably the lowest ever recorded for a large population. The fertility rates in Italy and Spain—both now at 1.2—are among the lowest on the continent; even Ireland, which traditionally featured the highest rate, has slipped below replacement to 1.9. These low rates can turn around, of course, although what will be necessary to produce such a change is not clear. Fertility was very low in the developed countries in the 1930s, recovering after the Second World War but resuming its decline over the past thirty years. Government policies to encourage higher fertility in eastern Europe are regarded as having at best changed the timing of reproduction with little effect on total fertility.

The current annual rate of population growth in the United States is 1 percent; the rate of natural increase is 0.7 percent with the difference being the net balance of international migration. Thus, immigration currently accounts for nearly a third of annual population growth. The demographic effect over the long run is, of course, much greater since the fertility rate of the foreign-born population on the whole is higher than that of the native-born. Immigrants and their descendants will comprise more than 70 percent of population growth

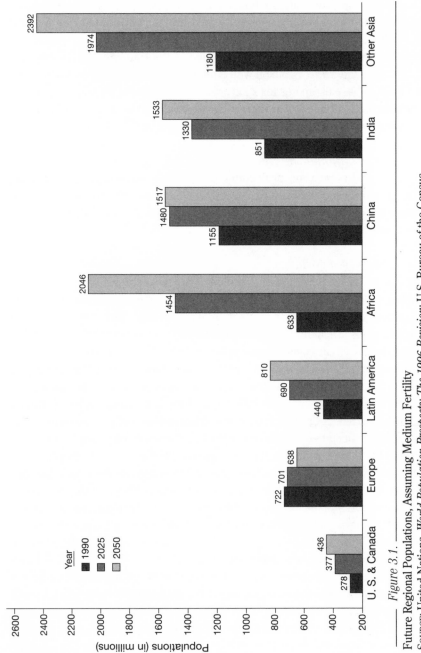

Figure 3.1.

Future Regional Populations, Assuming Medium Fertility

SOURCE: United Nations, *World Population Prospects: The 1996 Revision;* U.S. Bureau of the Census.

between 2000 and 2050, contributing some 88 million additional people to the midcentury total. The projected population of the United States in 2050 is nearly 400 million persons.

Latin America

The rate of population growth has declined in Latin America and the Caribbean, and fertility has fallen rapidly in the largest countries of the region. Brazil, which has the largest population, now has a TFR of 2.5, a rate that is probably still falling. The TFR in Mexico, the second-largest population, by now may have dropped below 3; and a similar picture is apparent in many other countries. Only several Central American countries along with Bolivia and Paraguay still show TFRs of more than 4. Despite these declining rates of growth, the U.N. medium projection shows that the population of Latin America will increase by 70 percent, from a total of 477 million in 1995 to 810 million in 2050.

Asia

There is a great amount of demographic heterogeneity on the Asian continent, ranging from countries that have all but completed the fertility transition (such as South Korea, Thailand, and Sri Lanka) to countries that have yet to begin the transition (such as Saudi Arabia, Iraq, Afghanistan, and Pakistan). China and India alone constitute 62 percent of the region's total population.

As is well known, the government of China, after some years of ideological ambivalence, has pursued a militant population policy designed to reduce fertility and hold the population to 1.2 billion. Because this total was exceeded in 1996, the one-child policy will probably be pushed even more aggressively. The projected population of mainland China for the year 2050 is 1.5 billion, even with a reported TFR below replacement.

The situation in India is quite different. There the government continues to be concerned about population, but its earlier experience with the political fallout of the sterilization campaigns has cooled the ardor somewhat. The population in 1998 is estimated at 982 million and is expected to exceed China's by the middle of the new century. The fertility rate has fallen to 3.4; it varies significantly between the north and the south.

The remainder of Asia is collectively projected to grow to 2.4 billion, nearly doubling its current numbers. The TFR for all of Asia is 2.8, reflecting several decades of decline. If China is excluded from that calculation, the TFR is 3.3.

Africa

Population growth is most rapid in Africa, especially in sub-Saharan Africa, where fertility remains very high (close to six births per woman). The average annual rate of growth in sub-Saharan Africa is just below 3 percent. Fertility has been declining for some years in northern Africa so that the rate of growth has dropped close to 2 percent in that region. In sub-Saharan Africa, the fertility rate shows signs of decline in several countries, notably Kenya and countries in southern Africa.

The total population of the continent is expected to reach about 2 billion by the year 2050 according to the U.N. medium fertility assumptions, with the TFR declining to replacement by 2040. If fertility were to remain constant over this time period, the population of Africa would reach 4.5 billion. Such a number equals the recent population number of the entire world, and it indicates dramatically that fertility must decline rapidly. The negative rates of economic growth in many countries in the region combined with the high rates of population growth underscore the dreary prospect of per capita income growth.

Nigeria is the most populous country in Africa, with an estimated 1997 population of 122 million persons. The fertility rate is more than six births per woman and shows modest declines only in the southern part of the country. Ethiopia with a population of 59 million has an even higher TFR of 7.0. In contrast, Egypt with 65 million has experienced a sharp decline in fertility to 3.6 partly as a result of government-supported family planning programs.

Public Awareness

One of the fascinating aspects of this massive unprecedented world population growth is how little concern or even awareness it has generated. Most people in the world are probably unaware of the magnitude of the growth, perhaps because the phenomenon is quiet and undetectable from day to day. If articulated at all, concern is likely to be expressed through frustrations about traffic jams, the density of city populations, suburban sprawl, smaller shares of land passed across generations, or the lack of jobs for young people. Most adults are probably vaguely aware that there are more people around today than in their parents' time, but that seems to be the limit of knowledge and concern. The process is largely invisible in the short run.

In more informed circles, population growth is largely one of those abstract considerations that is intellectually troubling but elicits a "what can we do about it" response. Since so many people are better off than in the past, perhaps there is no reason to be concerned anyway. With few exceptions, it is not high on the political agenda of many governments. In the United States, political campaigns never mention the subject, despite the high growth rate in this country compared with that of the rest of the developed world. We even see the subject of immigration discussed in the press and by the U.S. Commission on Immigration Reform without any reference at all to its important contribution to population growth. Even in international forums, such as the recent U.N. international population conference in Cairo, the issue of population growth was subordinated to a variety of women's issues in reproductive health and related subjects. It became politically incorrect to talk about numbers even in a U.N. meeting of governments specifically focused on population.

The low profile of population on the agenda of contemporary public concerns is itself an interesting subject for reflection. Maybe the reason lies in the deadening nature of large numbers, their abstract quality, or the subject's controversial dimensions. Whatever the explanation, it is clear that the subject does not generate much concern. The most likely explanation, however, is that each new generation adapts to its population environment, seeing it as perfectly normal, much in the same way that it adjusts to climate or topography.

Chapter 4

Jane S. De Lung

Population Growth

The Complicating Element

One of the primary missions of governments is to create an environment that will maximize economic and social systems that feed, educate, employ, and provide for the well-being of all of their citizens. The rapid growth of the world's population during the past fifty years is testing the ability of national governments and the world to meet this obligation.

Since 1950, the world has more than doubled from 2.5 billion to 6 billion people and is projected to grow by another 50 percent by 2050—from 6 billion to 9 billion. The 1.5 percent annual growth rate of global population masks significant differences among the regions of the world, with more than 90 percent of the growth occurring in the developing world. Over the next fifty years, the population of Europe and the United States is projected to grow by less than 1 percent per year. Deaths are projected to exceed births in Europe. Africa, however, one of the poorest continents in the world, is projected to grow from 750 million people to 2 billion people, almost 3 percent annually. Asia, excluding China, and Latin America are growing at just under 2 percent a year.

The natural, social, and economic environments of the nations of the world are affected by growth, but the impact depends upon a variety of factors, including the degree of economic and political development of the country and the natural resources of the nation and surrounding regions. Economic development, food security, global climate change and biodiversity, water, national sovereignty, labor force participation, and governance are among the systems influenced by population growth. Population growth is not the cause of problems in these systems, but it magnifies existing problems by making solutions more difficult, affecting the ability of both the public and private sectors to respond to these issues. The negative effects of poverty, poor government decisions, poor economic choices, and ill-conceived development and environmental schemes are magnified. Unintended consequences are harder to escape in a world of 8, 10, or 12 billion people because solutions are more difficult to implement.

Economic Development

Although the impact of population growth on economic development has been debated among economists, recent research advances the theory that the rapid decline in family size in eastern Asia was in part responsible for the Asian development miracle.[1] This decline resulted in dramatic increases in savings rates, providing the capital for simultaneous investments in manufacturing and a literate and productive work force, which, in turn, resulted in intergenerational economic growth. This was a critical element in the success story of the Little Tigers throughout Asia. This decline in family size was achieved through dramatic increases in contraceptive use, including abortion and sterilization. In the past forty years, no country has achieved sustained economic development without a fertility rate below 2.5 births per woman.

For the United States, world economic development assumes a special significance because of increasing globalization of markets. International trade is a major cause of high-wage job generation, with salaries 13 percent above the national average; but those jobs depend upon the fact that people throughout the world must become sufficiently affluent to purchase products produced in the United States. Currently less than 15 percent of all U.S. production is sold overseas.[2]

Slower population growth minimizes the devastation of economic turmoil, a major problem in the poorest countries of the developing world. If gross national product (GNP) declines by 3 percent and population grows by 3 percent, there is a 9 percent decline in per capita income. This is a major problem throughout sub-Saharan Africa, where population growth remains stubbornly high.[3]

Jobs and Wages

The relationship between population growth and employment is not direct, in part because of the lag time between the births that generate the growth and the entry of that cohort into the labor force fifteen to twenty years later. Throughout the developing world in the last half of the twentieth century, improvements in child survival have resulted in an ever-growing labor force.

The children born in the 1970s and 1980s, when the population growth rates were above 2 percent, are now entering the labor force. Today there are no undeveloped or unexplored areas of the world for this surplus labor to emigrate, as there were during the population explosion that occurred in nineteenth-century Europe due to advances in health care. An ever-increasing technological world demands an educated mind rather than a strong back, so unskilled immigrants are no longer welcomed. Governments with fragile economies have to grapple with the consequences of a large number of unemployed youth who, with time on their hands, seek remedies from government for legitimate grievances.

The challenge of creating jobs is a daunting task, made more difficult for countries with fragile economies. Perhaps the greatest test the nations of the world will face in the twenty-first century is to generate enough jobs for this large generation of young people. Unemployment in many countries of the developing world is as high as 30 percent. The International Labor Organization (ILO) reports that nearly one-third of the 1 billion unemployed adults are below the age of 25.[4]

The world labor force is projected to grow by 730 million people over the next twenty years, more than 90 percent in the developing world.[5] The world economy must generate 40 million additional jobs each year to keep pace with work force growth. This does not include generating the 1 billion jobs necessary to eliminate the current unemployment or underemployment. The United States, which has the world's largest economy yet only 5 percent of the world's population, generated 2.5 million jobs each year over the past four years. This is only 5 percent of the jobs that must be created to keep up with the annual growth in the world's labor force.

Job generation in the developing world affects the United States, where a major concern is growing income polarization and loss of high-wage manufacturing jobs to the developing world, where wages are significantly lower. While labor competition has not affected high-skill, high-wage jobs, blue-collar and less skilled jobs have been exported overseas.

Economists generally agree that increases in the size of a labor force tend to bring about decreases in average wages relative to capital costs. It follows that the surplus of labor throughout the world results in declining wages, particularly for the less educated. Improvement in communication and transportation options enables employers to seek the lowest, most productive wages. As jobs leave the United States to seek lower wages, particularly as more members of the developing world become educated, there will be more pressure on U.S. wages. While more jobs may be generated over the long haul, social tensions and dislocation occur in the short run. Those who lose their jobs may not benefit from or be able to participate in the new global economy. Slowing population growth today will not generate jobs but ultimately will result in a slowing of the increase in the number of people seeking employment, which can help raise wages, particularly for the less skilled.

Global Climate Change

The U.N.'s Intergovernmental Panel on Climate Change recently came to the conclusion that human activity (broadly defined) has contributed to the changes in global climate that have been recorded over the past one hundred years. There has been an increase in the average temperature of the globe of 0.6 degrees Celsius; Siberia is now warmer than at any time since the Middle Ages.[6]

Carbon dioxide has been tied to the warming of the planet because it traps heat within the atmosphere. The evidence that atmospheric CO_2 is rising is clear. By 1994, emissions of CO_2 were already as much as 55 percent above the 1990 level in some industrial nations, while in many developing countries emissions were up by 10 percent, 20 percent, and even 40 percent, a result of rising affluence combined with increase in population growth. This rise occurred despite the agreement in 1992 at the U.N.'s Conference on Environment and Development to stabilize CO_2 emissions at the level of 1990.[7]

At present there is no clearcut evidence of the consequences of an increase in the global temperature. Nevertheless, evidence points to the increase in water levels, which is flooding many coastal areas throughout the world; an increase in the world's temperature, resulting in the northward movement of the world's grain belts; and changes in ecosystems throughout the world.

Since one-fifth of the world's population lives on coastal plains, this increase in water levels could result in a major disruption of lives and industrial investment. While the increased food production that would result from the movement of the grain belt toward the north might benefit the United States and Russia, agricultural development in many marginal countries might be severely damaged.

There is some indication that global warming's disruption of atmospheric and oceanic systems that regulate weather may increase extremes in weather. More intense storms and increased devastation from cyclones, hurricanes, snowstorms, or droughts would be the result.

This is clearly an instance in which a lower rate of population growth would lessen the impact of the consequences of economic development. Currently, the developed world, with 25 percent of the population, consumes 75 percent of the world's energy. The United States is responsible for 25 percent of all air pollution. This will change rapidly as the fast-growing Asian countries begin to modernize and increase their manufacturing capacity, the number of cars in their economy, and the number of refrigerators.

The developed world cannot ask the rest of the world to forgo the standard of living presently enjoyed by the west, regardless of the potential consequences to the environment. Only through technological transfer, which may be difficult and expensive because of patent rights, or a reduction in the rate of population growth can the consequences of Impact = Population × Affluence × Technology be reduced.[8]

Water

Fresh water may be the ultimate barrier to human development. Although water is a renewable resource based on the hydrological cycle, freshwater supplies are limited. The amount of water that can be used sustainably is not greater today than it was 2,000 years ago, when the world's population was fewer than 9 million people.[9] The cost of desalination is currently too labor and energy intensive to increase the world's supply of fresh water.[10]

One result of economic development is an increase in demand for water from manufacturing and irrigation-dependent agriculture. While underdeveloped countries may not strain the water supply, that same supply will be inadequate as countries develop economically. Currently 400 million people live in thirty-one countries in which water is stressed; by 2020, more than 1.2 billion people will live in water-stressed areas. In 2025, two-thirds of Africa's population will live in water-stressed areas.

Water demand has a potential for international conflict in areas of great interest to the United States. Seven countries with high population growth all share the Tigris-Euphrates watershed. For the developed world dependent upon oil from these countries, the potential for conflict over water could have serious economic consequences.

In northern Africa, nine states share the waters of the Nile Basin. And while sub-Saharan Africa has less impact on U.S. interests, there are forty African countries with low rainfall sharing six rivers. The governments of these countries are all fragile, increasing the potential for conflict. Reducing the rate of population growth will provide time to develop creative solutions for water scarcity and give governments more maneuvering room.[11]

Food

Food security is emerging as a major international concern. World Watch Institute announced that there are only forty-nine days of grain supply in reserve.[12] Part of the reason for concern is that as incomes increase in the world's largest countries, consumption moves up the food chain from vegetables and grains to meat. One result of this progression is that more grain is necessary to produce meat to feed a human population, which increases grain prices.

For example, there is an escalating demand for food in China as the economy expands and 14 million people are added each year. Increasingly grain is being used to feed hogs, cattle, and chicken as the Chinese move from a grain-based diet to a meat-based diet. In 1990, China produced 329 million tons of grain and consumed 335 million. Demand is projected to rise to 479 million tons in 2030, based only on population growth, not on economic growth. If grain production does not rise, there will be a challenge to world grain markets.[13]

While this may benefit the United States and Russia because of their strength in the grain market, many poorer countries may be driven out of the grain markets or be forced to divert much-needed capital into food purchases rather than investment.

The amount of land devoted to farming is now expanding only one-eighth as fast as the population, compounded by growing affluence. While remarkable advances over the past forty years have increased the yields of crops and the size of animals, there is no indication that future scientific breakthroughs will result in similar productivity gains. A slower rate of population growth will make the problem more manageable and the consequences of the failure to develop technological fixes less dire.

There is a similar growing shortage of fish, a major source of protein throughout the world. One billion people in Asia rely on fish for animal protein. Fish account for 16 percent of animal protein and 5.6 percent of total protein consumed worldwide. The world's rivers, bays, and oceans are fully fished. The catch has fallen in all but two of the world's fifteen major marine fisheries, and aquaculture has failed to keep up with world population growth since 1989.[14]

Rising prices resulting in a declining per capita consumption of fish creates more problems for low-income earners who have traditionally used fish as a source of protein. While the declining fish catch in the oceans will create new jobs in aquaculture, this will result in higher prices for fish.

International Migration

Migration, both internal and international, will be one of the major political issues of the next decade. Despite the United Nations' statement that a fundamental human right is the right to emigrate, there is no corresponding right to enter any state. Nations maintain the right to control their borders and to choose whom they will admit as residents and citizens.

Increasing migration is a sign of a strengthening economy. It occurs when people are no longer focused on providing the basics of life but have growing expectations and increased awareness of economic development beyond the borders of their community. Migration generally occurs from rural areas to the urban areas within a country and then from a poor country to a rich country. Internal migration can exacerbate tensions between urban and rural areas and frequently reflects disparities in investments by governments between urban and rural areas.

In 1995, 43 percent of the world lived in urban areas. Fueled by high rates of migration, urban areas are growing 2.5 times faster than rural areas. This is an unprecedented growth of 3.5 percent a year for urban areas compared to an overall 1.9 percent growth for the world. By 2000, 48 percent of the world's population will live in urban areas. There is little guidance from history to aid the world in coping with this magnitude of growth.

There are 125 million people, including refugees, living outside their country of birth, one-half in the developing world. From 1985 to 1995, the number of refugees increased from 8.6 to 19 million, the majority in Asia and Africa. Although Europe has a smaller percentage of the world's refugees, there are more refugees in Europe today than there were after World War II. Refugees tend to be overwhelmingly women and children who have been driven from their country by war, famine, or environmental devastation.

International migration is a source of major conflict between the developing and developed areas of the world. Most migrants are male, over age 15, and economically active as they seek employment opportunities that are not available in their countries. The United States and Canada annually take in more than 40 percent of all immigrants who are admitted to a foreign country. Since 1980, the main receiving countries in the more developed regions registered a net migration of approximately 1.4 million persons per year, two-thirds of whom came from developing countries. This trend, however, is changing. Doors are being closed, and more than 40 percent of developed countries now have policies to lower immigration that will sharply reduce the flow of human beings throughout the world.

Governance and Population Growth

The economies of scale of a certain population size promote the efficiency of infrastructure and education investments and the diversification of manufacturing and agricultural development. Nevertheless, high rates of population growth raise the stress on fragile democracies.

High rates of population growth can produce demands on governments that cannot be met, and governments with limited experience will have trouble grappling with the diverse opinions and demands that citizens place on them.

In developing countries, growing scarcities may contribute to civil violence, such as the violence in Somalia, Haiti, Rwanda, and Liberia, all countries with high birth rates. In the former Yugoslavia, there was a great difference in the population growth rates between the Serbs and the Croats. The high rates of growth were not the only cause of the explosions that occurred in these countries, but they were a contributing cause.

Homer Dixon hypothesizes that one frequent characteristic of societies vulnerable to internal conflict is that those countries have limited access to critical natural resources such as water, farmland, forests, and fisheries. In these countries, there is subdivision, depletion, and degradation of the land. As a result of population growth, there are more people to divide a limited amount of land. One only has to look at the highlands in Kenya to see the consequences of continued division of land in a rapidly growing population. Growth and consumption patterns interact to create tensions; and higher densities result in more demands, more needs, more conflicts, more regulations, and more irritations, which result in the demand for more government.

One of the conundrums of the impact of population growth and size on issues of the day is the way in which population is woven into the fabric of every concern. The impact of people on even one aspect cannot be easily discerned, and the threshold of population size can be reached before we are aware of the consequences.

Our lack of knowledge about the interaction of human beings and nature, the economy, or the ecosystems places us at risk of crossing natural thresholds. For example, we do not know the maximum number of cars allowed on a given size road before tempers increase, the cost of delays impedes economic development, or gridlock is reached. As a result, only gridlock tells us that the maximum has been reached, and even then there are few ways to limit the number of cars on the road.

A similar lack of knowledge pervades many other vital issues, including questions about how many houses can be built before the aquifer is stressed or how many people can fish the waters before the stocks are depleted. We do not know how many is too many, and the challenge is that "how many" differs for each issue and may differ in each country.

Notes

1. Allen C. Kelley and Robert N. Schmidt, "Aggregate Population and Economic Growth Correlations: The Role of the Components of Demographic Change," *Demography* 32 (September 1995): 543–56.
2. U.S. Commerce Department, "Preliminary Data Release: U.S. Jobs Supported by Exports of Goods and Services" (Washington, D.C.: U.S. Commerce Department,

June 1996).

3. Kelley and Schmidt, "Aggregate Population," 1995.

4. Paul Kennedy, "The Jobs Crisis is Worldwide, Ominous and Growing," *Worldwatch* 9 (1996): 6.

5. Ibid., 3.

6. L. Brown, C. Flavin, and H. Kane, *Vital Signs, 1996* (New York: Norton, 1996), 38.

7. Ibid., 28.

8. Paul Ehrlich and Anne Ehrlich, *The Stork and the Plow* (New York: Putnam, 1995).

9. Robert Engleman and Pamela LeRoy, *Sustaining Water: Population and the Future of Renewable Water Supplies* (Washington, D.C.: Population Action International, 1993).

10. Ibid., 9.

11. Population Resource Center, "Water Scarcity, Population Growth and Development" (Princeton, N.J.: Population Resource Center, 1994).

12. Brown, Flavin, and Kane, *Vital Signs,* 41.

13. L. Brown, C. Flavin, and L. Stache, *State of the World, 1996* (Washington, D.C.: Worldwatch Institute, 1996), 72.

14. Ibid., 91.

Part III
People on the Move
Immigration and Migration

Chapter 5

Thomas J. Espenshade

The Challenge of Illegal Immigration

As it has numerous times before in the twentieth century, illegal or undocumented immigration to the United States is confronting the country with a significant public policy challenge. This time, however, the dimensions of the problem are substantially greater. The size of the population outside the United States hoping to gain access to U.S. labor markets and social amenities is larger than ever before; U.S. employers, faced with increasing global competition, are keenly aware of the need to hold down labor costs of production; and the number of undocumented migrants already living in the United States is at an all-time high. One might nevertheless ask whether the situation constitutes a problem. Presumably the illegal immigrants who live and work in this country are better off than they would be elsewhere; otherwise, they would leave. Employers who hire illegal workers must believe that such hiring is sound business practice, or they would search for better alternatives.

Illegal immigration presents several challenges. First, it challenges national sovereignty and the rule of law. By definition, undocumented migrants have no legal right to be in the United States, and the federal government's failure to keep them out fosters disrespect for U.S. laws governing immigration and possibly other areas of public life as well. Second, the effects that immigrants have on the native-born population are more negative than they would be if all immigrants were legal; and the progress that immigrants make moving into the mainstream of American economic, social, and political life may be slower because a substantial portion of overall U.S. immigration is undocumented. Third, because Americans have more negative attitudes about illegal immigration than they do about legal immigration, the presence of large numbers of resident unauthorized migrants in the United States creates more negative perceptions about overall levels of U.S. immigration.

The federal government has undertaken numerous initiatives in the second half of the twentieth century to reduce the number of undocumented immigrants entering the country and to lower the numbers already here. Apart from a few efforts that succeeded simply because illegal immigrants were relabeled "legal," these attempts have been largely unsuccessful. In some cases the incentives they embodied were perverse: illegal immigration increased as did the amount of time that undocumented migrants spent in the United States. Recently individual states, frustrated by what they perceive as the federal government's ineffectiveness, have attempted to implement their own policies to discourage the continued presence of illegal immigrants. Courts have thrown up numerous roadblocks to these initiatives. Moreover, it is not clear that the underlying premise on which some of the state efforts are based—namely, that illegal immigrants are attracted to the United States because of the generous provisions of the welfare state—is factually correct.

Policies to deal with migration need to take several issues into consideration: first, the demographic dimensions of undocumented U.S. migration; second, the determinants and consequences of these migratory streams; third, public attitudes toward illegal immigration, how they may influence people's opinions about desirable levels of U.S. immigration in general, and how illegal immigration compares in saliency with other matters that concern the American public; fourth, efforts to control undocumented immigration, focusing particularly on the latest federal initiative—the 1996 Immigration Reform Act; and finally, findings with respect to questions such as whether more needs to be done to control unauthorized immigration and what enforcement policies could be undertaken to lower undocumented immigration below current levels.

Demographic Dimensions of Illegal Immigration

The estimated size of the U.S. population in 1996 was 264.3 million persons, of whom 24.6 million (or 9.3 percent) were born outside the United States.[1] The foreign-born proportion has been rising steadily from 4.8 percent in 1970, although it was routinely 13 to 15 percent between 1900 and 1920. In October 1996 the U.S. Immigration and Naturalization Service (INS) estimated that there were 5 million illegal immigrants living in the United States.[2] Roughly one in every five foreign-born individuals is here without authorization, and on a broader scale nearly 2 percent of the entire population of the United States is undocumented.

The undocumented migrant population is unevenly distributed by country of origin. An estimated 2.7 million, or 54 percent of the total, are from Mexico. Another 335,000 are estimated to come from El Salvador. Other leading countries include Guatemala (165,000), Canada (120,000), and Haiti (105,000). An estimated 40 percent of all Mexicans living in the United States are here illegally, and the proportion among Salvadorans approaches one-half. With the exception of Canada, most of the illegal immigrants in the United States have come from poorer countries that have low average levels of educational attainment.

As of October 1996, California leads the nation with an estimated 2 million illegal residents, or 40 percent of the total illegal resident population. Other major destinations for undocumented migrants include Texas (700,000) and New York (540,000). Twenty-five percent of California's foreign-born population is estimated to be illegal, and 6.3 percent of its total population is unauthorized. Undocumented migrants consist of two large groups, depending upon their mode of entry into the United States. According to new INS estimates, 59 percent of the total illegal population, or 2.9 million, entered the country without inspection or with false documents, whereas 41 percent, or 2.1 million, entered legally on a temporary basis and overstayed the terms of their visas. Between 80 and 85 percent of unauthorized migrants living in California and Texas entered without inspection (EWI). By contrast, more than 90 percent of New York's undocumented population consists of visa overstayers.

The undocumented population has been getting larger over time. In April 1980 its estimated size was between 2.5 and 3.5 million; it increased to between 3 and 5 million by June 1986; then it declined sharply as close to 3 million undocumented migrants received amnesty and legal permanent resident status as a result of the 1986 Immigration Reform and Control Act (IRCA).[3] The INS estimates that the net annual growth in the size of resident unauthorized population is currently 275,000, with Mexican migrants accounting for more than half of this annual increment.[4]

Data on the number of border patrol apprehensions of persons attempting to enter the United States illegally also convey the impression of accelerated growth in the undocumented alien population. These data are not a good proxy for the size of the gross undocumented flow, but they have proven to be a reasonably reliable indicator of changes in flow levels.[5] During the 1980s the number of apprehensions rose steadily from fewer than 1 million each year at the beginning of the decade to more than 1.75 million during 1986, prompting Congress to pass IRCA. Following the act's implementation, the number of apprehensions subsided to fewer than 1 million in 1989.[6] Since then, however, there has been a substantial turnaround, aided by the Mexican peso devaluation in December 1994, so that during 1996 the number of border patrol apprehensions was 1.55 million, or about 129,000 per month.[7]

Determinants and Consequences of Unauthorized Migration
Determinants

Several theories have been suggested to account for the rise in undocumented migration to the United States. These can be divided into explanations for the initiation of international population movements and those that sustain and expand these movements once they have begun.[8] The former category emphasizes economic approaches to international migration, including neoclassical theory, the new economics of migration, dual labor market theory, and world systems theory.

Neoclassical approaches view potential migrants as rational economic actors who are motivated to seek out the highest income levels for their services. Because rapid population growth in developing countries exerts downward pressure on wage levels, this theory predicts that most international migration will be from poorer third world countries to more advanced industrialized ones. The micro counterpart to this macro theory views individuals as the relevant decision makers who weigh the present value of expected future income streams at a variety of potential destinations against the income expected at the origin. Expected income depends upon anticipated wage levels, unemployment levels, and (in the case of undocumented migrants) the probability of going undetected in the host country.[9] The new economics of migration literature differs from neoclassical economic theory in two important respects. First, families or households, not individuals, are seen as the relevant decision-making units because the survival strategies of families include but often supersede those of individuals. Second, family behaviors are better understood in terms of efforts to minimize risk rather than to maximize income. One way for families in poorer countries to do this is to send target earners to other countries. Risks can be diversified provided labor market conditions in the receiving country are uncorrelated or negatively correlated with those in sending countries.[10]

Dual labor market theory highlights the role of industrial capitalists and their chronic demand for foreign workers.[11] Employers have a natural incentive to use capital to meet the most stable portions of demand for their products (because the cost of idle capital falls on the owners of capital) and to employ labor to satisfy the more unpredictable portions.[12] Workers in the secondary sectors of an economy often face job insecurity, low wages, and little chance of upward mobility. According to this theory, native workers have the greatest incentive and ability to find employment in the primary sectors of an economy, leaving employers to turn to foreign labor to meet the less stable portions of demand. World systems theory argues that owners of capital, in a never-ending search for lower labor costs and higher profits, will be driven to expand beyond the bounds of industrial economies and to penetrate smaller economies on the margin of the world economy. These entrepreneurial forays into poorer countries often result in dislocations to local indigenous labor, which in turn now has a greater incentive to search elsewhere for work—sometimes in urban areas of laborers' own countries, sometimes in other countries.[13]

Once migration has begun, several factors help to perpetuate it. One is the set of previous migrants, including family members and close kin, on whom current and prospective migrants can count for financial help and information about jobs and housing. A second is the role of institutions. In the United States these include the sanctuary movement supported by local churches, a black market in false documents, and the use of coyotes (hired smugglers) who help undocumented migrants avoid the INS authorities. Migrant networks and institutions supporting undocumented migrants pave the way for more migration by lowering both the costs and the risks associated with unauthorized migration, a process that Myrdal and Massey have called the cumulative causation of migration.[14]

Empirical research on the causes of undocumented Mexico-U.S. migration has identified demographic, economic, and policy variables as important determinants. The flow is accelerated by Mexican population growth among young adults, by an improvement in U.S. labor market conditions relative to those in Mexico, and by the planting and harvesting seasons in U.S. agriculture. These factors, together with a series of policy variables related to the passage and subsequent implementation of the 1986 IRCA, account for roughly 90 percent of the variation in illegal alien flows to the United States between 1977 and 1988.[15] Household data collected from sending communities in Mexico shed light on some of the individual determinants of illegal immigration. Probabilities of making an undocumented trip to the United States are highest for Mexican males between the ages of 15 and 29; are lowest prior to 1940 and then rise, showing no tendency to fall following the passage of IRCA; and are higher for rural residents than for urban dwellers.[16]

Consequences

The consequences of illegal immigration that usually are of greatest concern have to do with labor market and fiscal impact. Most research has concluded that undocumented workers are paid less than other workers are, and the explanations tend to revolve around reduced labor-market experience, fewer job-related skills, and outright employment discrimination.[17] For example, Borjas and Tienda found that, although illegal immigrants have high rates of labor force participation, they typically earn about 30 percent less than do their legal counterparts from the same region of the world.[18] Despite the fact that most undocumented migrants face downward economic mobility when they first enter the U.S. labor market, added labor market experience usually reverses this pattern. For instance, among a sample of Hispanic men who applied for amnesty under the 1986 IRCA, nearly two-thirds confronted downward occupational mobility immediately after migrating to the United States, but half then moved up the occupational ladder in the period leading up to legalization.[19] The acquisition of English-language ability was an important predictor of subsequent mobility.

A topic that many believe has even greater public policy significance is the potential impact of undocumented workers on the earnings and employment opportunities of native workers. One of the alleged adverse labor market implications of illegal immigrants is that they take jobs away from U.S. citizens or otherwise lower the wages and working conditions for U.S. workers. The weight of empirical evidence, however, provides little support for this belief. Numerous studies have found that the labor market effects of unauthorized immigrants are either small or nonexistent, and sometimes they are positive.[20] A reasonable interpretation of these findings is that undocumented workers typically hold jobs that other workers find unattractive. Only case studies of a single labor market or of specialized industries or occupations tend to find support for the prevailing popular belief. Martin, for instance, found evidence of job displacement in agriculture, food processing, and construction and argued that processes of network recruitment and subcontracting effectively excluded American citizens and legal residents from many workplaces.[21]

Issues surrounding the fiscal impact of illegal immigrants center on the question of whether these individuals receive more in publicly provided goods and services, such as education and health care, than they pay for with their taxes. One review found that the costs associated with immigrants fall most heavily on state and, especially, local governments. Only when the United States is considered as a whole and estimates are aggregated across federal, state, and local governmental levels is there almost no evidence to suggest that immigrants impose a net fiscal burden on other taxpayers.[22]

Research that has focused explicitly on illegal immigrants has tended to support these generalizations. The Internal Services Department of Los Angeles County estimated in 1992 that the net county fiscal burden associated with undocumented migrants was about $440 per person.[23] Estimates for San Diego County suggest that the net fiscal cost equals $730 per capita when both county and state data are included.[24] These estimates include the costs for items such as education, public health, criminal justice, and social service delivery. The estimated fiscal burden in San Diego County rises to $1,110 per capita when the additional expenses for transportation, employment training, development services, and police protection are included.[25] Because most unauthorized migrants have below-average incomes and above-average numbers of children, it is understandable that they pay less in taxes than other households and also receive more in public benefits (especially educational services). These are the two most important factors accounting for the fiscal burden that undocumented migrants impose on other taxpayers. Clark et al. prepared estimates of the public revenues and expenditures associated with illegal immigrants in the seven states in which such individuals were the most numerous.[26] They included in their estimates the costs of incarceration and public education and the revenues from state, sales, and local property taxes. Nevertheless, because the authors did not include all revenue and expenditure items, it is impossible to draw conclusions about the net fiscal effects of undocumented workers.

Public Opinion about Illegal Immigration

American public opinion about immigration in general and undocumented immigration in particular has changed substantially during the twentieth century. Negative views about the consequences of U.S. immigration gained prominence after 1875, when the first restrictionist immigration rules were introduced.[27] These attitudes persisted until after World War II, when the public adopted more liberal attitudes toward foreign immigration as evidenced by results of public opinion surveys showing smaller proportions of the population who felt that immigration should either be zero or at least less than the current level.[28] Beginning in the late 1970s, however, these more tolerant attitudes were replaced by a wave of neo-restrictionist sentiment.[29] For most of the period since 1980, more than half of American adults interviewed in a wide variety of opinion polls say they think that immigration to the United States should be reduced.[30]

Numerous reasons have been advanced for the rise in neo-restrictionism, including concerns over job security, a perception that immigrants have undesirable cultural traits, and simple racism stemming from the fact that the 1965 amendments to the Immigration and Nationality Act had the effect of admitting many more legal immigrants from Asia and Latin America than had previously been possible.[31]

But another part of the explanation is likely to be the rise in undocumented immigration over the same period. Referring to the prevailing situation in the early 1980s, Passel noted, "One important characteristic that distinguishes contemporary immigration from previous waves of immigration is the presence of significant numbers of undocumented, or illegal, immigrants."[32] Espenshade and Hempstead found that respondents to a 1993 *New York Times/CBS News* poll were more likely to believe that the volume of immigration to the United

States should be reduced if they also felt that most recent immigrants were in the country illegally.[33]

Espenshade and Belanger examined responses to more than three hundred opinion poll questions that had to do with U.S. immigration and that appeared on national surveys conducted by nine different polling organizations during the thirty-year period between 1965 and 1995.[34] Their results support two broad conclusions. First, Mexican migrants in particular, and migrants from the Latin America/Caribbean area more generally, rank at the bottom in terms of how immigrants from different parts of the world are viewed. Asian immigrants are viewed in somewhat more favorable terms, and European immigrants are prized above all others. In relation to Latin American migrants, Asian immigrants are viewed as less likely to use welfare and commit crimes and more likely to work hard and do well in school. Only in terms of being overly competitive are Asians viewed less favorably than Hispanic immigrants. Although the American public feels that the United States is admitting too many immigrants from both Latin America and Asian countries, they are more likely to feel this way about Hispanic migrants.

Second, illegal immigration is a significantly more important concern to Americans than legal immigration is. In a national poll taken in September 1993, 15 percent of respondents said that the presence of legal aliens in the United States concerned them a great deal, but half gave this response when the question was asked about illegal aliens. A separate survey conducted the same month asked how big a problem legal and illegal immigration were. Legal immigration was viewed as a major problem by 30 percent of respondents, whereas nearly two-thirds considered illegal immigration a major problem. These sentiments are partly fueled by misperceptions about the relative importance of illegal immigration. Nearly half of all participants to a June 1986 national poll believed that most recent U.S. immigrants were in the country illegally. By June 1993 the proportion had risen to two-thirds. By the best estimates, however, net illegal migration accounts for only 30 percent of net total yearly U.S. immigration.[35]

Americans feel that the federal government can and should be doing more to control undocumented migration into the country. By margins of roughly nine to one, they believe that stricter control of our borders and coastlines is a good idea. Support begins to waver, however, once specific measures are proposed. There is widespread support for initiatives that are likely to be least effective (such as increasing the size of the border patrol) and only minimal consensus behind measures that might be expected to cut rather deeply into illegal immigration (such as constructing a wall along the entire border with Mexico). Many of the latter initiatives are seen as too harsh and are not supported.[36]

Subsequent analyses of national-level public opinion surveys point to two additional conclusions.[37] First, American attitudes often appear ambivalent. Slight changes in question wording can frequently produce sharply different responses. Some words or phrases, in fact, appear to have acquired symbolically important meanings to many Americans, and invoking these phrases can lead to predictable responses. Four critical axes have been identified: children versus adults as populations targeted for cuts in social services, legal versus illegal immigrants as potentially affected groups, education and health benefits versus welfare benefits, and citizens versus noncitizens. In each of these paired comparisons, items or individuals included in the first group tend to receive preferential treatment in attitudinal surveys. For example, proposals to reduce immigration flows or benefits to immigrants typically receive less support when they are viewed as negatively affecting children, legal immigrants, education and health services, and citizens.

Second, after examining the relevance of public opinion to U.S. immigration policy, Pascual-Moran concluded that (1) foreign policy considerations usually exert greater influence, especially if public opinion is not tightly organized into powerful pressure groups; (2) the cumulative and steady expression of public opinion is more effective than sporadic outpourings; and (3) the state of the macroeconomy, especially as it relates to levels of unemployment, affects policymakers and public opinion on immigration matters.[38] Since the 1970s U.S. public opinion on immigration has not been well organized or effectively articulated. Some authors have even argued that the public's attitude on illegal immigration is both inconsistent and lacking in intensity.[39] The analysis by Espenshade and Belanger supports Harwood's conclusions.[40] Despite professing a strong concern with immigration issues, especially when illegal immigration is cued as a problem for survey respondents, the general public is substantially less worried about immigration than it is about crime, job opportunities, and family economic security. When respondents are asked open-ended questions about the most important problem facing the United States today, illegal immigration usually ranks with "too much sex on TV" and well behind "don't know."

Policy Attempts to Control Undocumented Immigration
Historical Perspectives

The United States did not have an undocumented migration problem before 1875. Until then anyone who managed to come to the United States was permitted to enter.[41] The country's first immigration exclusion law, which barred prostitutes and convicts from the United States, was passed in 1875. Specific concerns about illegal immigration were reflected in legislation in 1888 and 1891 that permitted the deportation first of workers and then of anyone who had entered the country illegally. Coincidentally, the Bureau of Immigration (the forerunner of today's INS) was also born in 1891.

Congress extended its control over immigration policy in the early part of the twentieth century by introducing the first quantitative restrictions on immigration. These national-origin quotas, combined with the outbreak of the Mexican Revolution in 1910, intensified illegal immigration. In response, Congress in 1924 created the U.S. border patrol as the enforcement arm of the INS, responsible for protecting 6,000 miles of land borders with Mexico and Canada against the entry of undocumented migrants.

Labor shortages during World War II and a desire to legalize and control the flow of Mexican agricultural workers led Congress in 1942 to inaugurate the Bracero guest-worker program. Through a series of bilateral agreements primarily involving Mexico, the United States admitted temporary agricultural workers to pick perishable crops in western states. But this program apparently did little to stem the flow of illegal farm workers. The number of illegal immigrants apprehended by the border patrol totaled 1.4 million during the 1940s in contrast to fewer than 150,000 during the 1930s. By the early 1950s growing pressure to revisit U.S. immigration policy led to passage of the 1952 Immigration and Nationality Act (INA). Among other things, the INA stipulated penalties for persons found guilty of harboring illegal aliens. Interestingly, employing undocumented aliens was not the same as harboring them. In an apparent concession to agricultural interests, the Texas proviso exempted employers of illegal aliens from the INA's fines and imprisonment.

By 1954 the unauthorized immigration situation was deemed so serious that the INS launched Operation Wetback during which more than 1 million undocumented Mexican migrants, together with some who were U.S. citizens, were caught and deported back to Mexico. These events had a momentary chilling effect on subsequent flows of undocumented migrants, but the movement across the border did not stop completely. The Texas proviso constituted at least one loophole, and in the 1960s apprehensions of illegal immigrants once again began to grow. The growth accelerated after Congress terminated the Bracero program in 1964 in the face of public opposition to conditions under which migrant workers were forced to live. When the program ended, Mexican migrants who had grown accustomed to working in the United States found that they no longer had a legal means of entry, but their motivation was so strong that many continued to arrive, albeit now illegally. In this way, the agricultural workers who came from Mexico following World War II, some legally as Braceros and others illegally, can be seen as the predecessors of today's undocumented migrants.

Throughout this and subsequent periods the number of apprehensions of illegal immigrants rose steadily, reaching a total of 8.3 million for the 1970s and continuing to rise throughout the 1980s to an all-time annual peak of 1.8 million in 1986. This was the same year that the U.S. Congress, determined once again to do something about illegal immigration, passed IRCA. The act's principal objectives were to reduce, if not eliminate, the flow of illegal immigrants into the United States and to lower the number of undocumented migrants who had already taken up residence in the country. To accomplish these goals, IRCA expanded resources for border enforcement, outlawed for the first time the willful hiring of undocumented workers, and extended amnesty to those undocumented migrants who had lived continuously in the United States since the beginning of 1982. IRCA's effect on the flow of undocumented migrants was measurable but temporary.[42] In the long run, IRCA succeeded in reducing the stock of unauthorized U.S. resident migrants through the amnesty program, which converted the status of nearly 3 million illegal immigrants to legal permanent residents.

The 1996 Immigration Reform Act

The 1997 Omnibus Consolidated Appropriations Act was signed into law by President Clinton in September 1996. This measure incorporates the Illegal Immigration Reform and Immigrant Responsibility Act of 1996 (the Immigration Reform Act, or IRA). IRA is a reinvigorated version of IRCA with technology from the 1990s added. In an effort to restrict illegal entry, the act directs the attorney general to increase the number of border patrol agents by 5,000 by the year 2001 and augment INS support personnel by 1,500 persons. IRA also strengthens the ability of the attorney general to request available fixed-wing aircraft, helicopters, night vision equipment, four-wheel-drive vehicles, and other resources from other agencies, and it provides funds to construct a triple fence along the Mexican border starting at the Pacific Ocean and extending fourteen miles inland. Civil and criminal penalties for illegal entry, assisting illegal entry, and using false documents are also stiffened. Finally, the act requires new border-crossing cards to carry biometric identifiers and orders the INS to develop an automated entry- and exit-control system for all aliens.

IRA takes new steps to accelerate the departure, either voluntarily or involuntarily, of undocumented migrants living in the U.S. interior. These include added staff to detect employment eligibility violations and visa overstayers, new identification documents that are harder to manufacture illegally, plans to record the fingerprints of all illegal or criminal aliens arrested in the United

States, and pilot programs using the latest technologies to increase employment eligibility verification in states with high numbers of illegal immigrants.

One way to evaluate the potential effectiveness of IRA is to compare its implications in 2001 (assuming full implementation of its enforcement provisions) with those for 1996 with respect to a range of INS performance indicators. Prior research has indicated that the monthly gross flow of undocumented migrants across the southern U.S. border typically ranges between 75,000 and 300,000.[43] Based on 1996 levels of border patrol officer hours and INS capital expenditures for unattended ground sensors, lighting, transportation vehicles, and the like, as the monthly flow of undocumented migrants rises from 75,000 (typical of November and December) to 300,000 (more common in the spring and early summer months) we may expect the following:

1. The probability of being apprehended at the border on any single attempt to enter clandestinely falls from 0.51 to 0.37.
2. The monthly number of total apprehensions increases from 77,800 to 177,500.
3. The average number of attempted border crossings needed to enter the United States declines from 2.0 to 1.6.

These apprehension probabilities are above historical averages from the 1980s, but not by much. The full funding of the IRA by 2001 suggests that apprehension probabilities will fluctuate between 0.66 and 0.77, the total number of monthly apprehensions will vary between 253,000 and 578,000, and the average number of border crossings needed to enter the United States will run between 2.9 to 4.4.[44]

Even a monthly flow of undocumented migrants at the low end of our range (75,000) would generate more than 3 million apprehensions per year. This number is twice the 1996 volume and would be unprecedented. It is not known how the border patrol would cope with this quantity of arrests and detentions, whether apprehension probabilities in the vicinity of 0.7 could be achieved and maintained, and whether having to try three or four times to cross the Mexico-U.S. border before entering successfully would discourage a large number of would-be undocumented migrants from attempting a trip to the border in the first place. Before this happens, however, migrants are likely to react to increased levels of INS enforcement in ways to offset the impacts of higher apprehension probabilities by, for example, shifting their customary routes of entry along the border to places that are less heavily patrolled or by crossing when and where there are larger numbers of undocumented migrants who are also attempting entry so that the apprehension probability for any one migrant is reduced. At the same time, the number of apprehensions by the year 2001 could reach more than 5 million annually if there were an average of 150,000 undocumented crossings each month. This number of apprehensions would quickly overwhelm the ability of the INS to process all the detainees, clog the system to the breaking point, and result in a decline in INS productivity. In short, there is a feedback operating on the process of apprehension that sets a limit to how high apprehension probabilities can go regardless of the level of INS enforcement.[45] Equally important, related research has indicated that increases in the probability of being apprehended along the border were not sufficiently high during the late 1970s and most of the 1980s to have an influence on the numbers of undocumented migrants who attempted a trip to the United States.[46]

In the past few years the INS has expanded its efforts to locate and deport unauthorized migrants who have been living and working in the United States. By 1996, the number of deportable aliens apprehended by the INS Investigations Unit reached 94,500. But when this number is matched with the estimated 5 million resident undocumented migrants in the country, the result suggests that the chances that an undocumented migrant will be apprehended after entering the United States are roughly 2 percent annually, not much greater than they were in 1993. The IRA includes provisions to help locate and remove illegal aliens from the United States. As I noted earlier, 1,200 additional INS employees are authorized to investigate employment eligibility and visa overstays. Despite representing a 150 percent growth over the eight hundred INS staff who were charged with these responsibilities in 1996, the absolute numbers are still small in relation to the size of the problem and the number of U.S. employers. So far, the extra money to hire the additional staff has not been appropriated by Congress.

Reductions in the net flow of undocumented migrants to the United States below the current estimate of approximately 275,000 per year would have several advantages. First, it would improve the functioning of U.S. immigration overall. To illustrate, New Jersey has been identified as a state in which immigration is proceeding relatively smoothly both in terms of the impact that immigrants have on the native population and in terms of how quickly immigrants are moving into the economic, social, and political mainstream.[47] Three keys to successful immigration to New Jersey have been identified: an immigrant population that is well educated, diverse with respect to sending countries, and essentially legal. Undocumented U.S. migrants typically lack these three essential characteristics. Consequently, reductions in illegal immigration could help to create a more favorable climate for the immigrants we accept legally.

Second, fewer undocumented migrants would ease the fiscal impact on the average native-born taxpayer because illegal immigrants tend to pay below-average levels of state and local taxes and use above-average levels of state and local services, especially educational services. Of course, undocumented migrants also contribute to the local economy by creating jobs; working for lower pay, which results in lower prices for some goods and services; and filling jobs that some natives may be unwilling to take. So it is not obvious what the total economic impact of fewer illegal immigrants would be. Finally, fewer illegal immigrants could generate greater respect for the rule of law, especially if the number were reduced through greater enforcement of new and existing laws rather than by a deterioration in the position of the U.S. economy relative to that in Mexico and in other countries that send unauthorized migrants.

My review of previous attempts to control illegal immigration raises serious questions about the efficacy of border enforcement. Selective interior enforcement has a better chance of working. The 1996 IRA takes small, tentative steps toward improved worksite enforcement. Many of these are in the experimental or design phase rather than capable of becoming fully operational anytime soon. Ultimately, two elements will be required for employer sanctions to be successful. First, employers must be able to distinguish simply and accurately between those who have a legal right to work in this country and those who do not. This is an area in which improved documents and innovative technologies can help. Second, employers must have an incentive not to hire unauthorized workers. Only more widespread and consistent employer oversight can make this happen. A policy that relies primarily on voluntary compliance, backed up by only token or symbolic enforcement measures, seems destined to be ineffective.

If the trial employment verification program, new identification cards, and the entry- and exit-tracking systems are all put into place, and if these programs become mandatory in every state, these steps will likely go much farther in reducing illegal immigration than will increased border enforcement. In the past, there has been great resistance among employers to stiffer employment eligibility criteria on the grounds that it imposes too great an administrative burden on businesses. As long as Congress is sympathetic to these concerns, it is unlikely that truly effective employment verification measures will be instituted. If the goal of lawmakers is to deter illegal migration, overcoming obstacles to worksite enforcement may be the single biggest hurdle.

Notes

Partial research support for this chapter was provided by a grant from the Andrew W.

Mellon Foundation.

1. Kristin A. Hansen and Carol S. Faber, "The Foreign-Born Population: 1996," *Current Population Reports,* P20–494 (Washington, D.C.: U.S. Bureau of the Census, March 1997).

2. U.S. Immigration and Naturalization Service (INS), "Estimates of the Unauthorized Immigrant Population Residing in the United States: October 1996," *Backgrounder* (Washington, D.C.: U.S. Office of Policy and Planning, 1997).

3. Michael Fix and Jeffrey S. Passel, *Immigration and Immigrants: Setting the Record Straight* (Washington, D.C.: Urban Institute, 1994).

4. INS, "Estimates of the Unauthorized Immigrant Population," 1997.

5. Thomas J. Espenshade, "Using INS Border Apprehension Data to Measure the Flow of Undocumented Migrants Crossing the U.S.-Mexico Frontier," *International Migration Review* 29 (Summer 1995): 545–65.

6. U.S. Immigration and Naturalization Service (INS), *Statistical Yearbook of the Immigration and Naturalization Service, 1995,* M–367 (Washington, D.C.: U.S. Government Printing Office, March 1997).

7. U.S. Office of Management and Budget, *Budget of the United States Government: Fiscal Year 1998* (Washington, D.C.: U.S. Government Printing Office, 1997), appendix.

8. Douglas S. Massey, Joaquín Arango, Graeme Hugo, Ali Kouaouci, Adela Pellegrino, and J. Edward Taylor, "Theories of International Migration: A Review and Appraisal," *Population and Development Review* 19 (September 1993): 431–66.

9. J. R. Harris and Michael P. Todaro, "Migration, Unemployment, and Development: A Two-Sector Analysis," *American Economic Review* 60, no. 1 (1970): 126–42; Michael P. Todaro and Lydia Maruszko, "Illegal Migration and U.S. Immigration Reform: A Conceptual Framework," *Population and Development Review* 13, no. 1 (1987): 101–14.

10. J. Edward Taylor, "Differential Migration, Networks, Information, and Risk," in *Research in Human Capital and Development,* vol. 4, *Migration, Human Capital, and Development,* ed. Oded Stark (Greenwich, Conn.: JAI, 1986), 147–71; Douglas S. Massey, "Social Structure, Household Strategies, and the Cumulative Causation of Migration," *Population Index* 56 (Spring 1990): 3–26.

11. Michael J. Piore, *Birds of Passage: Migrant Labor in Industrial Societies* (Cambridge: Cambridge University Press, 1979).

12. Massey et al., "Theories of International Migration."

13. Immanuel Wallerstein, *The Modern World System: Capitalist Agriculture and the Origins of the European World Economy in the Sixteenth Century* (New York: Academic Press, 1974); Douglas S. Massey, "International Migration and Economic Development in Comparative Perspective," *Population and Development Review* 14 (September 1988): 383–413.

14. Gunnar Myrdal, *Rich Lands and Poor* (New York: Harper and Row, 1957); Massey, "Social Structure."

15. Thomas J. Espenshade, "Undocumented Migration to the United States: Evidence from a Repeated Trials Model," in *Undocumented Migration to the United States: IRCA and the Experience of the 1980s,* ed. F. D. Bean, B. Edmonston, and J. Passel (Washington, D.C.: Urban Institute, 1990), 159–81.

16. Katharine M. Donato, Jorge Durand, and Douglas S. Massey, "Stemming the Tide? Assessing the Deterrent Effects of the Immigration Reform and Control Act," *Demography* 29, no. 2 (1992): 139–57.

17. For information on undocumented workers' wages, see Deborah A. Cobb-Clark, Clinton R. Shiells, and B. Lindsay Lowell, "Immigration Reform: The Effects of Employer Sanctions and Legalization on Wages," unpublished manuscript, Illinois State University, 1994.

18. George J. Bojas and Marta Tienda, "The Employment and Wages of Legalized Immigrants," *International Migration Review* 27 (Winter 1993): 712–47.

19. Sherrie A. Kossoudji and Deborah A. Cobb-Clark, "Finding Good Opportunities Within Undocumented Markets: U.S. Occupational Mobility for Latino Workers," unpublished manuscript, University of Michigan, 1993.

20. Frank D. Bean, Edward E. Telles, and B. Lindsay Lowell, "Undocumented Migration to the United States: Perceptions and Evidence," *Population and Development Review* 13 (December 1987): 671–90; Thomas Muller and Thomas J. Espenshade, *The Fourth Wave: California's Newest Immigrants* (Washington, D.C.: Urban Institute, 1985).

21. Philip L. Martin, "Illegal Immigration and the Colonization of the American Labor Market," CIS paper, no. 1 (Washington, D.C.: Center for Immigration Studies, 1986).

22. Eric S. Rothman and Thomas J. Espenshade, "Fiscal Impacts of Immigration to the United States," *Population Index* 58, no. 3 (1992): 381–415.

23. Manuel Moreno-Evans, "Impact of Undocumented Persons and Other Immigrants on Costs, Revenues and Services in Los Angeles County," report prepared for the Los Angeles County Board of Supervisors (Los Angeles: Los Angeles County, Internal Services Department, November 6, 1992).

24. Auditor General of California, "A Fiscal Impact Analysis of Undocumented Immigrants Residing in San Diego County," report C-126 (Sacramento: State of California, Office of the Auditor General, August 1992).

25. Louis M. Rea and Richard A. Parker, "Illegal Immigration in San Diego County: An Analysis of Costs and Revenues," report to the California State Senate's Special Committee on Border Issues, September 1993.

26. Rebecca L. Clark, Jeffrey S. Passel, Wendy N. Zimmermann, and Michael E. Fix, "Fiscal Impacts of Undocumented Aliens: Selected Estimates for Seven States," project report (Washington, D.C.: Urban Institute, September 1994).

27. Rita J. Simon, *Public Opinion and the Immigrant: Print Media Coverage, 1880–1980* (Lexington, Mass.: Heath/Lexington Books, 1985).

28. Milton D. Morris, *Immigration: The Beleaguered Bureaucracy* (Washington, D.C.: Brookings Institution, 1985).

29. Edwin Harwood, "American Public Opinion and U.S. Immigration Policy," in "Immigration and American Public Policy," ed. Rita J. Simon, *Annals of the American Academy of Political and Social Science* 487 (September 1986): 201–12.

30. Thomas J. Espenshade and Katherine Hempstead, "Contemporary American Attitudes Toward U.S. Immigration," *International Migration Review* 30 (Summer 1996): 535–70.

31. Thomas J. Espenshade, "Unauthorized Immigration to the United States," *Annual Review of Sociology* 21 (1995): 195–216.

32. Jeffrey S. Passel, "Undocumented Immigration," *Annals of the American Academy of Political and Social Science* 487 (September 1986): 181–200.

33. Espenshade and Hempstead, "Contemporary American Attitudes."

34. Thomas J. Espenshade and Maryann Belanger, "U.S. Public Perceptions and Reactions to Mexican Migration," in *At the Crossroads: Mexican Migration and U.S. Policy,* ed. Frank D. Bean, Rodolfo O. de la Garza, Bryan R. Roberts, and Sidney Weintraub (New York: Rowman and Littlefield, 1997), 227–61.

35. Fix and Passel, *Immigration and Immigrants.*

36. Espenshade and Belanger, "U.S. Public Perceptions and Reactions."

37. Thomas J. Espenshade and Maryann Belanger, "Immigration and Public Opinion," in *Crossings: Mexican Immigration in Interdisciplinary Perspectives,* ed. Marcelo M. Suarez-Orozco (Cambridge, Mass.: Harvard University Press, 1998), 365–403.

38. Vanessa Pascual-Moran, "The Shadow of Public Opinion and Various Interlocking Issues on U.S. Immigration Policy: 1965–1982," Ph.D. diss., Columbia University, 1987.

39. Harwood, "American Public Opinion."

40. Espenshade and Belanger, "Immigration and Public Opinion."

41. Thomas J. Espenshade, "Policy Influences on Undocumented Migration to the United States," *Proceedings of the American Philosophical Society* 136, no. 2 (1992): 188–207.

42. Espenshade, "Undocumented Migration to the United States."

43. Ibid.

44. Thomas J. Espenshade, Jessica L. Baraka, and Gregory A. Huber, "Implications of the 1996 Welfare and Immigration Reform Acts for U.S. Immigration," *Population and Development Review* 23 (December 1997):759–801.

45. Ibid.

46. Thomas J. Espenshade, "Does the Threat of Border Apprehension Deter Undocumented U.S. Immigration?" *Population and Development Review* 20 (December 1994): 871–92.

47. Thomas J. Espenshade, ed., *Keys to Successful Immigration: Implications of the New Jersey Experience* (Washington, D.C.: Urban Institute, 1997).

Chapter 6

William H. Frey

Immigration and Demographic Balkanization

Toward One America or Two?

Current debates about the future of immigrant assimilation or an emergent multiculturalism in America overlook an important new demographic divide across the nation's geography.[1] This divide may soon supplant other well-known demographic divides across space: rural versus urban, city versus suburb, and the sharp racial cleavages across neighborhoods. The new divide is separating those regions of the country that continue to serve as immigrant gateways from the rest of the national territory in which the new immigration makes much smaller or negligible contributions to growth. The former areas are becoming increasingly younger, multi-ethnic, and culturally diverse—a demographic profile that shows little signs of spilling over into the whiter or white-black regions of the country with older and more middle-class populations.

The new demographic division has been exacerbated over the past decade and shaped by the larger numbers and increased dominance of immigrants with Latin American and Asian origins. This change in national immigrant stock, which is likely to continue, has roots in the formal and informal movements between Latin America and the United States that have evolved over several decades as well as in a fundamental change in American immigration policy beginning in 1965.[2] Legislation in that year overturned national origin quotas that favored European immigrants, replacing it with a more open system that emphasizes migrant family reunification. While the nationwide impact of this immigration policy has been subject to much scholarly and official conjecture, most of the debate has focused on its economic impact rather than its effect on the nation's social and political geography.[3]

Current immigration along with ongoing domestic migration forces are creating a demographic balkanization that portends increasing divisions across broad regions of the country. If the new trends continue, today's multi-ethnic immigrant gateway regions may very well turn into individual melting pots in which different Hispanic, Asian, African American, Native American, and Anglo groups coexist and intermarry while still retaining some elements of their own national heritage. Although this ideal image of "one America" may be approximated in these regions, it will be less achievable nationally. In the rest of the country, which will look demographically quite distinct, different political agendas will come to the fore, and there will be a lower tolerance for the issues and concerns of ethnically more diverse populations in other regions.

There is important evidence that demonstrates a new kind of demographic divide. It identifies key immigrant gateway regions of the country and how they are becoming distinct in terms of their racial/ethnic makeup, dual economy character, uniquely different poverty profiles, age-dependency characteristics, and patterns of interracial marriage. Current trends, if projected into the future, will imply why the ideal of "one America" nationwide might be difficult to maintain through the next century.

Immigrant Concentrations

For most of America's history, immigrants flocked to cities, attracted by jobs and the existence of like nationality groups that formed enclaves providing both social and economic support. These same cities also attracted large numbers of domestic migrants from smaller communities and rural areas, again because of the availability of jobs that tended to concentrate in immigrant gateways such as New York, Chicago, and Boston.[4]

Today's immigrants also cluster in major gateway areas; two-thirds of immigrants arriving between 1985 and 1996 located in just 10 of the nation's 280 metropolitan areas. Although this may seem natural and consistent with the past, it is inconsistent with the fact that the nation's employment opportunities and population in general have become much more dispersed across all regions of the country. Today, only about a quarter of the native-born U.S. population resides in these ten gateway areas.

The continued concentration of immigrants to the United States is an important ingredient of the emerging demographic balkanization. Despite the dispersion of jobs to other parts of the country, immigrants continue to concentrate in metropolitan areas. Evidence suggests that much of this concentration is influenced by the strong family reunification provisions of the post-1965 immigration law, which reoriented dominant immigrant origins toward Latin American and Asian nations. Family reunification immigration tends to occur in chains that link family members and friends to common destinations.[5] This is especially the case for lower-skilled immigrants since they are more dependent on social capital and kinship ties for assistance in gaining entry to informal job networks that exist in port-of-entry areas.[6]

Research by Borjas and a National Academy Panel points up an increasing gap in the education attainment of immigrants as compared with the native population.[7] Although the education attainment of immigrants is bimodal, with higher percentages of Ph.D.s and high school dropouts than exist in the native population, it is the lower end of the educational distribution that dominates recent immigrant streams. Thirty-seven percent of working-aged immigrants over the 1985–1990 period had not completed a high school education compared with 15 percent of native-born working-aged residents.

The concentrating effects of Latin American and Asian origins as well as lower skill levels for recent immigrants are supported in a study by Liaw and Frey.[8] The study examines state destination patterns for 20- to 34–year-old U.S. immigrants and finds that 76 percent of all Hispanic immigrants locate in just five states (California, New York, Texas, Florida, Illinois) and that 59 percent of Asians are similarly concentrated (California, New York, Texas, New Jersey, Illinois). Within each group, those with less than high school educations are the most highly concentrated: 81 percent of such Hispanics, and 64 percent of such Asians are located in just five states. This clustering is consistent with findings from an earlier study of immigrant destinations in the 1970s.[9] Liaw and Frey's further statistical analyses show that the attraction of a state's racial composition (Hispanic, Asian, white, or black) as a proxy for the influence of friends and relatives is more important than the state's employment growth or income levels, and this is especially the case for immigrants with high school educations or less.

Not only do recent immigrants continue to select the same immediate destinations upon arrival, but they have a tendency to remain there. The strong influence of friends and relatives is particularly important for immigration from Latin America and Asia because of their native language commonalities. Massey makes the case that the new immigration differs from earlier periods in that it is more concentrated linguistically as well as geographically.[10] Other studies show that when Hispanic and Asian migration within the United States does occur, it is highly channelized and follows the same race and ethnic networks.[11] The lack of a broad dispersal of foreign-born ethnic groups via internal migration is borne out in specific studies based on the 1980 and 1990 censuses.[12] These studies show that continued concentration is especially evident among foreign-born residents with lower education levels. Moreover, a plethora of recent research suggests that the post-1965 immigrants are not spilling into other parts of the country at a very rapid pace. In fact, they remain largely confined to their original ports of entry.

Immigrant Magnets, Native Magnets

In contrast to the post-1965 immigrants, native-born Americans, especially whites and blacks, are far more footloose. That is, their economic and social circumstances do not as heavily constrain them to particular parts of the country, and their migration patterns are dictated much more strongly by the pushes and pulls of employment opportunities and, to some degree, by quality-of-life amenities.[13] While for most of this century domestic migrants have been urbanizing and moving to the same metropolitan destinations as immigrants, this trend has changed in the past decade.[14]

Has the change occurred because domestic migrants are fleeing immigrants? Not generally, although this appears to be true for a segment of the population. (See my discussion later in this chapter.) Rather, it is because the focus of opportunities has shifted away from the more expensive, densely populated coastal metropolises such as New York and Los Angeles to less dense, faster-growing, more entrepreneurial regions of the country. These include large metropolitan areas in the southern Atlantic region and in western states surrounding California. They also include smaller-sized places in nonmetropolitan territory within these fast-growing regions. Because the current magnets and growth for domestic migrants are, largely, different from the immigrant gateway metropolises, it is possible to classify most states and many large metropolitan areas by their dominant migration source.

Table 6.1 shows the states and metropolitan areas that can be classed as either "high immigration" areas or "high domestic migration" areas for the first part of the 1990s. What is striking is that these areas are fairly easy to classify because recent population change in each is dominated by one kind of migration or the other. Exceptions for the early 1990s are the states of Florida and Texas and the Dallas metropolitan area. Florida, for example, is classed as a high domestic migration state because its domestic migration substantially exceeds its immigration levels. Within Florida, however, one can distinguish between the high immigration Miami metro area and high domestic migration metros such as Tampa and Orlando (not shown).

An important point to be made is that the high immigration states and high immigration metros in the 1990–96 period were the same states and metropolitan areas that received most immigrants during the 1980s and, in most cases, earlier decades.[15] This is consistent with my previous discussion, indicating that post-1965 immigrants have continued to land and stay in these traditional port-of-entry regions. It is also important to emphasize that domestic

——— *Table 6.1* ———
Migration Classification of U.S. States and
Metro Areas, 1990–1996

	Contribution to 1990–96 Change	
State	*Immigration*	*Net domestic migration*
High immigration*		
California	1,571,491	(1,855,045)
New York	728,754	(1,225,379)
Texas	474,376	426,696
Illinois	232,612	(344,018)
New Jersey	225,023	(251,013)
Massachusetts	100,606	(200,884)
High domestic migration[†]		
Florida	363,389	714,224
Georgia	65,714	424,892
Arizona	73,629	380,719
North Carolina	35,598	354,236
Washington	84,208	296,331
Colorado	40,064	282,759
Nevada	27,986	280,655
Tennessee	17,298	265,136
Oregon	40,833	211,867

(continued)

migration for these immigrant magnet areas changes over time in accordance with the economic upturns and downturns of region-based economic growth. For example, although Texas shows a great deal of domestic migration gain in the 1990s, plummeting oil prices in the 1980s drove a sharp domestic out-migration from the state.[16] In contrast, California's economy was relatively robust in the late 1980s but experienced a sharp downswing in the early 1990s as a result of defense cutbacks, a severe recession, and various natural disasters.[17]

Because of these economic shifts, the list of high domestic migration states and metro areas for the 1990s looks somewhat different from the way it did in the 1980s. While strong southern Atlantic job-generating engines such as Atlanta, Raleigh, and Charlotte attracted substantial domestic migration throughout, western and Rocky Mountain region metros such as Las Vegas, Phoenix, Portland, and Denver have improved their rankings. This resurgence of the west involved, in some cases, overcoming extractive industry declines of the late 1980s and the rise of new growth industries associated with computers, telecommunications, and entertainment/recreation.[18] What these areas have

——— *Table 6.1* ———
Migration Classification of U.S. States and
Metro Areas, 1990–1996 (continued)

	Contribution to 1990–96 Change	
Metro Area	*Immigration*	*Net domestic migration*
High immigration		
Los Angeles CMSA	939,438	(1,305,950)
New York CMSA	930,783	(1,331,740)
San Francisco CMSA	311,092	(303,615)
Chicago CMSA	232,528	(28,455)
Miami CMSA	224,630	(339,470)
Washington D.C. CMSA	165,781	(121,675)
Houston CMSA	148,101	51,286
San Diego MSA	109,948	114,723
Boston NECMA	108,278	(182,216)
Dallas CMSA	95,249	(180,645)
High domestic migration		
Atlanta MSA	49,812	319,100
Las Vegas MSA	19,324	259,402
Phoenix MSA	43,581	239,096
Portland, Oregon CMSA	34,500	157,864
Denver CMSA	31,977	136,522
Seattle CMSA	16,163	111,837
Austin MSA	52,797	107,735
Raleigh MSA	9,139	105,490
Orlando MSA	23,889	93,376
Tampa MSA	8,952	91,423

SOURCE: Compiled from U.S. Census postcensal estimates.

* States with largest immigration (except Florida, where domestic migration substantially dominates).

† States with largest net domestic migration, substantially exceeding immigration.

in common is that they are growing, largely, from domestic migration; immigrants and most of the recent foreign-born population remain confined to the more traditional port-of-entry regions.

Another domestic redistribution trend that has come to the fore in the 1990s is the new rural renaissance, in which smaller communities and nonmetropolitan areas are experiencing a resurgence of growth.[19] Unlike the rural renaissance of the 1970s, which resulted largely from the downsizing of urban manufacturing jobs and an OPEC-induced demand for oil, the current trend appears to be more permanent and sparked by advances in telecommunications, giving rise to more diversified economies in smaller places that tend to be more amenity-laden and high-ranking on quality-of-life measures.[20] This trend, along with the regional and new metropolitan gains I have highlighted, is almost totally the product of domestic migration.

Race and Space

It is important to separate areas whose current demographic change is dominated by immigration rather than domestic migration because a host of demographic characteristics differs sharply between the two groups. Probably the most important of these attributes is the race-ethnic composition of the groups. During the 1980s and early 1990s, the combined legal immigration to the United States was largely comprised of persons of Latin American and Asian origin—estimated to be 85 percent.[21] When illegal immigration is included, Mexico becomes the dominant country of origin of all immigrants. While it is true that the particular mix of national origins differs with each port-of-entry area, the non-Hispanic white component of immigrants to all of these areas is relatively small.

In contrast, domestic migrant streams among states and metropolitan areas are largely white or white and black. So areas that gain population mostly from domestic migrants are not increasing their multi-ethnic populations to a great degree via the migration component.

The high immigration parts of the country will show the most accentuated change in their race-ethnic composition. Of course, particular areas will have different mixes of race and ethnic groups, but it is clear that immigration and domestic migration patterns for the past two decades have clustered Hispanics and Asians into distinct regions of the country.

Immigrant Flight

The picture painted in the previous sections is one in which immigrants continue to be attracted to the same metropolitan regions based on the strong pulls of family and friendship networks that provide entrée to economic opportunities, which for them appear to be out of reach elsewhere. At the same time, domestic migrants are much more footloose and tend to follow the money, or at least job opportunities, coupled with amenities that may be available in any part of the country. In short, these patterns are portrayed as somewhat independent. While this is true to a large extent, the fact that most high immigration metros are also losing domestic out-migrants gives rise to the theory that some immigrant flight may be occurring.

In fact, research focusing on migration patterns from the 1990 census and for the 1990s indicates that immigration does provide a push for a significant segment of domestic out-migrants—those with lower skills and lower incomes.[22] The accentuated out-migration of less-skilled native-born residents is a relatively unique phenomenon because domestic migration within the United States has typically selected from the *most* educated professional members of the work force, a group that tends to be well apprised of nationwide geographic shifts in employment opportunities.[23] Normally, areas that sustain economic downturns will see highest out-migration rates among their college graduates and white-collar workers. Similarly, areas that experience employment growth will see the greatest rates of in-migration among highly educated workers.[24]

The fact that this standard model is not the case for high immigration states and metropolitan areas is new and noteworthy. It is consistent with the view that the concentrated influx of lower-skilled immigrants to these areas leads to their displacement from jobs as the immigrants bid down wages below those that native-born workers would accept.[25] This kind of pattern exists in almost all high-immigration metropolitan areas.[26] Moreover, statistical analyses that take into account other migration-inducing factors show that immigration exerts an independent effect on the net out-migration of less-skilled residents.[27]

Frey and Liaw have conducted simulation analyses to investigate how increases or decreases in current immigration levels would affect domestic migration of low-skilled residents. They find that, in California, a 50 percent decrease in immigration would reverse the outward flow of low-skilled, working-aged residents.[28] The net out-migration of 59,000 persons with a high school education or less would become a gain of 44,000 under a reduced-immigration scenario. On the other hand, if immigration were doubled, net out-migration would increase to 249,000. Similar although somewhat less dramatic findings are shown in each of the high immigration states according to this analysis. The study also shows that within the low-skilled segments of these populations, the domestic out-migration responses to immigration are most heightened for persons in poverty, especially for poverty whites. This domestic migration response to immigration on the part of less-skilled and poorer native-born residents also appears irrespective of the overall economic conditions in the area.

There is another aspect to the immigrant-induced domestic out-migration from port-of-entry areas: the spillover effects as less-skilled and poorer residents are exported to other parts of the country. In the case of California, much of this spillover is directed to nearby states.[29] In fact, between 1985 and 1990, California exported a net of approximately 10,000 poverty migrants each to the states of Oregon, Washington, and Arizona and nearly 9,000 to Nevada. (During the same period, California actually gained 3,000 poverty migrants from the rest of the United States.) From the perspective of these destination states, California exports are a mixed blessing. For example, about a third of Nevada's overall migration gains comes from exchanges with California, but 62 percent of its poverty gains comes from this exchange. Still, the domestic out-migration from California, Texas, New York, and other high immigration states is serving as a boon to growth, new jobs, and the repopulation of some areas that have been stagnant. Recent evidence suggests that a good part of the emerging rural renaissance is being fueled by working-aged, lower-skilled, lower-middle-income domestic out-migrants from the high immigration regions.[30]

The major reason that most observers have given to explain this low-skilled demographic displacement in high immigration regions has been tied to the economic competition that recent immigrants represent.[31] Still, job displacement is only one of several possible ingredients. Another impetus for moving may lie with a common public perception among residents in these states that immigrants are imposing an array of social and economic costs (including higher crime rates, watered-down services, and increased taxes) that are especially absorbed by poorer and middle-class residents. The appeal of California's Proposition 187, which restricts illegal immigrants' claim on state services, and anti-immigrant sentiments expressed in public opinion data suggest that there are broader concerns than simply job displacement.[32]

Finally, racial and ethnic prejudice may also be operating for low-skilled domestic out-migration from the increasingly multi-ethnic regions. Prejudice against people from unfamiliar backgrounds has long been known to affect local moves across neighborhoods and between cities and suburbs—as when earlier immigrant waves entered port-of-entry cities and, in the 1950s and 1960s, as middle-class whites located away from black neighborhoods and central cities.[33] Since an increased multi-ethnic presence now encompasses entire metropolitan areas in today's port-of-entry regions, lower- and middle-class native-born residents who cannot afford to live in gated communities are engaging in a new form of white flight.[34]

Consequences of Demographic Balkanization

The significance of this newly emerging demographic division across regions lies with the consequences it holds for the high immigration regions themselves and for new social and demographic cleavages that will develop across the nation.

Dual-Economy Gateways

One consequence of the focused immigration of a relatively large, unskilled population is the emergence of "hourglass economies" within major port-of-entry areas. That is, not only do the new immigrants take existing low-skilled service sector and informal economy jobs, but they have the effect of creating more of these jobs as employers respond to the existence of large pools of relatively low-paid labor. By the same token, complementary effects are generated because the kinds of services and occupations taken by the new immigrants tend to benefit industries and administrative activities that tend to attract professionals (mostly native born). The emergence of world cities that serve as corporate headquarters in the global marketplace while also attracting unskilled immigrants has been written about elsewhere.[35]

What is not as well appreciated is the ensuing race-class bifurcation that will emerge in these areas as middle- and lower-income domestic migrants elect to locate outside of these areas and the jobs at the lower rungs of the economic ladder become increasingly dominated by foreign-born and new ethnic minorities. In the past, less-skilled immigrants were able to bootstrap their way up the ladder by taking advantage of ethnic niches in the local economy in order to gain wealth and further advancement.[36] For some groups and highly motivated individuals, this process can still occur.[37] But the obstacles to such gains are likely to become more insurmountable for large numbers of unskilled residents residing in dual-economy metropolitan areas with financially strapped public education systems. In an economy in which education beyond high school is the key toward advancement, the prospects for breaking down this emerging race-class bifurcation in our large gateway regions is not promising.

Poverty Displacement

My earlier discussion of demographic displacement within high immigration regions indicated that the most affected groups were residents with low skills and low incomes. The implication that this holds for addressing the needs of poverty populations both in high immigration and low immigration regions is worthy of some discussion. State officials in high immigration regions are well aware that immigration contributes substantially to the size of the poverty population in their states, and the implications for federal welfare programs have been the subject of much debate.[38] Much less appreciated is how the demographics of the poverty populations in these high immigration regions will differ from other parts of the country as a result of both new immigrants in poverty who are arriving *and* poor domestic residents who are departing.

One group that is especially worthy of focus is the child poverty population. This population will continue to increase nationally, both because of the rise in the number of children and because of high rates of child poverty.[39] The geographic mobility dynamics of families with poor children are also important because they affect the sizes and demographic attributes of poverty children in different states.

There is a broad difference that is emerging between the child poverty populations in high immigration versus other parts of the country, according to 1996 Current Population Survey data. Fewer than half (47 percent) of poor children living within the ten high immigration metropolitan areas were native born by native parentage compared with four out of five poor children in the rest of the country. Almost half of the former poor children (46 percent) were Hispanic compared with 20 percent in the rest of the country. In Los Angeles, more than half of the children living in poverty (51 percent) lived in married-couple families compared with only 22 percent in large metropolitan areas that were not one of the ten immigrant magnets. These distinct demographics emerging with the child poverty populations in high immigration regions of the country hold implications for the kinds of schooling and social services required to serve these populations in contrast to the child poverty populations in other parts of the country. In the former areas, greater emphasis might be given to assimilation and bilingual education in the schools. In the latter areas, special problems associated with female-headed families who are gaining access to schooling and jobs might be emphasized.

Population Aging: The Racial Generation Gap

One demographic attribute of the immigrant population that makes an immediate impact on its destination area is its younger age distribution. The lion's share of immigrants, at their time of arrival, is comprised of young adults and their children. In noting these patterns, commentators and scholars have suggested that continued immigration may lessen the impending age-dependency burden after the baby boomers retire in the year 2012, when a "nation of Floridas" is expected to emerge.[40] What would seem to be a sensible solution to the age-dependency crisis from a national perspective fails to consider two items. First, immigration's impact will be much more dominant in the high immigration regions, both in its magnitude and in how it affects the racial-ethnic composition of the future working-aged population. Second, ethnic minorities, which make up large shares of the new immigrant waves, may be less concerned about elderly dependency than they are about child dependency in light of their own demographic patterns.

It appears likely that, for the foreseeable future, Hispanics, Asians, and blacks will be more concerned about taking care of their children than their elderly. How willingly will working-aged Hispanics, Asians, and even African Americans contribute local, state, and federal funds to support the elderly population's welfare concerns? The sharp racial-ethnic demographic distinctions that are emerging in the working-aged populations *and* the voting-aged populations hold important implications for a variety of national issues that will take on strong region-based constituencies.

New Marital States

Discussions of immigrant assimilation adhering to the melting pot metaphor often point to the increased tendency of groups to intermarry as a signal that assimilation is taking place.[41] It is not surprising, therefore, that commentators and academics are watching the extent to which the new immigrant minorities (Hispanics and Asians) have begun to intermarry with members of the largely native-born white and black population. Although mixed-race marriages for these groups are still quite rare, signs that they are increasing are taken as evidence that these groups are becoming part of the American melting pot.[42] This "blending of America" has been characterized as a quiet demographic counterrevolution.[43] Recently, the National Academy Panel on Immigration observed that the boundaries between such groups may blur in the future and that the core American culture has absorbed a number of groups that were defined as racially different in the past and may do so again in the future.[44]

Observations that some mixed-race marriages are occurring among Hispanics and Asians and that this may portend their further assimilation do not necessarily conflict with my view that distinctly different immigrant, foreign-born–dominant regions will develop apart from other areas of the country. Indeed, one might expect high levels of intermarriage between these and other groups *within* the high immigration regions of the country. Here, groups will be more likely to interact in school and workplaces and become more appreciative of their different backgrounds and life-styles. The kind of melting pot that one identifies with early twentieth-century immigrants in urban areas such as New York or Chicago may well replicate itself in much of California, Texas, and southern Florida. The question remains as to whether such intermarriage patterns will be both prevalent and acceptable in those parts of the country that remain largely white or white and black.

Clearly, the phenomenon of mixed-race marriages involving new immigrant groups is just beginning to emerge and undoubtedly will be the subject of considerable future research. The evidence that exists now makes plain that the vast majority of these marriages occur in California, the nation's premiere immigrant state, and that the remaining marriages are highly clustered in other immigrant magnets.

Toward One America or Two?

The incorporation of the nation's new immigrant ethnic minorities into a single "one America" melting pot will be forestalled by the continued clustering of immigrant groups within broad regions of the country that are no longer attracting large numbers of domestic migrants and longer-term residents. The populations of these high immigration regions will become increasingly multicultural, younger, and bifurcated in their race and class structures. In contrast, regions that are gaining population largely from domestic migration and those with stagnating populations will become far less multicultural in their demographic compositions and will differ in other social, demographic, and political dimensions as well.

While immigrant minorities have historically clustered in individual neighborhoods or inner cities, the new demographic balkanization is significant because of its geographic scope. The emergence of entire metropolitan areas or labor market regions that are distinct from the rest of the country in their race-ethnicity, age, and class profiles represents a new dimension and one that is not likely to change in light of the nation's ongoing immigration and settlement patterns.

While this new demographic balkanization serves as a *regional* divide, my use of this term is not meant to imply that increased divisions will occur between different race and ethnic groups. In fact, the concentration of large numbers of new race and ethnic minorities along with whites and blacks within the high immigration regions should lead to a greater incorporation of these groups into new American melting pots that will emerge distinctly within these regions. The nature of this incorporation involving a large number of groups as diverse as Mexicans, Central Americans, Koreans, Indians, Vietnamese, and others may take a form different from the familiar patterns of the Irish, Italians, Poles, and Jews at the turn of the twentieth century. The higher levels of residential segregation for these new groups within port-of-entry regions, their entrenchment in well-defined occupational niches, and, for some groups, extremely low levels of political clout will make their road to full economic and political incorporation long and arduous.[45] Still, the increasing levels of intermarriage that appear to be occurring within high immigration regions and evidence that second-generation children are more likely to speak English well and identify as hyphenated Americans suggest a potential for acculturation and mobility beyond segmented residence and workplace environments.[46] The increased interaction between these groups and longer-term resident whites, blacks, and other racial-ethnic minorities will bring about conflict but also will create new melting pots that will exist *only* within these broader high immigration regions—and the mix will take different forms in each region.

In contrast, the rest of America will include booming economic growth engines that attract large numbers of domestic white and black migrants such as those that now exist in much of the southern Atlantic region and in the Rocky Mountain states as well as in other parts of the country that are experiencing stagnating growth. The demographic profiles of both will be largely older, whiter, and more middle class than the more vibrant, younger, multiethnic regions I have described. New region-based political constituencies will emerge that place greater emphasis on middle-class tax breaks and the solvency of the Social Security system and that cast a wary eye on too much federal government regulation. Already these regions are becoming more conservative and more likely to vote Republican.[47] Their residents will become far less energized over issues such as preserving affirmative action laws, extending the federal safety net to new foreign-born generations, or maintaining bilingual education in the schools. Taking cognizance of this new geography, marketers will need to pay just as much attention to metropolitan and regional demographics as they do to local zip codes when targeting advertisements to consumers. More important, the new sensitivity to racial-ethnic blending that will begin to percolate in the high immigration regions will spill over only marginally, if at all, into this other America.

Some readers may view this new demographic balkanization with trepidation since it does not conform to the single "one America" ideal that we have held for much of the nation's history. They may wish to propose solutions to this "problem." Yet the most obvious solutions would take draconian measures that are almost impossible to execute in the realpolitik of today's America.

One such measure would be to drastically alter immigration to the United States in such a way that it would reduce the large number of less educated migrants who are most prone to become anchored in the low-skilled service and manufacturing economies of high immigration regions. This would mean either reducing the overall number of immigrants, changing the countries of origin of immigrants, or altering the preference system in such a way that low-skilled immigrants do not form a large segment of the immigrant pool each year. Although there may be some sentiment toward lowering the overall immigration levels, it is not likely that there will be a constituency willing to retreat from the more open country-of-origin provisions instituted in 1965. Likewise, there is little support to drastically alter the family reunification provisions of current immigration law that account for at least two-thirds of legal immigrants and has been purported to contribute to the declining relative education attainment of the overall immigrant flow.[48] Finally, illegal immigration has contributed significantly to the flow of lower-skilled immigrants, especially in California. Several legal mechanisms, most notably the 1986 Immigration Reform and Control Act (IRCA), have attempted to curtail illegal immigrants through employer sanctions, increased border enforcement, and other means. Nevertheless, the lack of strong enforcement and the availability of only modest government resources have rendered these measures relatively ineffective.

The simple fact seems to be that there are enough interest groups and constituencies—employers, consumers, and co-ethnics—who are benefiting from existing inflows of low-skilled immigration so as to curtail measures that would substantially alter the provisions of legal immigration or drastically reduce illegal immigration.[49] Local political interests are also weighed. California governor Pete Wilson took an anti-immigrant stance for his largely white, native-born constituency in the mid-1990s; at the same time New York City mayor Rudolph Giuliani took a pro-immigrant stance to receive support from his increasingly large foreign-born constituency. Beyond what may or may not be accomplished through changes in immigration laws or enforcement, an extended network of immigration is already established between selected origin and destination communities in Mexico and the United States, having evolved over decades with strong economic and social roots.[50] These flows are likely to expand over time rather than diminish in response to any token changes in U.S. immigration policy.

The second set of policy measures that would need to be enacted to curtail the demographic balkanization patterns now in place would involve Herculean federal efforts to prepare new waves of immigrant children for mainstream jobs that are available outside of their established ethnic enclaves and employment niches. Unlike large earlier immigrant waves, new immigrants and their children face a two-tiered economy in which a college education is essential for upward mobility. Yet the economies of immigrant regions are highly bifurcated. As has been shown, foreign-born workers fill well over half of all service and blue-collar jobs in the Los Angeles metropolitan region but hold fewer than one-fifth of professional or managerial positions. This picture will only change for future generations if drastic measures are introduced in local high schools and community colleges to prepare the children of the next generation to move not only upward but outward from the unique port-of-entry labor markets that surround them. Yet here again, the current political climate favors devolution of federal and even state responsibilities for education and social services to the local communities. Because these communities bear the greatest financial burdens and receive precious little of the financial benefits of new immigrant waves, measures to improve their upward mobility are not likely to be put into place any time soon.

It appears inevitable that the demographic balkanization scenario portrayed here will continue and become more entrenched over the decades ahead. The new high immigration zones will be distinct and constitute the twenty-first century version of America's melting pots—ensconced largely in California, Texas, and the southwest; southern Florida; the upper eastern seaboard; and Chicago. The cultural and demographic tapestry evolving in this America will differ sharply from the older, more middle-class, and whiter—indeed, more suburban—America that exists elsewhere. The distinctly different social geographies of these two Americas are not widely appreciated by commentators and scholars. Both the recommendations of a bipartisan Commission on Immigration Reform and an influential book argue that the Americanization of new immigrants should get high priority, emphasizing greater efforts toward immigrant naturalization, English literacy, and the primacy of individual over group rights so as to achieve a common civic culture.[51] Yet these pronouncements make no mention of the fact that much of mainstream America represents another America that lies well beyond the settlements of most new immigrants. To achieve these laudable goals and to understand the nation's evolving demographic realities of the twenty-first century, scholars and policymakers will need to reconcile how the two Americas portrayed in this chapter will relate to each other socially, economically, and politically.

Notes

1. Georgie Ann Geyer, *Americans No More* (New York: Atlantic Monthly Press, 1996); Nathan Glazer, *We Are All Multiculturalists Now* (Cambridge, Mass.: Harvard University Press, 1997); Peter D. Salins, *Assimilation American Style* (New York: Basic Books, 1997).
2. David Heer, *Immigration in America's Future* (Boulder, Colo.: Westview, 1996).
3. Julian Simon, *The Economic Consequences of Immigration* (Cambridge, Mass.: Blackwell, 1989); George J. Borjas, "The Economics of Immigration," *Journal of Economic Literature* 32 (December 1994): 1667–1717; U.S. Commission on Immigration Reform, *Becoming an American: Immigration and Immigrant Policy* (Washington, D.C.: U.S. Commission on Immigration Reform, 1997); James P. Smith and Barry Edmonston, *The New Americans: Economic, Demographic, and Fiscal Effects of Immigration* (Washington, D.C.: National Academy Press, 1997).
4. Joseph P. Ferrie, "Immigrants and the Natives: Comparative Economic Performance in the U.S., 1850–60 and 1965–80," working paper series on historical factors in long-run growth, no. 93 (Cambridge, Mass.: National Bureau of Economic Research, 1996).
5. Douglas S. Massey, Joaquin Arango, Graeme Hugo, Ali Kouaouci, Adela Pellegrino, and J. Edward Taylor, "An Evaluation of International Migration Theory: The North American Case," *Population and Development Review* 20, no. 4 (1994): 699–751; Silvia Pedraza and Ruben G. Rumbaut, *Origins and Destinies: Immigration, Race and Ethnicity in America* (Belmont, Calif.: Wadsworth, 1996).
6. Alejandro Portes, "Economic Sociology and the Sociology of Immigration: A Conceptual Overview," in *The Economic Sociology of Immigration,* ed. Alejandro Portes (New York: Russell Sage Foundation, 1995), 1–41.
7. Borjas, "The Economics of Immigration"; Smith and Edmonston, *The New Americans.*
8. Kao-Lee Liaw and William H. Frey, "Destination Choices of 1985–90 Young Immigrants to the United States: The Importance of Race, Education Attainment, and Labor Force," *International Journal of Population Geography* 4(1998): 49–61.

9. Ann P. Bartel, "Where Do the New Immigrants Live?" *Journal of Labor Economics* 7, no. 4 (1989): 371–91.

10. Douglas S. Massey, "The New Immigration and Ethnicity in the United States," *Population and Development Review* 21, no. 3 (1995): 621–52.

11. Frank D. Bean and Marta Tienda, *The Hispanic Population of the United States* (New York: Russell Sage Foundation, 1987); Kevin E. McHugh, "Hispanic Migration and Population Redistribution in the United States," *Professional Geographer* 41, no. 4 (1989): 429–39; Pedraza and Rumbaut, *Origins and Destinies.*

12. Ann P. Bartel and Marianne J. Koch, "Internal Migration of U.S. Immigrants," in *Immigration Trade and Labor Market,* ed. J. M. Abowd and R. B. Freeman (Chicago: University of Chicago Press, 1991), 121–34; June Marie Nogle, "Internal Migration Patterns for U.S. Foreign-Born, 1985–1990," *International Journal of Population Geography* 3 (1997): 1–13.

13. Larry Long, *Migration and Residential Mobility in the United States* (New York: Russell Sage Foundation, 1988); Patricia Gober, "Americans on the Move," *Population Bulletin* 48 (1993): 2–40.

14. William H. Frey, "Immigrant and Native Migrant Magnets," *American Demographics* (November 1996). The terms *domestic migration* and *internal migration* are used interchangeably to note migration with the United States as contrasted with immigration. Net domestic migration (or net internal migration) refers to a residual of in-migrants to an area from another part of the United States minus out-migrants from an area to another part of the United States. Most domestic (or internal) migrants were born in the United States, although, due to data limitations, these statistics include a small number of foreign-born domestic migrants. Separate analyses (not shown) indicate that the general patterns for all domestic migrants reflect those for native-born domestic migrants, and I interpret the former patterns as if they pertain to the latter.

15. William H. Frey, "Immigration, Domestic Migration and Demographic Balkanization in America: New Evidence for the 1990's," *Population and Development Review* 22, no. 4 (1996): 741–63.

16. Diane Jennings, "Job Seekers Making Tracks to Texas Again," *Dallas Morning News,* September 5, 1994, p. 1.

17. Stuart A. Gabriel, Joe P. Mattey, and William L. Wascher, "The Demise of California Reconsidered: Interstate Migration over the Economic Cycle," *Economic Review* [Federal Reserve Bank of California] 2 (1995): 30–45.

18. Kenneth Labich, "The Geography of an Emerging America," *Survey of Regional Literature* 28 (June–September 1994): 23–28.

19. Glenn V. Fuguitt and Calvin L. Beale, "Recent Trends in Nonmetropolitan Migration: Toward a New Turnaround?" CDE working paper, no. 95–07 (Madison: University of Wisconsin, Center for Demography and Ecology, 1995).

20. William H. Frey, "The New Geography of Population Shifts: Trends Toward Balkanization," in *The State of the Union,* vol. 2, *Social Trends,* ed. Reynolds Farley (New York: Russell Sage Foundation, 1995), 271–336; William H. Frey and Kao-Lee Liaw, "The Impact of Recent Immigration on Population Redistribution within the United States," in *The Immigration Debate,* ed. James P. Smith and Barry Edmonston (Washington, D.C.: National Academy Press, 1998), 388–448; William H. Frey and Kenneth M. Johnson, "Concentrated Immigration, Restructuring, and the Selective

Deconcentration of the U.S. Population," in *Migration into Rural Areas: Theories and Issues,* ed. Paul J. Boyle and Keith F. Halfacre (London: Wiley, forthcoming).

21. Philip Martin and Elizabeth Midgley, "Immigration to the United States: Journey to an Uncertain Destination," *Population Bulletin* 49, no. 2 (1994): 1–47.

22. William H. Frey, "The New White Flight," *American Demographics* (April 1994): 40–48; William H. Frey, "Immigration and Internal Migration 'Flight' from US Metropolitan Areas: Toward a New Demographic Balkanization," *Urban Studies* 32, nos. 4 and 5 (1995): 733–57; William H. Frey, Kao-Lee Liaw, Yu Xie, and Marcia J. Carlson, "Interstate Migration of the US Poverty Population: Immigration 'Pushes' and Welfare Magnet 'Pulls,'" *Population and Environment* 17 (July 1996): 491–538; Frey and Liaw, "The Impact of Recent Immigration"; Kao-Lee Law and William H. Frey, "Interstate Migration of Young American Adults in 1985–90: An Explanation Using a Nested Logit Model," *Geographical Systems* 3 (1996): 301–31.

23. Long, *Migration and Residential Mobility.*

24. William H. Frey, "The Changing Impact of White Migration on the Population Compositions of Origin and Destination Metropolitan Areas," *Demography* 16, no. 2 (1979): 219–38.

25. Vernon Briggs, Jr., *Mass Immigration and the National Labor Market* (Armonk, N.Y.: Sharp, 1992); George J. Borjas, Richard B. Freeman, and Lawrence F. Katz, "Searching for the Effect of Immigration on the Labor Market," working paper, no. 5454 (Cambridge, Mass.: National Bureau of Economic Research, 1996).

26. Frey, "Immigration and Internal Migration 'Flight'"; Frey and Liaw, "The Impact of Recent Immigration."

27. This research shows that, when other relevant economic and amenity variables are added to the analysis, immigration shows a significant independent effect on domestic out-migration. Studies of 1985–90 net domestic migration for metropolitan areas (Frey, "Immigration and Internal Migration 'Flight'") and for states (William H. Frey, "Immigration Impacts on General Migration of the Poor: 1990 Census Evidence for U.S. States," *International Journal of Population Geography* 1 [1995]: 51–67) show that immigration exerts a significant effect on out-migration, which is strongest for persons in poverty and with less than a college education. More rigorous analyses, which separate the explanation of migration departures out of a state from the explanation of migrants' destination selections (Frey et al., "Interstate Migration"; Frey and Liaw, "The Impact of Recent Immigration"), show that immigration's impact is greater on the departure part of the migration process, providing support for the view that it is more likely to serve as a push rather than reduced pull.

Other studies use similar analysis techniques for migration: for the late 1970s, see Robert Walker, Mark Ellis, and Richard Barff, "Linked Migration Systems: Immigration and Internal Labor Flows in the United States," *Economic Geography* 68 (1992): 234–248; Randall K. Filer, "The Effect of Immigrant Arrivals on Migratory Patterns of Native Workers," in *Immigration and the Work Force,* ed. George J. Borjas and Richard B. Freeman (Chicago: University of Chicago Press, 1992), 245–70; and Michael J. White and Lori Hunter, "The Migratory Response of Native-Born Workers to the Presence of Immigrants in the Labor Market," paper presented at the annual meeting of the Population Association of America, Cincinnati, April 1993. For the 1980s, see Michael J. White and Zai Liang, "The Effect of Immigration on the

Internal Migration of the Native-Born Population, 1981–90," working paper (Providence, R.I.: Brown University, Population Studies and Training Center, 1994). These studies show general but not uniformly consistent support for an immigration effect on internal out-migration of less-skilled residents. One study of net migration for metropolitan areas between 1985 and 1990 shows inconsistent effects that depend on the nature of the specification (Richard A. Wright, Mark Ellis, and Michael Reibel, "The Linkage Between Immigration and Internal Migration in Large Metropolitan Areas in the United States," *Economic Geography* 73, no. 2 (1997): 232–52).

28. Frey and Liaw, "The Impact of Recent Immigration."
29. William H. Frey, "Immigration and Internal Migration 'Flight': A California Case Study," *Population and Environment* 4 (1995): 353–75.
30. William H. Frey and Kao-Lee Liaw, "Immigrant Concentration and Domestic Migrant Dispersal: Is Movement to Nonmetro Areas 'White Flight'?" *Professional Geographer* 50, no. 2 (1998): 215–32.
31. Borjas, Freeman, and Katz, "Searching for the Effect of Immigration."
32. Philip Martin, "Proposition 187 in California," *International Migration Review* 29 (1995): 255–63; Thomas J. Espenshade and Charles A. Calhoun, "An Analysis of Public Opinion toward Undocumented Immigration," *Population Research and Policy Review* 12 (1993): 189–224.
33. Stanley Lieberson, *Ethnic Patterns in American Cities* (New York: Free Press, 1963); Karl E. Taeuber and Alma F. Taeuber, *Negroes in Cities* Chicago: Aldine, 1965); Douglas S. Massey and Nancy Denton, *American Apartheid* (Cambridge, Mass.: Harvard University Press, 1993).
34. Jonathan Tilove and Joe Hallinan, "Whites Flee Immigrants: Flee White States," *Newark Star Ledger,* August 8, 1993, p. 1; William H. Frey and Jonathan Tilove, "Immigrants In, Native Whites Out," *New York Times Magazine,* August 20, 1995, pp. 44–45.
35. Saskia Sassen, "Immigration in Global Cities," *Proceedings of the International Symposium on Immigration and World Cities* (New York: American Planning Association, 1996), 3–9; Roger Waldinger, "Immigration and Urban Change," *Annual Review of Sociology* 15 (1989): 211–32; Roger Waldinger, "Conclusion: Ethnicity and Opportunity in the Plural City," in *Ethnic Los Angeles,* ed. Roger Waldinger and Mehdi Bozorgmehr (New York: Russell Sage Foundation, 1996), chap. 15; Walker, Ellis, and Barff, "Linked Migration Systems"; White and Hunter, "The Migratory Response of Native-born Workers."
36. Waldinger, "Conclusion: Ethnicity and Opportunity."
37. Dowell Myers and Seong Woo Lee, "Immigration Cohorts and Residential Overcrowding in Southern California," *Demography* 33, no. 1 (1996): 51–65.
38. Thomas MaCCurdy and Margaret O'Brien-Strain, *Who Will Be Affected by Welfare Reform in California?* (San Francisco: Public Policy Institute of California, 1997).
39. Children's Defense Fund, *The State of America's Children Yearbook: 1997* (Washington D.C.: Children's Defense Fund, 1997).
40. Ben J. Wattenberg, "The Easy Solution to the Social Security Crisis," *New York Times Magazine,* June 22, 1997, pp. 30–31; Smith and Edmonston, *The New Americans;* Peter G. Peterson, *Will America Grow Up Before It Grows Old?* (New York: Random House, 1996).

41. Milton M. Gordon, *Assimilation in American Life: The Role of Race, Religion and National Origins* (New York: Oxford University Press, 1964).

42. Zhen Chao Qian, "Breaking the Racial Barriers: Variations in Interracial Marriage between 1980 and 1990," *Demography* 34, no. 2 (1997): 263–76; Roderick J. Harrison and Claudette Bennett, "Racial and Ethnic Diversity," in *State of the Union,* vol. 2, ed. Farley, 141–201; Reynolds Farley, "Increasing Interracial Marriage: Trends Revealed by the Census and Census Bureau Surveys," unpublished manuscript, University of Michigan, Population Studies Center, 1996.

43. Rochelle L. Stanfield, "Blending of America," *National Journal* 29, no. 37 (1997).

44. Smith and Edmonston, *The New Americans.*

45. William H. Frey and Reynolds Farley, "Latino, Asian, and Black Segregation in U.S. Metro Areas: Are Multiethnic Areas Different?" *Demography* 33, no. 1 (1996): 35–50; William A. Clark, "Residential Patterns: Avoidance, Assimilation, and Succession," in *Ethnic Los Angeles,* ed. Waldinger and Bozorgmehr; Waldinger, "Conclusion: Ethnicity and Opportunity"; Leo F. Estrada, "Demographic Limitations to Latino Political Potential in San Diego," in *Latino Politics in California,* ed. Anibal Yanez-Shavez (San Diego: University of California, Center for U.S.-Mexican Studies, 1996), 73–87.

46. Alejandro Portes and Ruben G. Rumbaut, *Immigrant America: A Portrait,* 2d ed. (Berkeley: University of California, 1996), chap. 7.

47. Michael Barone, "Divide and Rule." *National Journal,* July 12, 1997.

48. Borjas, "The Economics of Immigration"; Smith and Edmonston, *The New Americans.*

49. Waldinger, "Conclusion: Ethnicity and Opportunity."

50. Massey, "The New Immigration and Ethnicity."

51. U.S. Commission on Immigration Reform, *Becoming an American;* Salins, *Assimilation American Style.*

Part IV
Demographics, Income, and Economic Mobility

Chapter 7

Frank Levy

How Big Is the Income Dilemma?

The U.S. standard of living was a major, and expected, theme of the 1996 presidential campaign, although the lineup of partisans was a little unusual. There was, to begin with, President Clinton; call him the Democratic center. In 1992, Candidate Clinton had argued from the then conventional Democratic position that most people in the country suffered from declining wages and stagnant incomes. In 1996, however, President Clinton argued that these problems had now turned the corner and that wages and living standards for most persons were growing once again.[1]

In firm agreement with the president (on this point, if not much else) were a number of economic conservatives, who had argued for some time that the "stagnant incomes" story had been wrong from the beginning. A good example is Steve H. Hanke, a professor of economics at Johns Hopkins University and a columnist for *Forbes Magazine:*

> But there is an even better gauge of monetary well-being, and it is no surprise that the prophets of doom try to ignore it: real per capita personal income. It includes wages, rents, interest, profits and government transfers, less taxes paid—per person. This measure avoids the problems of household income data because the economic unit is fixed at one person. From 1973 to 1993, real per capita personal income registered steady improvements, increasing by 1.4% annually.[2]

To contrast with the president's optimism, his opponent, Senator Bob Dole, adopted what had once been the standard Democratic line—that most people continued to suffer from stagnant declining wages—except that now Bill Clinton's policies were to blame. Dole, too, had a number of unusual bedfellows, including liberal Democratic economists Lester Thurow of the Massachusetts Institute of Technology and Lawrence Mishel and Jared Bernstein of the Economic Policy Institute. Also in Dole's bed were a group of writers who argued that we were doing badly not because the numbers said so but because the numbers did a bad job of measuring how we were doing. For example, some people claimed that sales of Prozac or anti–car theft devices were signs of national problems and should not be counted in national output. Three among this number—Clifford Cobb, Ted Halstead, and Jonathan Rowe—had created a minor stir in October 1995 when their article was featured on the cover of the *Atlantic Monthly* under the provocative headline "If the Economy Is Up, Why Is America Down?"[3]

Some of this disagreement was standard posturing, but even a neutral voter would have had trouble determining the truth. In practice, the government publishes a number of different income statistics. The most widely used annual income statistics (from the Bureau of the Census's *Current Population Survey*) define income as pretax money receipts. As such, these statistics err on the high side by not subtracting taxes paid and err on the low side by not including the value of nonmoney income such as the value of employer-provided health insurance or Medicaid or Medicare. A second widely used statistic, the Department of Commerce's measure of disposable income per capita, corrects for all these problems but is only constructed as a single economy-wide average so says nothing about how living standards are distributed.

Some of the confusion can be resolved by sketching the path of living standards as average husband-wife families have experienced them over the past fifteen years. Most (but not all) government income measures can be shown to be consistent with public opinion and consistent with each other.

After reviewing problems with two commonly used statistics, one can see that people are less unhappy with the economy than the *Atlantic* headline suggests. A careful examination of polling data around the time of the *Atlantic* article shows that a majority of people perceived a slow growth in their living standards rather than a steady decline. A proper interpretation of the relevant economic data verifies this slow growth for a set of typical husband-wife families. These data do not point to any golden age. Improvement in living standards is slow enough that people are sensibly agnostic about the future—especially their ability to recover from a layoff or other income loss—even as they see moderate progress in the recent past.

This analysis relies on both the *Current Population Survey* and a set of auxiliary estimates that the Bureau of the Census has been making annually since 1979. These estimates include the value of federal and state income taxes and payroll taxes, the value of employer-provided fringe benefits, and the value of noncash government programs such as Medicare for every household in the *Current Population Survey* sample. Using these estimates, it is possible to construct the paths of a family's census income (pretax money income) and a measure close to its disposable income per capita, the Department of Commerce measure. Taken together, the two numbers provide a better understanding of a household's living standards. They also shed light on why different government statistics seem to tell different stories. A look at income trends among elderly families will demonstrate that rising incomes for the elderly, like increased income spent on medical care, may not translate into feelings of increased satisfaction in the polls.

A final note. All trends in living standards depend on how one adjusts for inflation. Unless otherwise noted, all government income measures have been adjusted to 1994 dollars using the implicit personal consumption expenditure (PCE) deflator of the gross domestic product accounts as it existed in 1994. This is a middle-of-the-road measure of inflation that keeps the focus on choosing the right income measures rather than on choosing inflation adjustments.[4] In addition, terms such as *disposable income per capita* and *wages* will refer to these variables expressed in 1994 dollars using the PCE.

Two Commonly Used Income Statistics and Their Problems

Perhaps the most widely used measures of national well-being are the Department of Commerce series on personal income per capita (before tax) and disposable income per capita (after tax).[5] Each series has the advantage of measuring both money income and nonmoney income, including employer-provided health insurance, Medicare, food stamps, and the imputed rent from home equity.[6] Moreover, because each measure is expressed in per capita terms, it automatically adjusts for demographic factors such as changes in family size. The two series, however, share two limitations.

The first involves the distribution of income. Both series are derived from the national income and product accounts, the aggregate accounts of the nation's gross domestic product. Because the series come from aggregate estimates rather than household interviews or tax returns, they contain no basis for examining the distribution of personal income or disposable income over different kinds of families. Put differently, personal income per capita says nothing about the personal income of the average person.[7]

The second limitation involves interpreting growth in either series. Consider the example of disposable income per capita, the measure used in the Hanke quotation at the beginning of this chapter. The measure can be rewritten like this:

$$\frac{\text{Disposable income}}{\text{Full-time equivalent workers}} \times \frac{\text{Full-time equivalent workers}}{\text{population}}$$

It follows that disposable income per capita (that is, per man, woman, and child) can grow either because the disposable income per full-time equivalent (FTE) worker is growing or because a greater fraction of the population is working.[8] The first case usually means that wages are rising, which should translate into increased national optimism. The second case is more ambiguous.

Specifically, consider a situation in which a rising fraction of the population at work reflects more wives working outside the home. When a wife moves into the labor market, the family often loses either in-home work or free time. Because no government income statistic counts unpaid housework or free time, the family's loss goes unrecorded, and the wife's market earnings are counted as a pure income gain. In this case, the increase in disposable income per capita likely overstates the gain in living standards as the family sees it.[9]

The other widely used living standards data are earnings and household income numbers from the Bureau of the Census's *Current Population Survey* (CPS). CPS data are based on a random sample of households. Because the data are reported on an individual and a household basis, they can be used to construct earnings distributions across individuals and income distributions across families.

As I have mentioned, the major limitation of CPS data is their measure of income: pretax money income, excluding capital gains. Because this measure ignores taxes and the value of nonmoney income such as fringe benefits, it potentially obscures large changes in living standards as families see them.

A second limitation involves the way in which CPS data typically are used. A common demonstration involves comparing the median earnings of all men who worked year round and full time in 1994 with a similar median (say, 1984) in which both statistics come from the CPS. This comparison of counterparts—all men in one year versus all men in another—may not represent the path of earnings as the individual perceives them.

Figure 7.1 contains an age-earnings profile based on 1994 median incomes of all prime-age men who worked year round and full time. In that year, earnings rose with experience through about age 50, a product of job changes and promotions. Suppose that Figure 7.1 was an accurate picture of income *over time*, not just at a point in time. Each year, young men would enter at age 25 and start moving up, while older men would retire in their 60s. If the num-

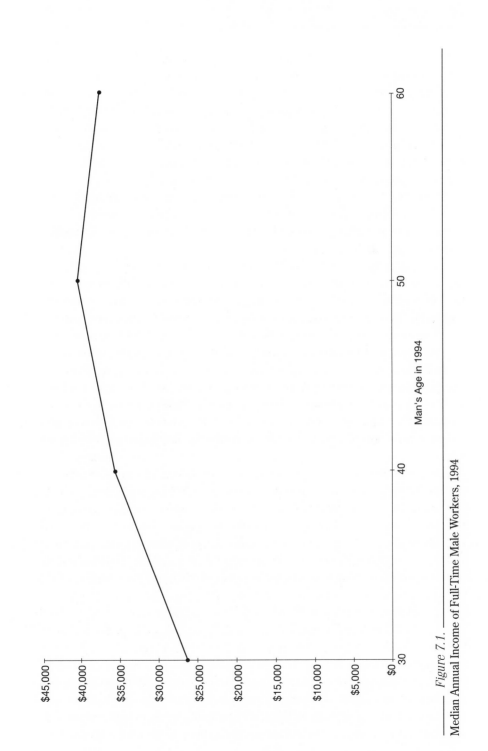

Figure 7.1.
Median Annual Income of Full-Time Male Workers, 1994

bers of men at each age were equal, the median earnings of all men, taken as a group, would never change. A description based on this median would point to stagnant earnings, but each man would experience rising earnings over much of his career.[10] In practice, this age-earnings profile may not exist for many men; there is no guarantee that in ten years today's 30–year-old will be earning as much as today's 40–year-old now earns. But earnings comparisons that fail to look for the profile risk a description of living standards that is different from what the individual sees.[11]

So what's a person to do? The Department of Commerce series on personal income per capita and disposable income per capita provide useful information on aggregate income, if not on its distribution across families. I examine these data later in the chapter.

The Bureau of the Census's CPS data suffer from the two problems I have described, but both problems can be more or less solved. With respect to the definition of income, as I have noted, since 1979 the census has produced a companion data set that contains the estimated value of federal and state income taxes and payroll taxes, the value of employer-provided fringe benefits, and the value of noncash government programs such as Medicare for every household in the CPS sample. Because the values are census-generated estimates rather than responses to household interviews, the census does not use them in its official release of numbers like median family income.[12] But beginning in 1979, the estimates can be combined with the standard CPS data sets to compute, on a family basis, an income measure roughly consistent with the Department of Commerce's measure of disposable income per capita.

The problem of the faulty comparisons can be solved by using several years of data to construct synthetic profiles: for example, the median income of male high school graduates who were ages 25 to 34 in 1979 followed by the median income of male high school graduates who were ages 35 to 44 in 1989 and so on. These are not true longitudinal data, but they give a better picture of people's experiences than does a comparison of counterparts. These synthetic profiles for different kinds of families are described later in the chapter.

What Do the Polls Really Say?

For many years, political scientists have noted the public's schizophrenic attitude toward Congress: people tell pollsters that they distrust Congress and congresspeople in general, but they think their own congressperson is fine.[13] There is evidence that a similar schizophrenia applies to opinions on the economy. In 1996, large numbers of Americans were "down" in the sense that they described the economy as being on the wrong track. When the question switched from the economy to their personal situation, people were more positive.

In an *NBC/Wall Street Journal* poll taken between January 13 and 16, 1996, respondents were asked the following question:

Would you say that you and your family are better off or worse off than you were four years ago?

Better off = 49%
Worse off = 25%
About the same (volunteered response) = 24%
Not sure = 2%[14]

A second question asked for similar information in a different form.

Please tell me if this is an area in which you feel very satisfied, somewhat satisfied, somewhat dissatisfied, or very dissatisfied: Your income is keeping up with the cost of living.

Very satisfied = 11%
Somewhat satisfied = 35%
Somewhat dissatisfied = 27%
Very dissatisfied = 25%
Not sure = 2%[15]

In each question, about one-quarter of respondents saw themselves as clearly worse off in President Clinton's first term. The remaining three-quarters saw themselves as keeping even or gaining some ground. The responses suggest a slow, general improvement in living standards: a few people doing very well; some people doing badly; most people holding their own or gaining a little, possibly by adding another earner or moving up an age-earnings profile (see Figure 7.1).

Should we take these answers seriously, or do people say whatever comes into their heads? The evidence suggests that the answers are serious. In 1992 the United States was in a recession (with an unemployment rate of 7.3 percent). In the first half of the year, the better-off, worse-off question was asked five times, and an average of 41 percent of respondents saw themselves as worse off than they were four years earlier. In January 1996 (when the unemployment rate was about 5.5 percent), 25 percent of respondents saw themselves worse off than they were four years earlier (the 1992 response). The fact that these responses track the business cycle indicates that people know what they are talking about. If most families were seeing declining living standards, their responses would be much more negative.

If people saw slowly rising living standards, does this mean that they were insulated from the layoffs that have characterized the economy? Answers to another question suggest not:

As you may know, in recent years, many businesses have had to lay off employees and restructure their company to make themselves more competitive. This process is often called "downsizing." Has this process of "downsizing" affected you personally?

Downsizing has affected personally = 30%
Downsizing has not affected personally = 69%
Not sure = 1%[16]

Being affected personally can mean different things: being laid off, having a friend or close relative laid off, and so on. But clearly many respondents have come face to face with economic restructuring. As one would expect based on media stories, this proportion rises with age, reaching 41 percent of workers between ages 40 and 64.[17] The sample's moderately positive response on living standards occurs in spite of this close contact.

A second characteristic of today's economy is the growing earnings gap between more and less educated workers. That gap appears in these responses but only in a limited way. In answer to the first question (Is your family better off or worse off than it was four years ago?), 50 percent of college graduates and 48 percent of persons with high school or less say they have been better off in the past four years. The sharp distinction is not among persons of different educational groups but among persons of different ages. Only 31 percent of retirees say their finances have improved in the last four years, a point to which I will return. College–high school differences are sharper when the question of living standards is posed in terms of income keeping up with the cost of living: 18 percent of college graduates are very dissatisfied versus 32 percent of those with high school or less.

College–high school distinctions are also larger in perceptions of respondents' current financial situation (how good it is rather than whether it has improved) and in opportunities for career advancement:

Please tell me if this is an area in which you feel very satisfied, somewhat satisfied, somewhat dissatisfied, or very dissatisfied:

Your financial situation.[18]

	High School or Less	College Graduates
Very satisfied	11%	21%
Somewhat satisfied	44%	51%
Somewhat dissatisfied	28%	21%

Very dissatisfied	16%	7%
Not sure	1%	—

Your opportunities for career advancement.[19]

	High School or Less	College Graduates
Very satisfied	13%	21%
Somewhat satisfied	27%	35%
Somewhat dissatisfied	19%	16%
Very dissatisfied	16%	9%
Not sure	25%	19%

Earlier, I argued that the poll results point to a slow, general improvement in living standards. These last responses refine that picture, suggesting that the improvement is distributed in ways that favor college graduates over high school graduates.

From these questions, we can see that a majority of people viewed their own recent experience as moderately favorable.[20] When questions turn from the recent past to the future, opinions became more pessimistic.

During the next year, do you think your own financial situation will improve, will get worse, or will stay about the same?[21]

	High School or Less	College Graduates
Will improve	35%	41%
Will get worse	8%	5%
Will stay about the same	54%	51%
Not sure	3%	3%

Do you expect your children's generation to enjoy a higher standard of living than your generation?[22]

	High School or Less	College Graduates
Expect children's generation to enjoy a higher standard of living	46%	33%
Do not expect children's generation to enjoy a higher standard of living	48%	60%
Not sure	6%	7%

With respect to the next year, the percent of people expecting their situation to improve lies about ten points below the percent who say their situation improved in the past four years. Looking further into the future, fewer than half of all respondents (including only one-third of college graduates) expect their children's generation to enjoy a higher standard of living than the current generation. Since the question refers to the next generation rather than one's own children, it may be biased downward from the general/personal schizophrenia that I have described. But whatever the source of this pessimism, the pessimism has increased over time: in 1990, 60 percent of respondents expected that their children's generation would live better than the current generation was.

On the whole, then, respondents were more pessimistic about the future than the past. This pessimism, too, is consistent with very slow growth of average wages. When average wages grow rapidly, they serve as a safety net for economic change.[23] This was the case through the 1950s and 1960s, when rapidly growing average wages

> helped to cushion the loss of "good jobs" that occurs even in periods of strong economic expansion. The loss of a good job often results in taking a different job at lower pay. . . . [W]hen real wages are growing throughout the economy, a worker can imagine regaining his old real wage in a few years and relative earnings declines need not lead to absolute earnings declines, at least in the long run.[24]

When average wages grow very slowly or stagnate, the economy is much less forgiving. Adults find it harder to recover from the wage loss of a layoff—not impossible, just harder.[25] Students find it harder to recover from a bad educational choice. In recent years, the economy's rapid restructuring has made such events more likely. Unease about the future has increased correspondingly. In sum, the same slow growth of living standards implied by people's reading of the recent past helps to explain why they are nervous about the future.

The Department of Commerce Measures: Personal Income per Capita and Disposable Income per Capita

I have argued that public opinion polls suggest a slow improvement in living standards that favors college graduates over high school graduates. Is this also what the data say?

The two Department of Commerce income measures, the before-tax personal income per capita and the after-tax disposable income per capita, are constructed as part of the department's national income and product accounts—the accounts of the country's gross domestic product. As we have seen, each measure includes both money income and nonmoney income including employer-

_____ Table 7.1 _____

Growth of Personal Income per Capita and per Worker (1994 dollars)

	1950	1960		1984	1994	
Aggregate personal income (billions)	$1,337	$1,928		$4,553	$5,702	
Population (millions)	151.7	180.8		236.4	261	
FTE workers (millions)	58.6	64.8		101.2	117.8	
			% change			% change
Personal income per capita	$8,814	$10,661	21.0	$19,260	$21,846	13.4
Personal income per FTE worker	$22,816	$29,746	30.4	$44,990	$48,402	7.6

SOURCE: National Income and Product Accounts.

provided health insurance and the imputed rent on home equity. This makes them comprehensive income measures. Because the numbers come from aggregate economic statistics rather than household-based data, they cannot speak to the distribution of that income. As such, they can say nothing about high school graduates versus college graduates, but they can begin to describe overall changes in the standard of living.

To put the measures in context, I contrast their performance in two decades: 1984–94 and 1950–60. The later decade was the most recent detailed data when this chapter was written. The earlier decade was one when, by all accounts, U.S. living standards were rising rapidly.[26]

When we use the 1950s as a standard, we can see that the recent growth of personal income per capita has been fairly strong: a 1984–94 increase of 13.4 percent, about two-thirds of the increase in the booming 1950s. This is something of a puzzle since neither the public opinion results nor most media stories suggest recent experience has been this good. The exception is the *Forbes* quotation that cites disposable income per capita (the after-tax equivalent) in an unqualified way.

The puzzle's explanation lies in Table 7.1's last line. Recall my earlier discussion, in which I said that personal income per capita can grow for different reasons. In the 1950s, labor productivity was growing rapidly, and average personal income per FTE worker grew by 30 percent. Personal income per capita grew at a slower 21 percent because the baby boom was causing the population (the number of capitas) to grow faster than the number of workers. In 1984–94, productivity growth was much slower. Personal income per FTE worker grew by only 7.6 percent, about one-fourth of its 1950s increase. But

_____ Table 7.2 _____
Growth of Wages, Salaries, and Benefits per FTE Worker

	1950	1960	% change	1984	1994	% change
Wage and salary income	$14,744	$19,831	34.5	$26,381	$27,835	5.5
Other labor income	$143	$814	468.7	$2,634	$3,234	22.8
Total compensation	$14,887	$20,645	38.7	$29,015	$31,070	7.1

SOURCE: National Income and Product Accounts.

personal income per capita still increased by 13 percent because the population was shifting toward more workers and fewer dependents: birth rates were low; more wives were in the labor force; the biggest baby boom cohorts were turning 21 and beginning their careers.

Table 7.2 sharpens the point by looking at two components of personal income: (1) wage and salary income and (2) other labor income, which represents the value of employer-provided fringe benefits.[27] Both numbers are calculated per FTE worker rather than per capita.

Department of Commerce estimates of wage and salary income are moderately more optimistic than estimates from other sources, and they show a total 5.5 percent increase over the past ten years.[28] The inclusion of fringe benefits increases the ten-year growth to 7.1 percent. Some observers suggest that the combination of wages and fringe benefits have increased much faster than wages per se. They overstate the point for recent years. Over the past five decades, fringe benefits have become a growing fraction of total compensation. But in the last decade, the fraction has grown slowly because higher health insurance costs have been offset by falling pension contributions.[29] As a result, total compensation (wages and salaries plus other labor income) did not grow much faster in 1984–94 than did wages and salaries per se.

I have noted that when a growing fraction of the population works, the rise in personal income per capita may overstate gains in living standards. The primary case involves more working wives and work lost inside the home. A more subtle case involves the median age of first marriage, which has risen by about three years since the early 1970s for both men and women. The result is a growing number of young singles who contribute to the growth of personal income per capita because they only have themselves to support. But many of these young singles expect to get married and to have children in the future. Correspondingly, their (temporarily) high personal income per capita may not translate into feelings of affluence in opinion polls.

In sum, the series on personal income per capita points to a steady rise in

———— *Table 7.3* ————

The Disposition of Personal Income among Taxes, Savings, and Consumption (in per capita terms, 1994 dollars)

	1950	1960	$ change	1984	1994	$ change
Real personal income per capita	$8,814	$10,661	$1,848	$19,260	$21,846	$2,586
Less contributions for social insurance	$112	$242	$130	$811	$1,078	$267
Less taxes	$778	$1,269	$491	$2,412	$2,843	$431
Equals disposable personal income	$7,924	$9,150	$1,226	$16,037	$17,924	$1,887
Less interest and net transfers	$104	$185	$81	$472	$491	$19
Less savings	$476	$537	$61	$1,355	$778	($577)
Equals personal consumption expenditure per capita	$7,456	$8,660	$1,166	$14,681	$17,733	$3,052
Taxes as a percent of all personal income	8.8	11.9		12.5	13.0	
Taxes plus contributions to social insurance as a percent of earned money income (excludes transfers and non-money income such as Medicaid and fringe benefits)	11.4	16.4		21.2	23.7	

SOURCE: National Income and Product Accounts.

average living standards over the past decade, but much of the rise is due to demographic rearrangements rather than increased compensation. As such, it likely overstates the gain in living standards that people experience. In this case, a better gauge of public sentiment may be the growth in personal income per FTE worker, and that statistic is consistent with the polling results I listed earlier. It is rising, not declining, but at a rate of less than 1 percent per year.

In the disposition of personal income (where all the money goes), taxes represent a potential disconnect between increased personal income per capita and increased feelings of affluence. If taxes take a growing bite out of increased income, people will feel stretched no matter what the pretax numbers say.

With respect to taxes (the difference between personal income per capita and disposable income per capita), the data in Table 7.3 paint a mixed picture. In these Department of Commerce data drawn from the national income and product accounts, average tax rates are higher in 1984–94 than they were in the 1950s: about 11 percent of all personal income in the 1950s versus 13 percent of all personal income in the past decade. At the same time, the *rise* in taxes during 1984–94 was not particularly large. In 1950–60, higher taxes absorbed about one-quarter of the increase in personal income per capita. In 1984–94, higher taxes absorbed about one-sixth of the personal income increase.

The tax rates in Table 7.3—for example, 13 percent in 1994—are well below tax rates as seen by a typical middle-income family. There are three reasons why. First, the national income and product accounts treat payments into Social Security, Medicare, and so on as contributions to social insurance rather than as taxes. Most people see those payments as taxes and count them as part of their tax burden.[30]

A second reason for the apparently low tax rates is that personal income per capita, the tax base in these calculations, includes nonmoney income: the value of employer-provided fringe benefits, the value of Medicare, the imputed rent received from an owner-occupied home. Most people do not see these items as income. More to the point, the Internal Revenue Service does not see these items as income and does not tax them. Since governments raise tax revenues raised from money income alone, tax rates are correspondingly higher.

Finally, not all forms of money income are taxed at the same rate. A primary example is government transfer payments: Social Security, Aid to Families with Dependent Children, unemployment insurance, federal workers' pensions, and so on. By 1994, these money transfers accounted for about one-sixth of all personal income, and a significant fraction were not taxed—partly by reason of legislation, partly because many of the payments went to households with very low incomes.[31] Here, too, raising a set amount of tax revenue from a smaller tax base (in this case, money income minus a significant fraction of money transfers) requires a higher tax rate.

If rough adjustments are made for these three factors, the perceived tax rate (see Table 7.3), which is the tax rate as seen by an average middle-income family on its money income, stood at 14 percent in 1950 and stands at about 23.5 percent today, a rate more in line with popular perception.[32]

With these corrections, however, the original conclusion of Table 7.3 stands. While average tax rates have risen over time, the recent modest growth of disposable income per capita did not reflect a sudden rise in taxes. Rather, the problem began with the fact that productivity growth was weak and pretax personal income per FTE worker did not grow very fast in the first place.

Table 7.3 contains a final point on consumption spending. We have seen that the period between 1984 and 1994 was marked by slow growth of income per worker. As Table 7.3 shows, it was also marked by a rapid decline in the savings rate. As a result of declining savings, and despite the slow growth of income, personal consumption expenditure per capita grew faster in 1984–94 (20.8 percent) than it did in 1950–60 (15.6 percent). One cannot be thrilled about the sources of this growing consumption, which is based on less savings and a greater part of the population working, but it is important to note the trend.

The Bureau of the Census Current Population Survey *(with Additional Estimates)*

Having looked at aggregate income trends, I turn to constructing the paths of living standards as seen by the following kinds of families:

1. Husband-wife families in which the husband has a high school diploma or GED (and no more) and was between the ages of 25 and 34 in 1979[33]
2. Husband-wife families in which the husband has a four-year-college diploma (and no more) and was between the ages of 25 and 34 in 1979
3. Husband-wife families in which the husband has a high school diploma or GED (and no more) and was between the ages of 35 and 44 in 1979
4. Husband-wife families in which the husband has a four-year-college diploma (and no more) and was between the ages of 35 and 44 in 1979[34]

The standard census income variable, which is the variable that appears in federal reports of median family income, is defined as pretax money income excluding capital gains. When a family's census income is combined with estimated variables (see note 34), the resulting definition is reasonably close to the more comprehensive Department of Commerce definition of disposable income.[35] This disposable income variable can then be divided by the number of persons in the family to produce an estimate of the family's disposable income per capita.

These census data come from annual random samples (the census does not follow the same families over time), so the fifteen-year paths of living standards for typical families are based on synthetic cohorts. The first example of younger families, in which the husband was a high school graduate, was constructed as follows:

- Begin with the group of all husband-wife families in which the husband was a high school graduate and was between the ages of 25 and 34 in 1979.[36]
- Compute the median census income (pretax money income) for this sample. Define *typical families* for the sample to be families whose incomes lie between +/–20 percent of the median: that is, families near the center of the sample's income distribution.

- Compute the mean value of each variable of interest for these typical families, including husband's income, wife's income, taxes paid, and so on.
- Repeat the process for all husband-wife families in which the husband was high school graduate and was between the ages of 35 and 44 in 1989. Repeat the process a final time for high school graduate husbands between the ages of 40 and 49 in 1994.[37]

The three samples—25– to 34–year-olds in 1979, 35– to 44–year-olds in 1989, and 40– to 49–year-olds in 1994—draw from roughly the same population of families as it ages. No account is taken of divorce or remarriage, and there is no guarantee that families near the group's average in 1979 will remain near the group's average in 1989. But the resulting picture of living standards over time is a better description of what typical families see than the standard story citing the year-to-year change in the median income of all U.S. families.

One caveat. The Census Bureau switched from paper-and-pencil interviews to computer-based interviews (CASIC) in January 1994. This switch may have created a modest shift in the data for 1993 versus previous years, which reflects changes in interviews rather than changes in the economy. I will return to this point in discussing the data. If the problem exists, it will affect all year-to-year analyses of CPS data—for example, the news story of year-to-year change in median family income.[38]

Young Families with High School Graduate Husbands

The first example describes a husband-wife family in which the husband is a high school graduate and was between the ages of 25 and 34 in 1979 (see Figure 7.2). This is a picture of a husband and wife who are passing from about age 30 to about age 45, a time in which the husband's income should be rising due to experience-based promotions (see Figure 7.1). In reality, much of the rise was undone by weak overall wage growth in the economy and the labor market shift against high school graduates. As the husband passed from age 30 to age 40, his average money income rose by 12 percent. But by age 45, he was earning slightly less (excluding fringes) than he had earned when he was 30. Because of the changes I have noted in CPS interview procedures, the size of the husband's earnings decline between ages 40 and 45 may be modestly overstated. But it is reasonable to say that he has seen very little net earnings gain in the past fifteen years.

While the husband's earnings showed no gain, the family's money income rose by 21 percent over the same period. The difference reflects the increasing contribution of the wife's earnings. In 1979, when these couples were in their late 20s and early 30s, half of all wives worked more than 760 hours per

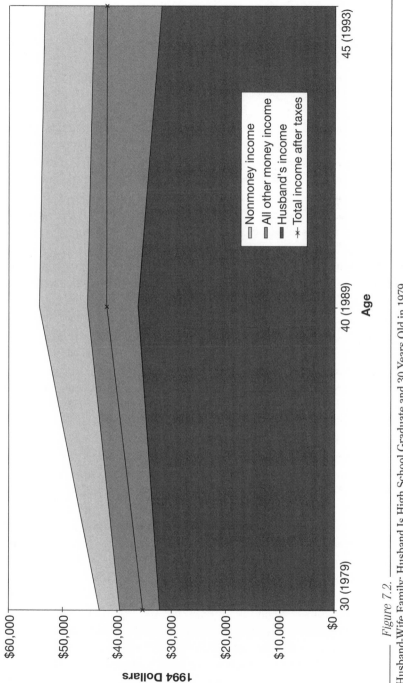

Figure 7.2.
Husband-Wife Family: Husband Is High School Graduate and 30 Years Old in 1979

year. By 1994, half of all wives in the sample (now in their mid 40s) worked more than 1,500 hours per year, something close to full time. Average wives' earnings rose from $7,600 to $14,000, and their increased earnings were the major source of the family's income gain.

The combination of federal income taxes, payroll taxes, and state income taxes absorbed about 20 percent of total money income, a fraction that was fairly constant over the period. Fringe benefits and, in some cases, programs such as Medicaid and food stamps increased after-tax money income by 7 percent in 1979, rising to 10 percent in 1994 (line d). The imputed rent from home equity increased after-tax money income by 3 percent in 1979 and by 9 percent in 1994, reflecting the rising values of homes. When the income and tax numbers are combined with numbers on family size, they show that both disposable income and disposable income per capita grew by about 29 percent over the fifteen years. The fact that both numbers grew at the same rate reflects a constant family size over the period.[39]

If you look at Figure 7.2, you can see how a family might be agnostic about the future even though its disposable income per capita has grown fairly well over the past fifteen years. The husband is earning no more (adjusted for inflation) than he earned fifteen years ago. Nonmoney income, including imputed rent from home equity, has raised the family's income by about 8 percent, but this is income that is hard to see. The biggest increase in the family's income has come from the wife's extra work—a source of growth that, as I argued earlier, probably overstates living standard gains. Equally important, about half of all wives in this sample are now working close to full time, meaning that if a husband is laid off in the future, there is little more that these wives can add to the family's budget. All of this is consistent with the *NBC/Wall Street Journal* poll responses.

What about younger high school graduate families who are starting out today? Will they follow the same path? We can see the beginning of an answer by comparing younger high school graduate families in 1979 with younger high school graduate families in 1994, which are counterpart families starting out in different years. As I suggested earlier, comparing counterparts does not say much about how individual families experience living standards over time, but it does say something about economic trends.

These data, summarized in Figure 7.3, offer a second reason explaining why people may be agnostic about the future. While the 1979 and 1994 young high school graduate families have similar total and per capita incomes, they derive those incomes in different ways. As I have noted, labor market conditions since the early 1980s have worked against high school graduates. Changing conditions usually have their biggest effects on new entrants, persons unprotected

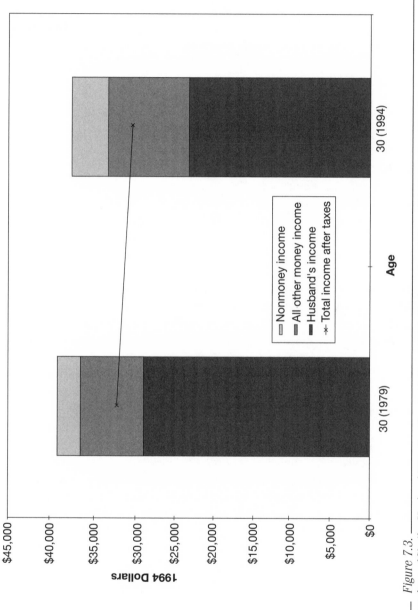

Figure 7.3.

A Comparison of Similar Husband-Wife Families in 1979 and 1994: Husband Is a 30-Year-Old High School Graduate

by seniority. This can be seen in Figure 7.3, in which 1994 high school graduate husbands start out with incomes about $6,000 less than their 1979 counterparts, a decline that may be exaggerated slightly by census interview changes. The two groups' family incomes are similar only because half of all 1994 wives are already working more than three-fourths time, a level that 1979 wives did not reach until later in their careers. For the 1979 family, increased wife's work was the major source of family income growth. For the 1994 family, that source has been tapped, and the family's future income growth is less certain.

Young Families with College Graduate Husbands

The second group set of families includes younger husband-wife families in which the husband was a four-year-college graduate rather than a high school graduate (see Figure 7.4). Here the picture is more optimistic. As the husband passed from age 30 (in 1979) to age 45, his earnings (excluding fringes) rose by about one-third. Among these families, too, wives' hours of work increased over time; but here the wives' earnings represented a second source of income growth rather than the only income growth or an offset to falling husband's earnings.

The combination of rising husbands' income and more wives' work raised household money income by 53 percent over the fifteen years. Total disposable income rose slightly faster because nonmoney income (including imputed rent on home equity) more than doubled, while taxes took a constant 23–24 percent of money income.[40] Disposable income per capita grew at a slower 31 percent because many of the families were having children over these years. As shown in the figure, most of these families should be able to say that their recent living standards have improved.

How do today's young college graduate families compare to those who started out in 1979? Broadly speaking the two groups begin from similar positions (see Figure 7.5). Husbands in 1979 and in 1994 have similar incomes. Wives in 1994 work longer hours; but as a result, 1994 families have higher family incomes. Total disposable income in 1994 is about 10 percent higher, and disposable income per capita is 19 percent higher, reflecting fewer children in the 1994 families.

While this chapter is not explicitly about inequality, one aspect of inequality is implicit in my discussion: the gap between the family incomes of high school and college graduates that will expand as these families age.

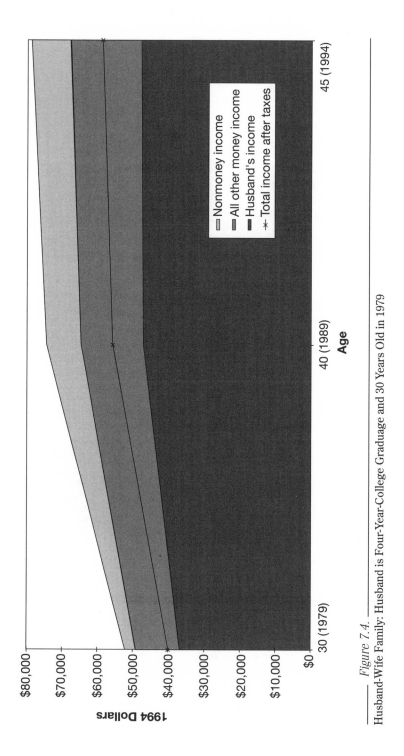

Figure 7.4.

Husband-Wife Family: Husband is Four-Year-College Graduage and 30 Years Old in 1979

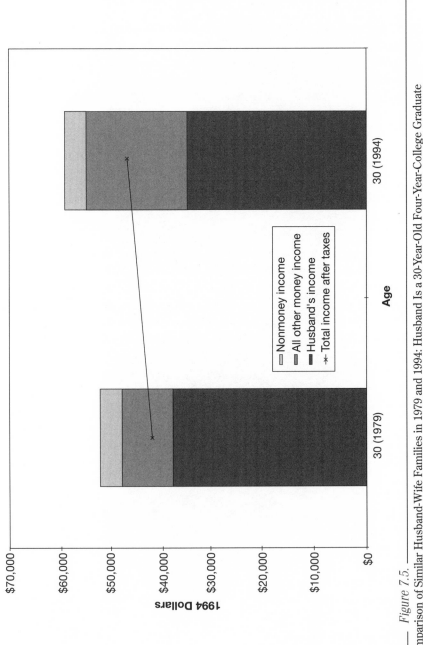

Figure 7.5.

A Comparison of Similar Husband-Wife Families in 1979 and 1994: Husband Is a 30-Year-Old Four-Year-College Graduate

Middle-Aged Families with High School Graduate or College
Graduate Husbands

Figures 7.6–7.9 repeat these pictures for high school and college graduate husband-wife families in which the husband was between the ages of 35 and 44 in 1979. Why look at 40–year-olds after having just looked at 30–year-olds? The answer lies in the age-earnings relationship sketched in Figure 7.1. As workers age, they run out of promotional opportunities; and if all else remains constant, the age-earnings relationship flattens out.

As we have seen, economic conditions over the past fifteen years have worked against younger high school graduates. Their flat earnings (see Figure 7.2) reflect a standoff between bad economic conditions and the normal earnings rise in the early part of one's career. Forty-year-olds are later in their careers. They cannot expect this normal earnings rise, so bad economic conditions will put greater downward pressure on their earnings.

The data confirm this story: as they moved from age 40 to age 55, middle-aged college graduate husbands saw relatively flat earnings, while middle-aged high school graduate husbands saw declining earnings, particularly after age 50. Among both sets of families, wives worked longer hours as the families aged. Among college graduate families, the wives' earnings were largely an addition to income. Among high school graduate families, wives' increased earnings were about enough to keep total family income constant over the past fifteen years.

How would such families respond to an *NBC/Wall Street Journal* poll? Middle-aged college graduate families have seen rising disposable income over recent years, a judgment that holds even if the wife's income gain is overstated. But the husband's paycheck per se has not improved much, so the husband (and his family) remain vulnerable to future layoffs. These families, too, are consistent with the pattern of poll responses: things have improved in the recent past, but people are concerned about the future. Middle-aged high school graduate families tell a different story. Among these families, income trends are more pessimistic, particularly in the past five years. These families are reasonably among the quarter of respondents who say their finances have deteriorated over the past four years or the quarter who say they are just keeping even.

Today's families enter middle age in a weaker income position than did their 1979 counterparts: slightly weaker for college graduates and moderately weaker for high school graduates. In 1979, a 40–year-old high school graduate husband earned about $37,000 a year. In 1994, a 40–year-old high school graduate husband earned about $29,000 (a figure that may be biased downward by the changed census interview procedures). The decline in family

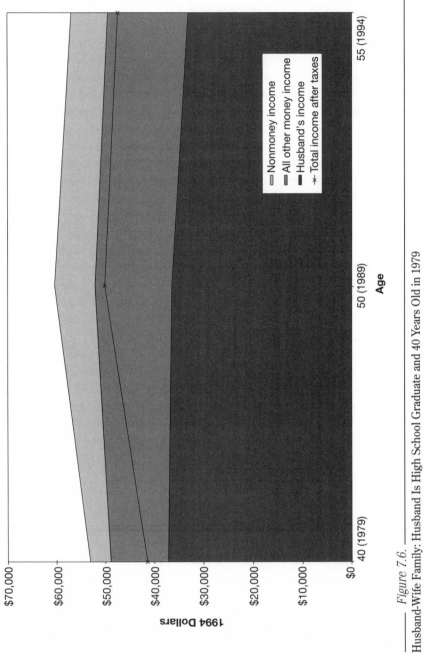

Figure 7.6.

Husband-Wife Family: Husband Is High School Graduate and 40 Years Old in 1979

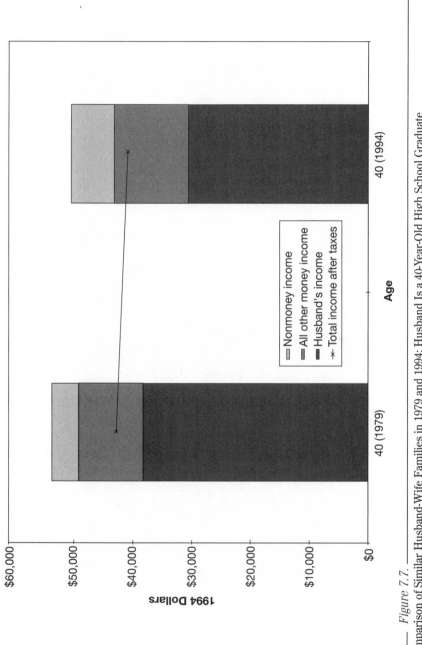

Figure 7.7.

A Comparison of Similar Husband-Wife Families in 1979 and 1994: Husband Is a 40-Year-Old High School Graduate

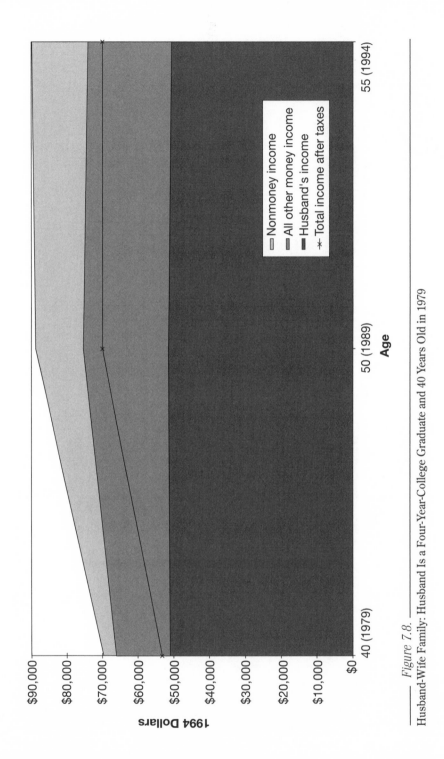

Figure 7.8.

Husband-Wife Family: Husband Is a Four-Year-College Graduate and 40 Years Old in 1979

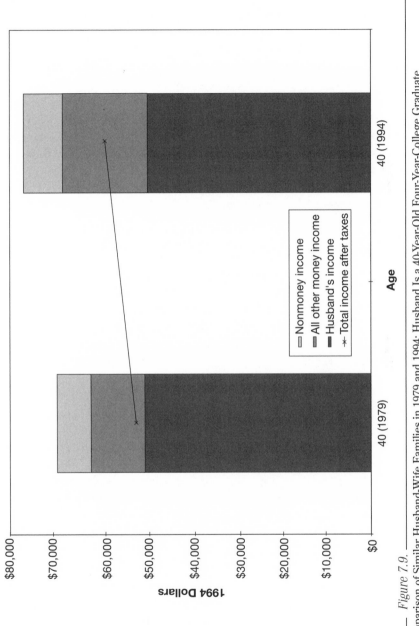

Figure 7.9.

A Comparison of Similar Husband-Wife Families in 1979 and 1994: Husband Is a 40-Year-Old Four-Year-College Graduate

incomes is smaller than the decline in husbands' earnings because the average wife in the 1994 family works about eight hundred more hours per year than her 1979 counterpart did (see Figure 7.7).

Today's 40–year-old college graduate husband also earns less than his 1979 counterpart did, but the difference is much smaller (about $50,800 versus $47,500). Thus, in these middle-aged college graduate families, increased wives' work has led to higher family incomes (see Figure 7.9).

Does the weaker position of today's middle-class families say something about the economy? Yes and no. People who were 40 in 1994 were born in 1954, near the peak of the baby boom. They belong to very large cohorts, and in an era of slow-growing wages we would expect them to have somewhat lower incomes than the smaller cohorts who preceded them and the smaller cohorts who follow them. But superimposed on these demographics is the growing income split between college and high school graduates, and this trend is unlikely to reverse anytime soon.

Incomes of Retired Families

Recall from my earlier discussion that the elderly were far less likely than younger persons to report a rise in their financial position over the last four years. At first glance, this is surprising since most income studies conclude that the elderly are far better off than they used to be and that the expansion of Social Security, Medicare, and other such programs is the Great Society's biggest success story.[41]

In practice, this may reflect another disconnect between rising incomes and public satisfaction. When we say that the incomes of the elderly have risen, we mean that today's elderly have higher incomes than did an earlier (different) group of elderly. But today's elderly may have little basis for making that comparison. Rather, they may compare their current incomes to the larger incomes they had when they worked. In this sense, rising elderly incomes are similar to the earlier case of money spent on medical care in which the persons receiving treatment today may not have a basis for knowing how much the treatment has improved in the past decade.

Table 7.4 compares the incomes of 65– to 74–year-old husband-wife families in 1979 and 1994. The comparison includes all families, regardless of the husband's education. It shows that elderly incomes have risen significantly over the past fifteen years, with disposable income per capita rising by one-third over the period. While this does not prove the point, it is consistent with the argument and suggests another reason to explain why rising per capita income may not lead to great satisfaction in the polls.

_____ *Table 7.4* _____

Average Income of Recently Retired Couples; Husband's Age 65–74,
1980–1995 (1994 dollars)

	1980	1990	1994	1995
Household money income (census income)	$23,860	$30,376	$32,596	$28,726
Total household money income = census income + capital gains + EITC	$23,998	$30,607	$32,949	$28,966
Federal and state income taxes and federal payroll taxes	$1,131	$2,613	$3,113	$2,138
Noncash income, including health insurance	$3,189	$5,602	$6,571	$6,571
Imputed rent on home equity	$3,340	$5,158	$5,054	$5,117
Total household disposable income	$29,396	$38,754	$41,462	$38,516
Total household disposable income in per capita terms	$13,745	$18,032	$19,042	$18,203

SOURCE: Author's tabulations of CPS files.

When extensive debate fails to resolve a question, it is a good sign that the question is a close call. That is the case with the current debate over living standards. Recall that the headline for the *Atlantic* article proclaimed that American was down despite the fact that the economy was up. In reality, when economic variables are portrayed correctly, the economy is not so far up. And in the opinions that count, America is not so far down.

Do these drab results suggest that the income dilemma is overdrawn? I think not. The income question is a close call with respect to a rise or a fall, but nobody suggests that living standards have been growing briskly. Thus, most workers have little protection against job displacement and the income losses that accompany it. It is also clear that families headed by young high school graduates (families just now starting out) are doing significantly worse than their older counterparts were, with weak prospects for future income growth. The fact becomes particularly important when we remember that the number of such families is significantly larger than the number of families of similar age headed by a college graduate. If future incomes actually grow as slowly as it appears they will do, the issue of income inequality will become much more pressing in day-to-day life.

Over the recent past, however, a majority of families have managed to wring slowly rising living standards out of flat earnings. Over time, the family's disposable income has risen through wives' increased earnings as well as a modest gain in nonmoney income. In some cases, the family's disposable income per capita has risen faster than disposable income because the family's children are leaving the household, so income is divided among fewer mouths. Both statistics probably overstate living standard gains because they fail to adjust for lost work in the home when a wife takes a paid job. But even with this problem, both statistics reflect some progress.

Given these numbers, it is reasonable that Americans should not be so down about the economy's past performance. And in fact, as we have seen, they are not. But as is equally reasonable, they are agnostic about the future.

This is not a dramatic story—neither the best of times, nor the worst of times. But for those who want to understand the living standards of the typical U.S. family, this is where we are. Feeling their way through a period of slow growth and economic restructuring, many families are improving slowly, others are holding on, and some are falling behind. When looked at correctly, both government statistics and the poll numbers say as much.

Notes

Support for the work in this chapter came from the U.S. Department of Labor, the Competitiveness Policy Council, a grant from the Alfred P. Sloan Foundation to MIT's Industrial Performance Center, and the Rose Chair in Urban Economics. Kathy Yuan of MIT's Department of Urban Studies and Planning and David Murphy of MIT's Department of Electrical Engineering provided extensive and careful research assistance. Thanks go to Dave Iannelli of Coldwater Research in Ann Arbor, Michigan, and to David Wessel of the *Wall Street Journal* for discussion of polling data and for unpublished cross-tabulations of the *NBC/Wall Street Journal* poll of January 13–16, 1996, conducted by Peter Hart and Robert Teeter. Special thanks go to participants in a Competitiveness Policy Council review session, participants in the MIT Public Finance Lunch, and a number of friends who read earlier drafts of the chapter and provided insightful comments. A slightly different version was issued by the Competitiveness Policy Council in September 1995.
1. Council of Economic Advisors, *Economic Report of the President: 1996* (Washington, D.C.: U.S. General Printing Office, 1996).
2. Steve H. Hanke, "The Stagnation Myth," *Forbes,* April 22, 1996, pp. 145–46.
3. Clifford Cobb, Ted Halstead, and Jonathan Rowe, "If the GDP Is Up, Why Is America Down?" *Atlantic Monthly* 2276 (October 1995): 59–78.
4. For the period under study, the implicit PCE deflator used here is similar to the revised, chain-weighted PCE deflator that was part of the 1996 national income and product account revisions. Incomes deflated by the standard consumer price index would grow more slowly than those presented here. Incomes deflated by the revised consumer price index proposed by the Boskin Commission would grow much faster. See Robert J. Gordon, "The American Real Wage Since 1963: Is It Unchanged

or Has It More Than Doubled?" unpublished manuscript, Northwestern University, December 17, 1995, for more discussion of this point.

5. The measure comes from the national income and product accounts, the accounts that underlie the nation's gross domestic product. See, for example, Council of Economic Advisors, *Economic Report of the President: 1996,* tab. B27.

6. In the national income and product accounts, persons who live in owner-occupied homes are credited with imputed rent (an estimated amount of income equal to what they could receive if they rented their homes to others) less depreciation. The concept is legitimate; but imputed rent, like employer-provided health insurance, is not an item most people think of as income.

7. Personal income per capita is an arithmetic mean: total personal income divided by the total population. The personal income of the average person would be *median* personal income per capita—the amount such that half of all people have more while the other half have less. This median only could come from household-based data such as surveys or tax returns.

8. The number of FTE workers is calculated by taking the total number of hours worked in the economy and dividing by 2,000, the number of hours worked in a full-time year. Income per FTE worker has a clear interpretation. Income per actual worker is harder to interpret because, other things equal, we would expect part-time workers to earn less than full-time workers, and the mix of full-time and part-time workers shifts from year to year.

9. See Robert Eisner, *The Total Incomes System of Accounts* (Chicago: University of Chicago Press, 1989), for an estimate of the value of household production. In "If the GDP Is Up?" Cobb, Halstead, and Rowe raise this point as well.

10. Put differently, a standard demonstration of stagnant wages shows that a 30–year-old man today earns no more, adjusted for inflation, than a 30–year-old man earned ten years ago. To the individual, the more important question is whether a *40–year-old man* earns more today than a 30–year-old man earned ten years ago.

11. A third widely quoted number is the Bureau of Labor Statistics's series on average hourly earnings of production and nonsupervisory workers. According to this series, the average hourly earnings of nonsupervisory workers, adjusted for inflation, were 13.3 percent lower in 1995 than in 1973 (see Council of Economic Advisors, *Economic Report of the President: 1996,* tab. B43). For many authors, the statistic demonstrates declining wages for the majority of the population (for example, see Simon Head, "The New Ruthless Economy," *New York Review of Books,* February 29, 1996, pp. 47–52).

There are, however, problems with this interpretation. First, the Bureau of Labor Statistics's wage series comes from a sample with potential bias (see Katherine G. Abraham, James P. Spletzer, and Jay C. Stewart, "Divergent Trends in Alternative Real Wage Series" (Washington, D.C.: Bureau of Labor Statistics, October 19, 1995). Second, the series suffers from potential composition problems. Between 1973 and 1995, the number of employed women increased much faster than the number of employed men. During these same years, women typically earned 60 to 70 percent as much as men. Taken together, these trends create a situation in which men's wages and women's wages could both be constant (or rising), but the *average wage for all workers* could fall because an increasing share of all workers were women.

The wages earned by many individuals may indeed be stagnant or declining, but this Bureau of Labor Statistics series is not an acceptable basis for examining the proposition.

12. The census uses the estimates to show the effect of different income definitions. See, for example, U.S. Department of Commerce, Bureau of the Census, "Income, Poverty and Valuation of Noncash Benefits: 1993," *Current Population Reports,* P60–188 (Washington, D.C., 1995).

13. *NBC/Wall Street Journal* poll, January 13–16, 1996. Unpublished tabulations were provided by Coldwater Research in Ann Arbor, Michigan. Thanks go to David Wessel of the *Wall Street Journal* for sharpening the ideas in this section.

14. Ibid., question 12a (form b).

15. Ibid., question 13.

16. Ibid, question 16a.

17. I shall return to this point later in the chapter.

18. *NBC/Wall Street Journal* poll, question 12b.

19. Ibid., question 13.

20. But among those who believe the economy has improved, not all attribute the improvement to Bill Clinton.

21. *NBC/Wall Street Journal* poll, question 12c.

22. Ibid., question 14.

23. In terms of Figure 7.1, a rising average wage would mean that the whole curve would shift upward over time: that 30–year-olds in 1989 would earn more than 30–year-olds earned in 1979, that 40–year-olds in 1989 would earn more than 40–year-olds earned in 1979, and so on.

24. Frank Levy and Richard C. Michel, *The Economic Future of American Families* (Washington, D.C.: Urban Institute, 1991), 10.

25. In "Job Insecurity: What Underlies the Perception" (Library of Congress, Congressional Research Services, March 15, 1996), Linda Levine reports unpublished Bureau of Labor Statistics data showing the February 1994 status of full-time workers who lost their jobs in 1991–92: 40 percent were employed and earning more than their previous weekly earnings; 35 percent were employed and earning less than their previous weekly earnings; 25 percent were either unemployed or out of the labor force.

26. Frank Levy, *Dollars and Dreams: The Changing American Income Distribution* (New York: Russell Sage Foundation, 1987).

27. Other components of personal income include interest payments, dividends, pension benefits, Social Security benefits, the value of Medicare, and so on.

28. Department of Commerce estimates of annual wage and salary income are slightly higher than estimates from the Bureau of the Census's *Current Population Survey.* Estimates of hourly wages from the two sources differ more sharply because the Department of Commerce estimates fewer hours of work in the economy than the hours of work reported by respondents in the CPS. See Abraham, Spletzer, and Stewart, "Divergent Trends in Alternative Real Wage Series," for a discussion of these points.

29. Employer pension contributions in the 1980s fell for several reasons, including a smaller proportion of workers with any pension plan, more workers with 401K plans

rather than standard pensions, and strong pension fund performance that lowered employers' required contributions.

30. As several readers have pointed out, however, a world without Social Security would require higher out-of-pocket payments from adult children to their parents.

31. For example, consider legislation that excludes half of a person's Social Security benefit from taxation. Similarly, no part of Medicare coverage is counted as income.

32. Specifically, (1) count contributions to social insurance funds as taxes; (2) exclude the value of fringe benefits from disposable income per capita; and (3) make the extreme assumption that taxes are not paid on any government transfers. The perceived tax rate would be closer to 30 percent if I included the employer's contribution to Social Security, Medicare, and so on—a contribution that economists agree falls on the worker in the form of lower wages.

33. In 1992, the CPS changed the precise questions used to determine education. Before 1992, we can determine that an individual had completed twelve years of education (and no more), but we cannot determine whether the person actually received a high school diploma.

34. I choose 25– to 34–year-old and 35– to 44–year-old husbands because they represent two different segments of the age-earnings profile (see Figure 7.1), which usually flattens substantially as the individual ages. I choose both high school and college graduates because an important story of the 1980s labor market was the growth in the high school–college earnings gap.

The data source is the annual March demographic files of the CPS supplemented with census estimates of the following variables:
- Federal income and payroll taxes paid per household
- State income taxes paid per household
- Capital gains received per household
- The money value of employer provided health insurance
- The money value of noncash government benefits, including food stamps, Medicaid and Medicare, subsidized school lunches, and subsidized housing
- The money value of the imputed rent on home equity

35. One difference is the lack of estimated property taxes paid in the census data.

36. More precisely, the husband was 25 to 34 years old in March 1980, the time of the survey in which 1979 income information was collected. For clarity, however, I will refer to the husband's age as if it occurred in the same year as the income information.

37. A technical point: the CPS is a weighted sample, and sampling weights are used in computing all medians and means presented here.

38. A second caveat: to make this chapter as current as possible, it describes income patterns through the March 1995 CPS covering income for 1994. As the census released this data set, they discovered errors in their estimates of 1994 employer contributions to group health insurance. For purpose of this chapter, the 1994 contributions have been replaced by their 1993 values, computed for equivalent family types, and adjusted for 1993–94 inflation.

39. The combined growth rate of money income plus nonmoney income is about 29 percent. If family size were changing too, the growth rate of disposable income per

capita would be lower than 29 percent (if family size was increasing) or higher (if family size was declining as children left home).

40. This includes contributions to Social Security and so on.
41. For example, see Levy, *Dollars and Dreams.*

Chapter 8

Dowell Myers

Upward Mobility in Space and Time

Lessons from Immigration

Demography holds many valuable lessons for public policy. Of most general importance is its insight into dynamics of change over time. In contrast to the simple study of population characteristics or changes in overall characteristics from one decade to the next, demographers have developed methods for decomposing aggregate changes into separate components that drive changes over time. Behavior rates can be linked to the changing composition of the population, and the combination of the two are used to explain overall trends.

The recent rise in immigration to the United States has initiated rapid and dramatic changes in gateway regions in which immigrants have congregated. Nowhere is this more prominent than in southern California, home to one-quarter of all the immigrants in America. Several dimensions of change are at work. The rising volume of immigration has brought ever-larger waves of immigrants to join their predecessors, and the immigrants themselves change rapidly the longer they reside in the United States. At the same time, the growing prominence of the immigrant population is altering the average status attainment in the region. The complexity of these changes can be best explained through the tools of demographic analysis. In fact, close analysis of these immigration-based trends promises more general lessons because the rapidity of change brings into sharper focus ongoing dynamics involving the native-born residents as well.

Fostering upward mobility is a broad, overarching goal of social and economic policy. Upward mobility is central to the enduring American dream that everyone can get ahead by hard work in this country and that each generation will succeed more than the previous. Applying the demographic perspective to an analysis of upward mobility focuses on three indicators: mobility out of the central city, rising out of poverty, and movement into homeownership. Each of these three separate issues is an area of distinct policy interest, yet the three are related as parts of a common underlying process of upward mobility.

Immigration in America poses special challenges for local policymakers because its effects are highly concentrated in relatively few gateway regions. Local governments in those areas have struggled to finance the service needs of recent arrivals, including added expenditures for education, health care, and general municipal services. These services may be viewed as worthwhile investments in the production of valued citizens and workers, and our evidence shows that immigrants achieve substantial upward mobility. The immigrants, however, are also spatially mobile, and the city that finances the essential earlier investment in new immigrant arrivals may not enjoy the later benefits returned by those same immigrants when they become taxpaying homeowners and well-paid workers. Local officials face a dilemma of incongruence between investment in their local place, which is fixed in space, and in the local population, which is free to flow across boundaries. Thus, a few local governments bear the burden of incorporating the bulk of the new arrivals when they are most dependent, while the rest of the United States enjoys the benefits of that investment once the immigrants achieve their upward mobility.

A review of the growing importance of immigration in southern California, along with some potentially misleading conclusions about the state of upward mobility, can help us draw some insights from demography.

Waves of Immigrants to Southern California

Southern California is a large region extending from the Mexican border to Ventura County, north of Los Angeles. In 1990, 17.1 million residents lived in the region, 4.6 million of whom were foreign born (26.6 percent of the region's residents). The region has been a principal destination for new immigrant arrivals in the nation as a whole, comprising nearly one-quarter of the entire foreign-born population in the nation in 1990.

Accumulating Waves

The rapidity of change in southern California is indicated in Table 8.1, which shows the accumulating waves of immigrants. From 1.3 million new arrivals in the 1970s (prior to the 1980 census), immigration soared to 2.3 million arrivals in the 1980s. Following this period of rapid growth, the number

_____ *Table 8.1* _____
Accumulating Waves of Immigrants in Southern California

	1980	1990	2000	2010
Period of arrival:				
2000s	—	—	—	2,046,863
1990s	—	—	2,102,512	1,801,266
1980s	—	2,324,628	1,945,491	1,698,445
1970s	1,284,920	1,287,557	1,073,910	972,299
Pre-1970	1,086,180	942,721	635,595	472,663
Native born	11,112,100	12,550,692	15,266,830	17,496,829
Total population	13,483,200	17,105,598	21,024,339	24,488,366
	Percent of Population			
Foreign born	17.6	26.6	27.4	28.6
New immigrants	9.5	13.6	10.0	8.4
Newly arrived	54.2	51.0	36.5	29.3

SOURCE: Public use microdata samples, 1980, 1990; John Pitkin and Patrick Simmons, "The Foreign-Born Population to 2010: A Prospective Analysis by Country of Birth, Age, and Duration of U.S. Residence," *Journal of Housing Research* 7, no. 1 (1996): 1–31; author's step-down allocation to southern California.

of new arrivals may remain fairly steady in future decades.[1] Nevertheless, each new wave of arrivals accumulates on top of its predecessors, with the result that the total foreign-born population continues to grow.

One consequence of the rapid increase of immigrants is that a very large proportion has only recently arrived. At the time of the 1980 census, 54.2 percent of all the foreign-born residents in the region had arrived in just the preceding ten years. This fraction remained relatively unchanged in 1990 because the volume of new arrivals doubled in the 1980s. From that date forward, however, with a constant flow of new arrivals, the fraction of foreign born who are newly arrived should steadily decline.

Importance of Lengthening Duration of Residence

Recency of immigration indicates a relatively unassimilated population. As the duration of residence in the U.S. lengthens, however, substantial changes are expected in immigrants' status attainments. The Southern California Immigration Project has uncovered numerous advances that occur with increasing length of residence, including increased naturalization to citizenship, improved English proficiency, occupational mobility, rising income, declining poverty, less reliance on public transit and more commuting by solo car driving, greater homeownership, and mobility out of the central city.[2]

Each of the waves of immigrants can be imagined on a trajectory of assimilation with regard to the different outcome variables. The accumulating foreign stock thus consists of some who are newcomers and have yet to progress along with others who have immigrated earlier and are relatively established and accomplished in important aspects. The total status of the population as a whole depends on the mix of these different arrival cohorts along with their rates of status attainment at each stage in their lengthening residence.

Misleading Conclusions

Casual inspection of changing immigrant characteristics in the region could produce some misleading conclusions about important issues. Consider the following incorrect inferences drawn from true data pertaining to residence in the central city, escape from poverty, and attainment of homeownership.

Some might infer that immigrants have a growing preference for living in the city of Los Angeles, given that the percentage of city residents who are immigrants increased from 27.4 percent in 1980 to 37.7 percent for 1990. Others might take the same data as evidence that immigrants' upward mobility has been increasingly thwarted.

Many have assumed that immigrants are stuck in poverty and are doomed to a lifetime of dependence. They might point to data showing that 23.5 percent of new immigrants in 1980 were poor in southern California, increasing to 24.6 percent of new immigrants in 1990. This rising poverty trend is not a favorable omen, but we will see later in the chapter that it is a highly misleading indicator of immigrants' escape from poverty.

As a third example, many observers also fear that immigrants are failing to achieve homeownership, which may have a negative impact on the region's housing market. In 1980, 24 percent of new immigrants were homeowners in southern California, falling to 22.1 percent of new immigrants in 1990. Like the poverty trend, this does not appear to augur well, but a closer look at the data is warranted.

Insights from Demography

How rapidly immigrants succeed in upward mobility is an important concern for us all. Immigrants' escape from poverty benefits not only themselves but also the host society. Similarly, immigrants' purchase of homes provides needed buyers for more established residents who are seeking to sell. But casual analysis of data leading to the misleading conclusions I have mentioned is not sufficiently sensitive to yield reliable interpretations.

Application of some basic principles from demography can help. This field provides a specific framework for conceptualizing and measuring change, something well illustrated by the example of immigrant assimilation. Adoption of that framework can yield some fundamental insights useful to public policy.

Conceptualizing Change

The general insights from demography are simple but profound. Demographic analysis focuses on counting and describing people and directly studies the diverse elements of the population and their changes.

In addition, demography emphasizes quantitative changes over time more than any other discipline or profession. With their access to extremely rich data sets such as the decennial census data, current population surveys, and records of vital statistics, demographers emphasize direct measurement of population characteristics. The quantitative units of analysis in demography are years: years of age, years of history, and years in elapsed intervals of time. In contrast, the quantitative units in economics are dollars, used in incomes and prices, which are vital for accounting purposes. Economists, however, do not always specify changes over time because of theoretical emphasis on vagaries such as "long run," "permanent income," or the instantaneous and atemporal "equilibrium." Some economists do address time series analysis, conceived as a sequence of overall conditions at points in time. Demographers, however, analyze more complex temporal structures that trace changes in temporal variables, such as age, across points in time. Much could be gained by linking economic relationships with demographers' temporal framework for describing complexities of change.

Immigration calls for demographic treatment because it is all about time: changes in the volume of new arrivals from decade to decade, changes in the status attainment of immigrants as they reside longer or age through their life cycle, and changes between the attainments of successive arrival cohorts. Analysis of problems that are embedded in the context of these multiple temporal dimensions can certainly benefit from a demographic perspective.

Changes wrought by immigrants can be conceptualized as involving three key components:

- Differences in volume of immigrants in each wave, or arrival cohort
- Differences in the initial status of successive cohorts
- Progress over time, or upward mobility, within cohorts

First, the number of people in each cohort is of great importance, and rising immigration has increased the size of immigrant cohorts. With the increasing numbers of immigrants, and especially larger numbers of new immigrants, the average character of the overall population will be weighted toward the characteristics of immigrants. We might term this component the *cohort size effect*.

Second, the initial level of advantage or achievement held by immigrants at time of arrival is also important. Arrival of new cohorts that are less advantaged will depress overall status attainment levels in the population. This is particularly true if the successive new arrivals are larger in number. This component can be termed the *cohort succession effect*.

Third, immigrants' rate of advancement or improvement over the decade has a great impact on the overall status attainment. The population's average achievements can be sustained in the face of new immigrant arrivals (particularly if those cohorts are of larger size and lower achievement) only if previous arrivals advance themselves rapidly. This third component directly measures upward mobility and can be termed the *cohort progress* or *upward mobility effect*, but its measurement is often confused with the preceding two factors.

Tracing Cohorts

A key element of demographic analysis involves tracing cohorts through time. Dually identified cohorts are required for immigration research. One dimension is the arrival cohort, the wave of immigrants arriving in a specified period, such as the 1970s. In Table 8.1 these were displayed in rows that extend across time.

The second dimension is age, defined as all persons born in a given interval—a birth cohort—and who possess the same age as one another throughout their lives. A "double cohort" method has been developed to trace the progress over time of birth cohorts nested within immigrant arrival cohorts.[3]

Age is potentially a highly misleading variable because it is so familiar and universally regarded as important. The problem is represented by misuse of the term *age cohort*, which sounds like a birth cohort but is usually just an age group. (Over time, cohorts pass from one age group to the next.) Figure 8.1 underscores how much age groups and birth cohorts differ in their representation of changes over time. Two topics are analyzed: occupational participation as gardeners, and proficiency with the English language. In turn, two views are presented on each topic: one that represents a naïve age group perspective, and one that emphasizes the cohort perspective.

Gardening is a time-honored occupation for Asian men in southern California, one that is strongly related to age. The graph on the upper left side of Figure 8.1 suggests that the older these men become, the more likely they are to become gardeners. While we might readily suspect that this is an inappropri-

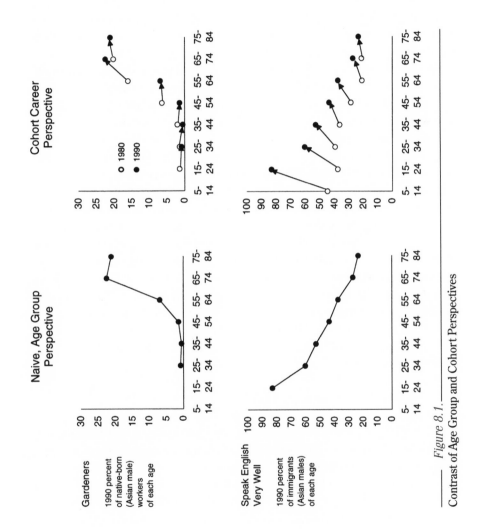

Figure 8.1.
Contrast of Age Group and Cohort Perspectives

ate conclusion when we view the data in graphic form, if age were included as a variable in a regression equation, its strong positive effect would be duly noted as significant and probably unquestioned. In contrast, the cohort career perspective links data for cohorts observed in both 1980 (white dots) and 1990 (black dots). The striking conclusion here is that cohorts are locked into life-long occupational careers. Most informative is the flat trajectory for men passing from ages 45–54 to 55–64. According to the cross-sectional age graph, their participation as professional gardeners should have turned upward; instead, the cohort retains a virtually constant percentage in the gardening occupation. When the data are viewed in cohort form, the appropriate conclusion to draw is that older Asian men were likely gardeners for their whole careers and that their sons or grandsons will never join them in that occupation.[4]

As a second example, the willingness and ability to learn English has been a key question in debates surrounding immigration. In the age group perspective, the naïve conclusion is that the older immigrants become, the less likely they are to speak English well, apparently losing ability held at younger ages (see Figure 8.1). In contrast, the more realistic cohort perspective shows that English-speaking ability grows markedly in every age group save the very oldest. On average, English proficiency accumulates over time and never declines.

In conclusion, it is apparent that cohorts need to be traced over time, not simply compared in one year. In addition, we need to keep track of multiple cohorts, each with a different arrival period and birth period. These cohorts are all at different stages in their careers, and each has a unique profile of characteristics and attainments. If we trace the cohorts over time, we can ascertain their true rate of upward mobility without being confused by other dimensions of change.

Indicators of Upward Mobility
Movement out of the Central City

The first indicator of upward mobility pertains to spatial location. In a real sense, all immigrants are spatially mobile, but we must focus on their re-location within the metropolitan region after arriving in the United States. (A small additional fraction of immigrants moves between states after arrival, but most remain located in the region of initial settlement due to the attractions of friends, relatives, and growing rootedness.) With our cohort method or census data in general, we cannot literally follow immigrants as they move around. But we can detect net shifts in the locations of immigrants over a decade's time. These net shifts contribute to overall changes in the population and are of greatest concern to policymakers.

Figure 8.2 displays the percentage of regional residents that lived inside the

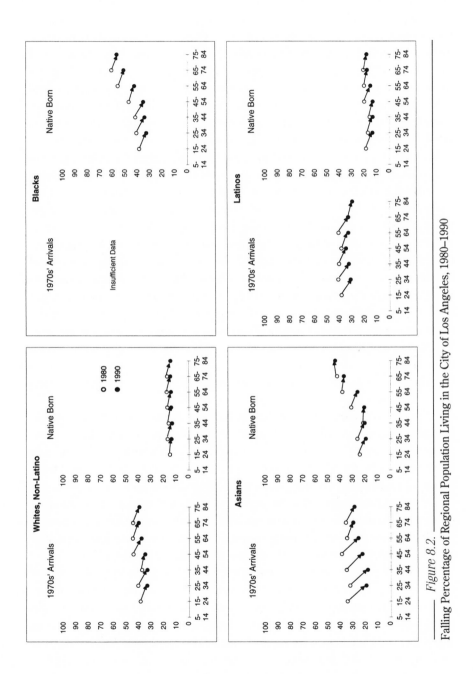

Figure 8.2.

Falling Percentage of Regional Population Living in the City of Los Angeles, 1980–1990

city of Los Angeles in 1980 and 1990. Four major race-ethnic groups are shown, with subplots for 1970s' arrivals, who were the newest immigrants in 1980, and for native-born members of the same group.[5] Within each plot, the arrows trace birth cohorts that are ten years older in 1990 than in 1980. With the series of white dots (1980) higher than the series of black dots (1990), all the cohorts trend downward. Black native-born residents are most likely to live in Los Angeles city; native-born white and Latino residents are least likely. Among the immigrants, the departure of Asians is most pronounced, with the rate of city residence falling nearly by half for some cohorts.

Overall, the pattern displayed is one of declining preference for living inside the city of Los Angeles. Immigrants may locate there soon after arrival, but after ten years of U.S. residence, substantial fractions have departed for the suburbs. Despite this clear trend, the population of the city of Los Angeles grew by half a million persons from 1980 to 1990. All of the net increase in residents was attributed to growing numbers of foreign-born residents. Thus, the departed upwardly mobile residents were replaced by a fresh wave of new immigrants, a group larger than before, that further increased the fraction of the city's residents who are foreign born. The growing percentage of foreign-born seems to indicate a growing preference for central city living, but the evidence in Figure 8.2 clearly shows dispersal out of the city. Only the growing volume of immigrants (the cohort size effect) kept the fraction of foreign-born from falling.

Escape from Poverty

The economic status of immigrants can be assessed in many ways. One of the most commonly used indicators is the poverty rate. This has two advantages. The poverty rate takes into account not only the total income of family members but also the numbers of mouths to feed. Thus, it provides a means of equating income and needs, although this formulation is far from perfect. A second advantage of using poverty rates is that they draw attention to those who are most disadvantaged—unlike mean household income, which is weighted upward by the minority of very high-income households, and median income, which draws attention to the middle-income level.

One of the major questions about immigrants is the extent to which they are mired in poverty and will remain a persistently dependent population. Examination of individual and family poverty rates in a cohort framework can help to answer this question quite directly. Figure 8.3 displays the percentage of southern California female residents living below the poverty line in 1980 and 1990. As in Table 8.2, four major race-ethnic groups are shown, with subplots for the newest arrivals in 1980 and, for comparison, for native-born members of the same group.[6] Although Table 8.3 shows only females, the two genders follow very similar poverty patterns, with the primary exception that rates for native-born black males are about 5 percent lower in the adult age range.

Most immigrant cohorts in every race-ethnic group arrive with about 20 percent of their individual members in poverty, while children and teens/young adults are quite a bit higher. Among native-born blacks and Latinos also, there is much higher poverty among the very young. This is followed by a deep decline into the middle adult years and then a modest upturn in elderly years.

The most striking aspect of Figure 8.3 is the steep downward plunge of poverty rates after immigrants have resided ten years longer in the United States. Among non-Hispanic white immigrants, poverty rates are cut to about one-third their initial level, and declines almost as great are observed among Asians. Poverty rates of Latinos also shift sharply downward. For example, of those between ages 15 and 24 in 1980, poverty was 26 percent, falling to 17 percent in 1990 at ages 25 to 34. The next older cohort shows a slower decline in poverty because this is the age range when family sizes are growing most rapidly for Latinos.

Indeed, the Latino success in escaping poverty illustrates a paradox. Among all foreign-born Latinos in the region, the poverty rate actually rose from 21 to 23 percent between 1980 and 1990, lending support to those who argue that immigrants are stuck in poverty. Yet we see plainly from Figure 8.3 that Latino immigrants markedly improved their situation over the decade. It is puzzling how this could occur for the cohorts displayed here at the same time as the total poverty situation worsened. Which measure best describes the Latino experience: rising or falling poverty?

The best explanation is that all Latino cohorts indeed reduced their incidence of poverty over the decade. Yet the arrival of a new wave of immigrants brought even larger numbers (the cohort size effect) with even higher initial poverty (the initial status effect). The net effect of the newcomers, even though all existing cohorts were rapidly improving themselves, was to push up the average number in poverty. This is not to say that these new arrivals will be doomed to poverty themselves. Instead, the likelihood is that they also will engage in upward mobility that leads them to escape from poverty. Thus, the answer to the question is that the cohort view best describes the experience of the average Latino.

Movement into Homeownership

The final indicator of upward mobility is homeownership. To many people, homeownership is the American dream: property ownership for family shelter representing the reward offered for hard work in this country. Recent

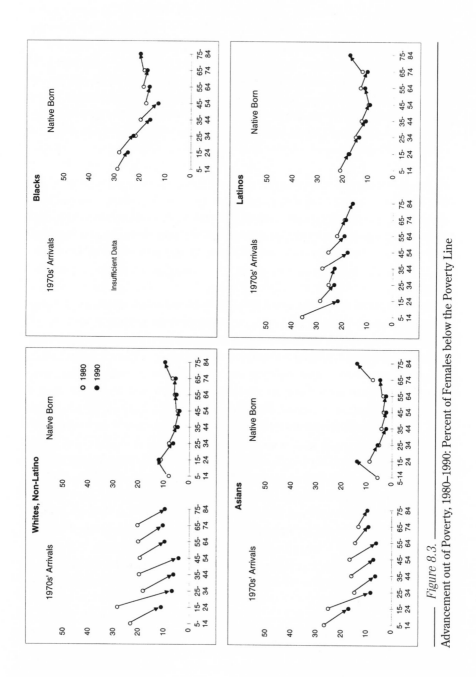

Figure 8.3.

Advancement out of Poverty, 1980–1990: Percent of Females below the Poverty Line

studies have highlighted the importance of homeownership to immigrants.[7] Unlike poverty, homeownership signifies a higher level of achievement, one approximating middle-class status. Homeownership is also often a lifelong cumulative investment, not something that changes from year to year. Accordingly, it indicates cumulative achievement of upward mobility as more of the population enters this status. Nevertheless, annual changes in economic conditions can markedly alter the rate of entry into homeownership, slowing the incremental accumulation of ownership attainment and hindering the progress of young adults.[8]

Figure 8.4 displays the progress of immigrants and native-borns into homeownership between 1980 and 1990. Like poverty, homeownership is a status shared by all members living in the household, although responsibility for the home is generally assigned to the household head or partners in the married couple who share responsibility. In the present case, the percentage of males who are homeowners is plotted.[9] Because of its cumulative lifelong quality, homeownership exhibits extremely strong age effects, with strong upward trajectories as people advance ten years further into their housing careers.

Among native-born residents, dramatic increases in ownership are observed between ages 20 and 50. Thereafter, the probability of homeownership continues to grow slightly and does not decline even among the elderly.[10] This basic pattern holds among all four major race-ethnic groups. The one partial exception is among blacks, where the upward trajectory that signifies entry into homeownership is stunted among young men. Whereas cohorts of middle-aged and older blacks achieved fairly high ownership levels, the trailing cohorts are tracking well short of those levels. For example, the cohort arriving at ages 35 to 44 in 1990 (black dot) has much lower ownership than the cohort previously located at ages 35 to 44 in 1980 (white dot). Comparison of only the age group rates in a single year would seriously mislead us about blacks' prospects for achieving homeownership as they grow older. In the naïve age-group perspective, one would assume that young blacks would leap upward to the ownership levels of older age groups (established by the higher-tracking, preceding cohorts) when they reach that advanced age. The cohort view, however, affords a more pessimistic and, unfortunately, more realistic assessment.

Immigrants deviate from this basic life-cycle pattern because their housing careers are disrupted by their international relocation. The disruption effects are most apparent for those who are middle aged upon arrival. From initially low levels, homeownership rates of all cohorts save the oldest surge upward, doubling in many cases. Substantial differences exist between the ownership levels of different immigrant groups, reflecting strong economic disparities between different immigrant flows.[11] Among Asians and white non-Hispanics

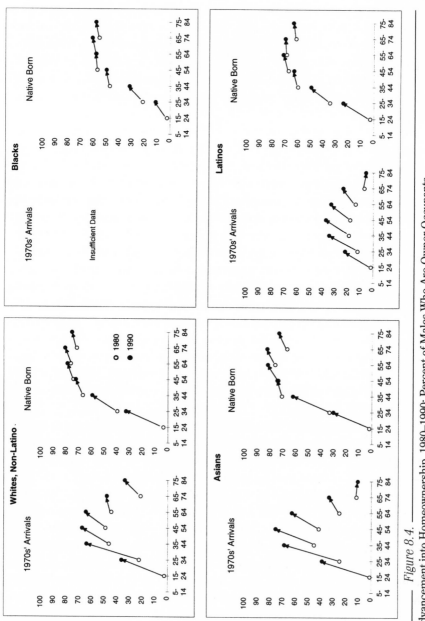

Figure 8.4.

Advancement into Homeownership, 1980–1990: Percent of Males Who Are Owner-Occupants

(which include Middle Easterners), many adult immigrants arrive with substantial savings and high earnings ability, providing them with favorable ownership opportunities from the beginning of their U.S. residence. Latino immigrants, however, are much less advantaged, possessing little wealth and low earnings ability. Their ownership rates are very low at the outset but increase markedly over a decade. Given their low advantage, Latinos' progress into homeownership is all the more remarkable, signifying a strong desire to participate in the American dream.

Implications for Public Policy

How should the preceding evidence on upward mobility be used to inform public policy? In general, the evidence that I have reported regarding immigrants' progress is positive and reassuring. Nevertheless, it also may create awareness of and appreciation for the complexity of some of the dilemmas involved. Several broad issues deserve discussion. Foremost is how better understanding of the dynamics of change is required before trends can be interpreted for effective evaluation and intervention. In addition, a focus on upward mobility also highlights certain conflicts between policies for places and policies for people. Finally, we raise several dilemmas faced by immigrant gateway communities in this era of devolution of responsibility from the federal to state level and from the state to localities.

Understanding Dynamics for Better Intervention

I presented three misleading conclusions about upward mobility in southern California: immigrants were more likely to take up residence in the central city; immigrants were increasingly poor; immigrants were less likely to attain homeownership. Which of the three key components for conceptualizing change were responsible for these conclusions? And what is the correct interpretation with regard to upward mobility? (see Table 8.2).

Central City Residence. Location in the central city was increased between 1980 and 1990 by the larger size of immigrant cohorts (the cohort size effect) because those immigrants were more likely than native-borns or longtime immigrant residents to live in the city. The newest arrivals, however, were less likely than their immediate predecessors to live in the central city (the cohort succession effect), suggesting declining preference for central city living. More important, the declining incidence of central city living within cohorts' residential careers shows that upward mobility was decreasing the likelihood of central city residence for immigrant cohorts the longer they lived in the United States (the cohort progress effect).

_____ Table 8.2 _____
Three Dimensions of Change

	Size of Cohorts	Starting Level	Rate of Change
Location in central city	More immigrants +	Fewer choose central city −	Fewer choose central city −
Poverty status	More immigrants +	Higher rate of poverty +	Falling rate of poverty −
Homeownership	More immigrants −	Lower rate of ownership −	Rising rate of ownership +

The misleading conclusion that preference was increasing did not separate out these different factors; instead, the growing size of immigrant cohorts in the region was implicitly allowed to dominate the calculation. It is not certain what policy objectives might be desired with regard to the central city concentration of immigrants. Policy initiatives intended to decrease central city concentrations of immigrants would need to reduce the overall size of immigrant waves (something controlled by federal, not local, policy, if at all), or they could attempt to accelerate the ongoing immigrant dispersal from the central city. If, on the other hand, greater central city concentration is desired, policy initiatives might include lobbying for even laxer immigration controls, advertising the virtues of the city to successive waves of new arrivals by offering relocation assistance, or establishing incentives to retain immigrants who are departing the city.

Escape from Poverty. Poverty increased because the larger size of recent immigrant waves raised the overall poverty rate to reflect new immigrants' own high poverty (which was substantially greater than that of native-borns or previous immigrants). In addition, the newest arrivals also were more likely than their immediate predecessors to be poor. Finally, the rate of change found within cohorts' careers shows that upward mobility decreased the likelihood of poverty for immigrant cohorts. The misleading conclusion of growing poverty was drawn by focusing only on the differences in the initial poverty level for successive waves of immigrant arrivals, not from their subsequent rate of progress. In fact, the poverty level of new immigrant households fell from 23.5 percent when first observed in 1980 to 16.4 percent in 1990 when they had lived in the United States ten years longer. Thus, the 1970s' arrivals became substantially less poor over time, regardless of the fact that the 1980s' arrivals were starting out at slightly higher poverty levels.

The misleading conclusion of growing poverty was reached by misusing the language of upward mobility to interpret changes between successive arrival cohorts that are entirely different groups of people. Tracking the same cohort over time yields a more meaningful expression of average individual experience. Policymakers should note the true trend in poverty experience and not be misled by other trends. If the goal, in fact, is to reverse the increase of poverty at arrival of recent cohorts, some kind of screening system would be required to ensure that immigrants entering the nation have sufficient skills and resources or that those entering the city can afford the available housing. Desires for such a screening system, however, are predicated on the assumption that the small upward shift in poverty across successive arrival cohorts foretells an immigrant population doomed to perpetual poverty. Instead, policymakers would do better to recognize the large improvements over time for existing residents and learn how to accelerate the upward mobility they are already experiencing.

Advancement into Homeownership. Attainment of homeownership was decreased by the larger size of immigrant cohorts because recent immigrants were less likely than native-borns or previous immigrants to be homeowners. In addition, the newest arrivals also were less likely than their immediate predecessors to be homeowners after arrival. On the other hand, and at the same time, we find strong evidence of increasing homeownership rates within cohorts, signifying their progress over time and, hence, upward mobility. As with poverty, the misleading conclusion was drawn by focusing only on the differences in the starting homeownership rate between successive waves of immigrant arrivals, not by measuring their subsequent rate of progress. Policy prescriptions resemble those for poverty: recognize the true rate of average individual progress, learn its mechanisms, and accelerate it.

Improvements for Places or People?

All of my discussion has assumed that upward mobility for persons is the primary criterion for successful public policy. Yet this objective may pose a conflict with public policy that is administered in specific places. A city's residents do not remain the same over time, and the lifetime trends experienced by residents can diverge greatly from the trends of the place. The result is that favorable trends recorded for either people or places may reflect the opposite for the other.

The potential conflict between place prosperity and people prosperity has long been recognized.[12] One problem is that place targeting of public programs (such as entitlement zones) is an inaccurate way to target people in need: "initially ineligible people become beneficiaries by their place of residence, while some intended beneficiaries are excluded for the same reason."[13] A second problem is that landowners can capitalize on the economic benefits targeted to places, leaving little net benefit to tenants who happen to live in the location. Alternatively, newcomers might arrive to take advantage of the place-targeted benefits, displacing the original residents for whom the programs were intended.

The people versus place distinction becomes more critical when changes are analyzed over longer time intervals. Roughly 20 percent of households change residence in a given year; taking account of repeated movers, after a decade the number of people continuing to reside in the same home may be whittled down to only a quarter or less of the original residents. Many of these movers relocate within the same city of residence, but others pass onward from city to suburb or migrate into the city from afar. Even if the city's population remains constant in size, the persons arriving in the city usually have characteristics that are systematically different from those that are departing. The result of all this mobility is that the residents at the end of a decade are substantially different people from those at the beginning. (Even those who have remained in place are ten years older than at the beginning of the decade.)

A focus only on changes in the average status of all the residents misses these dynamics of people passing through the city. Measurements of a city's residents' characteristics at specific points in time includes the most disadvantaged newcomers while overlooking the most advantaged "graduates" from the place. Thus, if either the influx of disadvantaged newcomers has been growing or the departure of upwardly mobile residents has been increasing, the city's average economic status will tend to fall over time. That downward trend for the place is a completely misleading indicator of the upward trend for the residents themselves.

This chapter has emphasized one major cause of the opposite trends for people and places: that upward mobility occurs across space as well as over time. As we have seen, upward mobility out of the central city implies that more successful residents are being lost to the suburbs. Instead, the city takes in a fresh wave of new residents who may be much less advantaged. The newcomers have much higher poverty rates than those who have resided longer, while the upwardly mobile residents who have escaped poverty and are buying homes are more likely to do so in the suburbs than in the city. The irony is that all the local residents may be upwardly mobile, but the arrival of a new, larger cohort combined with departure of many upwardly mobile residents depresses the average economic status of the city's residents.

This creates a dilemma for local officials who are responsible for well-being only in the present place and who seek evidence of positive change. What is a mayor to do? Take credit for all the successful residents who have moved out of his or her city? Or extol the virtues of less advantaged newcomers who are ready to draw upon the city's services?

Local officials who seek to elevate the status of a given place may do so contrary to the interests of initial residents. As Sawicki and Flynn allege, "public policy often aims at moving individuals in order to generate improvements in geographically-based indicators. For example, the *de facto* goal of a city policy often seems to be to displace poorer households with richer ones, thus raising the socioeconomic standards of the area."[14] Rising economic status has undeniable fiscal advantages, not to mention public relations value. On the other hand, officials in cities that operate more inclusively, incorporating waves of disadvantaged newcomers, may receive little credit for the services their cities perform or for the investments they make in upwardly mobile residents.

Intergovernmental Assistance for Immigrant Gateway Cities

Upward mobility is a primary goal of social and economic policy, and it is certainly a desired objective held out for new immigrants to the United States. Yet achievement of this upward mobility poses administrative problems when it crosses spatial boundaries. As I have shown, not only are the immigrants crossing international borders, but over time they also tend to move between cities and suburbs or, more generally, from gateway areas to more dispersed locations.

New immigrants concentrate in selected gateway communities where they receive essential support for establishing their new lives in America. Immigrants rely upon not only public services but also religious institutions and other nonprofit organizations as well as general social and economic structures of the community. Education of immigrant children and parents, job training, health care, and myriad other services all constitute essential investments made in the new residents. Through these investments immigrants become socially and economically adapted for productive lives in America and are incorporated into the mainstream. These investments make possible immigrants' subsequent upward mobility.

There has been substantial debate over the public fiscal costs of servicing the new immigrants. It is safe to say that all residents of cities are expensive, especially those with children to educate. Yet immigrants return substantial fiscal benefits paid through local property taxes, retail taxes, and state and federal income taxes. Consensus seems to be nearing that immigrants are a net fiscal benefit on the whole, but with one major discrepancy. The majority of the fiscal costs of immigrants are borne by the localities that provide education, health care, and general municipal services. Yet the majority of the fiscal benefits are received through income tax payments and Social Security payments to the federal treasury. Thus, there is a strong spatial mismatch between the costs and benefits of immigration.[15]

This imbalance between costs and benefits works to the great disadvantage of the gateway communities that are making the initial investments in new immigrants. Without this investment immigrants would be less upwardly mobile, yet the fruits of that investment are spread broadly to other jurisdictions. Not only does the federal government receive the majority of tax benefits, but even within the southern California region the economic benefits of upwardly mobile residents are dispersed beyond the gateway communities.

These spatial imbalances should be corrected by intergovernmental transfers from the federal government to the states and from the states to the counties and cities. Gateway communities such as the city of Los Angeles clearly deserve support for their essential investments in the nation's new immigrants. The simple principle of local taxation for local services for local residents is very shortsighted. That principle assumes that services are merely consumed in the present and are not investments in the future. It also assumes that residents will remain within their present community for life. My findings of upward mobility clearly undermine these assumptions: immigrants are highly mobile in both space and time.

Unfortunately, recommendation for intergovernmental assistance runs counter to the rising tide of support for devolution, a transfer of decision-making power and fiscal responsibility from higher to lower levels of government. A correlate of greater local control is loss of fiscal support. One great injustice posed by immigration is that localities have no constitutional right either to exercise their own immigration policy (only the federal government can control the international border) or to limit free movement between states and localities within the United States. Yet these powerless localities must foot the bill for human investment needed by any residents who choose local residence. Adding to the injustice, the fruits of that investment are then lost to the gateway communities when successful, upwardly mobile immigrants depart to other jurisdictions.

Upward mobility is a deeply valued objective in America, one pertaining to both native-born and immigrant residents. My analysis has explored three indicators of upward mobility that are highlighted by the rapid changes for immigrants: movement from central city to suburbs, escape from poverty, and attainment of homeownership.

One lesson is that measurement of trends with regard to these indicators can be confused by the interaction of three underlying components of change: the size of arriving cohorts, their initial status attainment relative to preceding arrivals, and immigrants' rate of progress over time. These components yield changes in population characteristics for places, often disguising the underlying changes for people themselves. Analysis reveals a substantial discrepancy between a focus on changes for places and changes for people. For example, places may be growing in poverty because of the size of arriving cohorts and their higher initial poverty, yet we find that the great majority of the residents are participating in upward mobility. Some of this upward mobility leads to spatial mobility, with the most successful immigrants dispersing to the suburbs.

A second lesson is that a focus on cohorts' progress through their careers holds the key to understanding changes for people as opposed to the places they occupy. Rather than compare places that are a mélange of different cohorts all at different career stages, we need to trace specific cohorts over time, not simply compare them in one year. In this manner we can ascertain the true experience of upward mobility without being confused by other dimensions of change.

The third lesson is that the policy conflicts between the place perspective and the people perspective can be profound. Population flows across borders and jurisdictional boundaries, acquiring investment from local services at one point in time and repaying benefits elsewhere at a later time. Local officials may despair that the population influx is driving down the city's average economic status, while spatial dispersal to the suburbs is robbing the city of its assets. Instead, they may wish to elevate their city's economic status by displacing the poor and impeding upward mobility of successful residents to the suburbs. Yet the laws of free movement prevail.

The final lesson is that a rational and fair solution requires intergovernmental transfers to spread the benefits and costs of immigration more evenly. At present the bulk of the tax benefits are received by the federal government, while the bulk of the service costs are borne by the gateway communities. Contrary to the spirit of devolution, every locality is not truly an island of self-accountability. Devolution accentuates the emphasis on enhancing the local place without regard to population movements across places. In contrast, free movement and upward mobility in America more likely require intergovernmental sharing of resources and responsibilities.

Notes

1. John Pitkin and Patrick Simmons, "The Foreign-Born Population to 2010: A Prospective Analysis by Country of Birth, Age, and Duration of U.S. Residence," *Journal of Housing Research* 7, no. 1 (1996): 1–31.
2. Conducted at the University of Southern California, with primary support from the Los Angeles–based Haynes Foundation, the Southern California Immigration Project has analyzed a broad set of indicators of immigrants' progress between 1980 and 1990. Exploiting a wide array of information collected by the decennial census, the study reports its principal findings in the following: Dowell Myers, "The Changing Immigrants of Southern California," research report no. LCRI–95–04R (Los Angeles: University of Southern California, School of Urban Planning and Development, 1995); Dowell Myers, Maria Yen, and Lonnie Vidaurri, "Transportation, Housing and Urban Planning Implications of Immigration to Southern California," research report no. LCRI–96–04R (Los Angeles: University of Southern California, School of Urban Planning and Development, 1996); Dowell Myers, Cynthia Cranford, Julie Park, Sarah Imber, and Lee Menifee, "Upward Mobility Through Los Angeles: Immigrant Trajectories of Poverty and Location, 1980 through 2020," research report no. LCRI–97–01R (Los Angeles: University of Southern California, School of Urban Planning and Development, 1997).
3. Dowell Myers and Seong Woo Lee, "Immigration Cohorts and Residential Overcrowding in Southern California," *Demography* 33, no. 1 (1996): 51–65; Dowell Myers and Cynthia Cranford, "Temporal Differentiation in the Occupational Mobility of Immigrant and Native-Born Latina Workers," *American Sociological Review* 63, no. 1 (1998): 68–93.
4. The small upward rise for men passing to ages 65 to 74 in 1990 likely reflects a shift in the worker population in retirement years. While men in some occupations retire at 65, thus dropping out of the labor force, gardeners are more likely to continue; therefore, the occupational percentage of all workers jumps.
5. Black immigrants to the United States are relatively small in number, and relatively few come to southern California, making up only 1 percent of the 1970s' arrivals. As a result, the sample is too small to reliably plot estimates by age.
6. Myers, "The Changing Immigrants of Southern California." This study also reports male rates.
7. *Fannie Mae National Housing Survey, 1995: Immigrants, Homeownership, and the American Dream* (Washington, D.C.: Fannie Mae, 1995).
8. James W. Hughes, "Economic Shifts and the Changing Homeownership Trajectory," *Housing Policy Debate* 7, no. 2 (1996): 293–325; Dowell Myers and Jennifer Wolch, "Polarization of Housing Status," in *State of the Union,* vol. 1, *Economic Trends,* ed. R. Farley (New York: Russell Sage Foundation, 1995), 269–334.
9. The result for the percentage of females is virtually the same because husbands and wives share ownership and nonmarried males have low ownership rates much like nonmarried females. If males and females are both counted, homeownership is double-counted for married couples; however, if only one person per household is allowed to be the homeowner, the maximum ownership rate for married couples falls to 50 percent, and the overall ownership level of the population appears much lower than is the case for their actual living situation. Although ownership rates are

plotted for only half the population, it should be understood that these mirror the other half as well.

10. The slight upturn in ownership rates among the oldest cohort does not reflect increased home buying at that advanced age but the higher mortality of renters, who are generally of lower economic status and in worse health than owners.

11. Roger Waldinger, "Ethnicity and Opportunity in the Plural City," in *Ethnic Los Angeles,* ed. Roger Waldinger and Mehdi Bozorgmehr (New York: Russell Sage Foundation, 1996), 445–70.

12. Louis Winnick, "Place Prosperity and People Prosperity: Welfare Considerations in the Geographic Distribution of Economic Activity," in *Essays in Urban Land Economics in Honor of the Sixty-Fifth Birthday of Leo Grebler,* ed. Real Estate Research Program (Los Angeles: University of California at Los Angeles, Real Estate Research Program, 1966), 273–83; Matthew Edel, "'People' versus 'Places' in Urban Impact Analysis," in *The Urban Impacts of Public Policies,* ed. Norman J. Glickman (Baltimore: Johns Hopkins University Press, 1980), 175–91; Roger Bolton, "'Place Prosperity vs. People Prosperity' Revisited: An Old Issue with a New Angle," *Urban Studies* 29, no. 2 (1992): 185–203; David S. Sawicki and Patrice Flynn, "Neighborhood Indicators: A Review of the Literature and an Assessment of Conceptual and Methodological Issues," *Journal of the American Planning Association* 64 (Spring) (1996): 165–83.

13. Edel, "'People' versus 'Places,'" 178.

14. Sawicki and Flynn, "Neighborhood Indicators," 175.

15. James P. Smith and Barry Edmonston, eds., *The New Americans: Economic, Demographic, and Fiscal Effects of Immigration* (Washington, D.C.: National Academy Press, 1997).

Part V
The Great American Family Dilemma

Chapter 9

Daphne Spain

Balancing Act

If You've Got the Money,
Honey, I've Got the Time

If you were a Willie Nelson fan during Jimmy Carter's presidency, you may remember the song that shares the name of my subtitle. Willie was singing about a broke cowboy looking for a date, but the title captures the balancing act that has existed in most families as recently as 1970, when 87 percent of families consisted of married couples and only 16 percent of married mothers were employed full time. Husbands made the money, and wives made the time for family life.

As we approach the twenty-first century, however, only about two-thirds of all families include both parents, and 38 percent of married mothers are employed full time. Since men have not taken on domestic responsibilities as vigorously as women have entered the labor force, we've seen a gradual erosion of family time. The great American family dilemma is that both women and men now have the money (although women earn only 71 percent of what men earn), but nobody has the time.

An exploration of changing demographic trends will show how they are related to the availability of family time. Most people today complain about being too rushed, having too little time to do the things they enjoy, or being overscheduled. Books such as Juliet Schor's *The Overworked American* and Steven Covey's *Seven Habits of Highly Effective People* reflect these concerns.[1] Even children are affected. The *Washington Post* recently ran an article about middle school students who were issued weekly appointment calendars along with their textbooks.

One reason that the shortage of time, especially "quality time," has become such an important issue is that *women's* time is now scarce. Women's role in the family has evolved from expressive to instrumental in several ways since the 1970s, and that change has created a time shortage with repercussions for the entire family.[2] It is necessary to examine how federal, state, and local policies can address the time needs of families.

How Families Have Changed

Families have changed radically since the baby boom era, when the typical woman married at age 20, had 3.5 children, and was unlikely either to work outside the home or experience divorce. But those years (which baby boomers are so nostalgic about) are a demographic anomaly. Age at first marriage and divorce rates were unusually low, while fertility was unusually high.

Focusing on changes in the family since the 1970s rather than the 1950s illustrates how much families have been transformed within one generation. The most obvious difference is that the traditional definition of *family* has been expanded to include those consisting of homosexual couples, cohabiting partners, single parents, or members blended together after remarriage. Three demographic trends have contributed to a time shortage for all types of families: the decline in the proportion of married-couple families, the rise of mothers' entry into the labor force, and the persistently gendered distribution of housework and child care.

Decline in the Proportion of Married-Couple Families

Since 1970, the proportion of all families consisting of two parents and their children has declined from 87 to 68 percent. Mother-child families have increased from 12 to 27 percent of all families, and father-child families have risen from 1 to 5 percent of all families.[3]

Family structure differs significantly by race and ethnicity. Married couples form about three-quarters of white families, about one-third of black families, and approximately two-thirds of Hispanic families. Single mothers account for one-fifth of white families, more than one-half of black families, and about one-third of Hispanic families.

The growth in proportions of single mothers results from high rates of divorce and out-of-wedlock births. Just as sex was separated from procreation with the introduction of effective contraception, marriage has become separated from family formation. While most sexual activity and marriages involve both women and men, however, it is still women who carry disproportionate responsibility for single parenting.

Indeed, father absence has been identified as a new social crisis. In *Life Without Father,* David Popenoe reports that the proportion of children who live apart from their fathers is now approaching one-third as a result of high rates of divorce, out-of-wedlock births, and cohabitation.[4] Popenoe suggests that men are abandoning fatherhood because economic, federal, and cultural trends are devaluing their role in the family, and he argues for various strategies that would reinforce men's commitment to traditional marriage and biological fatherhood. This approach, though, begs for a return to a narrow definition of family and to an outdated economic reality. It also implies, despite Popenoe's strenuous objections to the contrary, that women are somehow to blame for this sorry state of affairs. The subtext of his book seems to be that if only women would stay home and play their caregiving (expressive) role in the family, men could be more successful at the (instrumental) wage-earning role, and children would benefit from this arrangement. Popenoe is not alone in his tendency to target women as the source of family problems: welfare moms are subject to much harsher treatment under the new welfare reform act than are deadbeat dads.

Since it is unlikely that federal policies will quickly reverse a trend toward single-parent families, it is more productive to establish policies that address the time concerns of families as they currently exist. The increase in the proportion of single mothers has specific implications for the use of time. Even among married couples in which the wife performs most of the household chores and child care, the presence of another adult provides an alternative to constant responsibility for children. A single parent, however, is on duty twenty-four hours a day, seven days a week. The time demands of children vary with their ages: the youngest ones need supervision, and the older ones need to be driven to various places. If a single parent cannot personally provide for a child's needs, she must arrange to have those needs met by hiring someone to baby-sit, trading off sleepovers with a friend, or organizing transportation to soccer practice with a neighbor. These arrangements do not just happen; they take time.

Rather than being rewarded for taking care of their children, though, single mothers often are stigmatized while the fathers of their children pay few social or economic penalties. Child support from absent fathers, for example, is notoriously difficult to collect. The real question for the twenty-first century is not "what do we do about single mothers?" but "why are women still being blamed for raising children outside of marriage while men are rarely held accountable?"

The Rise in Mothers' Labor Force Participation

Women's greater economic responsibility for their families has led both unmarried and married mothers to enter the labor force in growing numbers since the 1970s. The proportion of married mothers in the labor force rose from 40 to 70 percent between 1970 and 1995. Among unmarried mothers, about one-half of those who never married were in the labor force in 1980 and in 1995. Greater changes occurred for widowed, divorced, or separated mothers: 61 percent were in the labor force in 1970 compared with 75 percent in 1995.[5]

Since unmarried mothers are more likely to be in the labor force than married mothers, their time is even more limited than that of wives. Unmarried mothers are fully responsible for the physical, emotional, and economic well-being of their children and must allocate time accordingly without a spouse to share tasks. The balancing act between family and employment obligations is challenging for most women, but single mothers experience even more difficulties.

Trend data for married mothers' labor force attachment illustrate that the greatest changes have occurred for women with preschoolers. The proportion of married mothers with children under age 6 who worked full time, year round tripled between 1970 and 1996, from one-tenth to almost one-third. The proportion of married mothers with school-age children who are employed full time has almost doubled, from 23 to 44 percent during the same time period (see Table 9.1).

The resulting "life without mother" at home takes a toll on families. Married couples in which both partners are employed spend less time with each other and less time with their children than do couples in which only one spouse is employed.[6] Time pressures on employed mothers differ somewhat from the pressures on mothers who work only in the home. Commuting, for example, becomes an issue. Women work closer to home than men, at least partially so they can be available for children's emergencies. Women are more likely than men to use public transit. Yet since the majority of mothers work part time, their commuting needs differ from the peak hours around which most public transit systems are arranged. Women also are more likely than men to "trip-chain," or combine work trips with household errands. It is not surprising, then, that the proportion of women using public transit and carpooling has declined while their use of private cars has increased.[7]

Women need the flexibility a car offers in order to reach their jobs, pick up the kids, buy groceries, and stop by the video store or library. It is not just that cars are more convenient than public transit; public transit often fails to go to all the places that women need to be. Zoning laws that separate residential from commercial districts make it unlikely that home, job, child care, and shopping facilities are in close proximity.[8] Public transit can also present actual obstacles to women. The escalators and turnstiles in subway systems, for example, are almost impossible to navigate with a baby stroller or toddler in tow.[9]

_____ *Table 9.1* _____
Married Mothers' Labor Force Attachment, 1970–1996

Status of Mothers	1970	1980	1990	1996
With children under age 18				
Percentage who worked last year	51	63	73	74
Percentage who worked full time,				
year round	16	23	34	38
With children under age 6				
Percentage who worked last year	44	58	68	68
Percentage who worked full time,				
year round	10	18	28	31
With children ages 6–17				
Percentage who worked last year	58	68	78	80
Percentage who worked full time,				
year round	23	29	40	44

SOURCE: U.S. Bureau of Labor Statistics, *Current Population Survey*, unpublished tabulations, 1970–90; Population Reference Bureau analysis of data from the March 1996 *Current Population Survey*, 1996.

NOTE: Data are for women age 16 and over who are married and living with their husbands.

The journey to work introduces a significant time pressure for mothers that did not exist twenty-five years ago. So, too, does the obvious fact that women spend less time in the home now. Whether women have entered the labor force out of choice or necessity is irrelevant to the loss of twenty to forty or more hours per week of time at home experienced by the majority of mothers. What gives in this scenario? Leisure activities are probably the first: birthday parties at Chuckie Cheeze instead of in the backyard, shorter vacations closer to home due to conflicting schedules, "bureaucratized play" organized for children whose parents probably never belonged to a soccer team. When baby boomers long for the lost family, they're forgetting how much of a mother's time was spent creating family events.

The Gendered Distribution of Housework and Child Care

The shortage of time created by changes in mothers' labor force participation rates has been exacerbated by the lack of change in the distribution of household and child care tasks. The amount of housework that men report doing has risen since the 1970s, and the amount that women report doing has declined, but women still perform twice the number of hours of housework as men. Although data for the 1990s are not yet available, data for the 1980s

_____ *Table 9.2* _____
Hours per Week Men and Women Spend Doing Housework,
1965, 1975, 1985

Gender/Characteristic	1965	1975	1985	Change 1965–85
Total, ages 18–65				
Men	4.6	7.0	9.8	+ 5.2
Women	27.0	21.7	19.5	– 7.5
Ratio of men to women	0.17	0.32	0.50	
Married				
Husbands	4.5	6.8	11.1	+6.6
Wives	31.6	24.2	22.4	– 9.2
Ratio of husbands to wives	0.14	0.28	0.50	
With preschool-age children				
Fathers	3.9	5.9	9.0	+ 5.1
Mothers	32.0	25.1	22.5	– 9.5
Ratio of fathers to mothers	0.12	0.24	0.40	
With school-age children				
Fathers	5.3	7.6	10.4	+ 5.1
Mothers	30.3	23.9	19.9	– 10.4
Ratio of fathers to mothers	0.17	0.32	0.52	

SOURCE: John P. Robinson, "Who's Doing the Housework?" *American Demographics* 10, no. 12: 24–28.

NOTE: Housework includes cooking meals, meal cleanup, house cleaning, doing laundry, outdoor chores, repairs, garden and animal care, and paying bills. It excludes child care.

suggest that women do about twenty hours of household work per week compared with ten hours for men regardless of marital status or presence and age of children (see Table 9.2).

These statistics exclude child care, which occurs increasingly outside the home: one-quarter of children whose mothers work full time and 15 percent of children whose mothers work part time are now in a group-care center compared with about half that proportion during the 1970s.[10] Travel to child care facilities generates one more time demand, often contributing to trip-chaining in a mother's journey-to-work commute. Interestingly, the Census Bureau collects data on child care arrangements only for the children of working mothers, not for working fathers, a clear signal that women are still overwhelmingly responsible for child care. An aging population means that care of the elderly may also soon fall to women, in which case we may see census statistics on parental care arrangements of working daughters.

Women perform a wider variety of tasks than men do: the majority of women are employed outside the home, and they retain primary responsibility for child care and housework within the home. These multiple obligations through which women "compose a life" may be inherently rewarding, but they also take time.[11] Several suggestions for public policies could address this shortage of time in ways that would improve the quality of life for all families.

Public Policies to Increase Family Time

Federal, state, and local policies could be implemented to increase time for women and their families. Some of these have historical precedents, while others require new solutions.

Federal Policies

In 1943 the federal Public Housing Authority built a new town for defense workers at the shipyards in Vanport City, Oregon. The entire project was completed in ten months by crews working around the clock every day of the week. Because many single mothers were doing double duty as Rosie the Riveter, child care facilities were an important part of the plan. Child care centers were located in a straight line between home and work to minimize travel time. They were open twenty-four hours a day, seven days a week (just like the shipyards), and provided infirmaries for sick children, bathtubs so mothers did not have to bathe children at home, and cooked food so mothers could pick up hot casseroles along with their children. The town, nicknamed Kaiserville after the industrialist who owned the shipyards, eventually housed 40,000 people.[12]

The example of Kaiserville suggests that the federal government can respond quickly to the needs of working families when the occasion demands it. An immediate threat to national security such as a war, however, has been replaced by the slow erosion of family time resulting from men's and women's involvement in the labor force and the absence of responsive public policies.

Kaiserville set a precedent for federal family policy, one that is now nearly erased from memory. Just as the United States has forgotten historical lessons, it also has ignored contemporary lessons from its international peers. All industrialized nations except the United States have generous maternity leave, child care, and subsidy policies that encourage women and men to combine employment with family responsibilities. Paid maternity (and sometimes paternity) leave in Europe varies from 8 weeks in Switzerland to 65 weeks in Sweden, low-cost or free day care is available, parents are encouraged to work fewer hours when their children are young, and families receive direct allowances based on the numbers and ages of children. By contrast, the Family and Medical Leave Act enacted in the United States in 1993 guarantees only twelve weeks of unpaid leave to male and female employees working in large firms.[13]

Redefining full-time work to mean thirty to thirty-five hours per week rather than thirty-five hours or more per week and adjusting benefits accordingly might be encouraged at the national level. The length of the work week has been modified historically to reflect changing technology, and computers are only the latest link in that long chain of development. Just as the federal bureaucracy took the lead in hiring women at the turn of the twentieth century, it could become a pioneer in promoting the shorter work week at the turn of the twenty-first century.[14] Both men and women would be eligible for reduced hours, and lower expectations for hours of paid employment among men might contribute to more evenly distributed chores within the home.

State Policies

Three policies that would create more time for families could be instituted at the state level. The first—modifying the school calendar—may seem counter-intuitive at first, yet lengthening the school day and the school year would benefit families in the long run. A school day that ends at 3:00 P.M. is based on the assumption that mothers (not fathers) will be home when children get out of school. This assumption is as outdated as the school year that lasts from September through June because children were once needed to plant crops in the summer. In other words, the hours of the day and the months of the year in which children attend school are driven by traditions that may have little to do with optimal learning conditions.

Educators and politicians have already begun to question whether our current educational system produces students who are competitive in the global market. If the school day and the school year are extended in the interests of the economy, one probable side effect is that mothers will be less constrained in labor force participation and career advancement. If school calendars were organized around adults' working hours instead of mothers' paid work being organized around children's school hours, the result could be more family time. Schools have already made some concessions to the rise in women's labor force participation by requiring children to enroll in school at younger ages and by providing after-school programs. Mandatory kindergarten was instituted almost twenty years ago, and after-school programs were organized more than ten years ago. It is now time to lengthen the formal school day to provide both instruction and supervision for the children of parents who work full time.

A second way in which states can increase the amount of time that families have together is through the coordination of child care facilities with transit stops. Maryland's Department of Transportation has cosponsored KidStop, a child care facility built in 1994 at a Montgomery County Metrorail station in the suburban Washington, D.C., area. Funding was provided by the Foundation for Working Families, a public-private partnership of county government, the school system, and eleven area companies. The foundation raised construction money that was matched by the state; the Washington Metropolitan Area Transit Authority gave the group a thirty-year lease on two acres for ten dollars, and corporate donations allowed firms to reserve slots at the center for employee's children for the next ten years. KidStop (dubbed "kiss and cry" rather than "park and ride" or "kiss and ride") served 60 children last year and has the capacity for 120. Similar efforts to simplify parents' schedules are being tried in Illinois and California.[15]

A third way in which states can address the family time issue is by implementing flex time for state employees. Since so much of state work involves secretarial/clerical skills and almost 80 percent of administrative support workers are female, a state-wide policy granting greater flexibility would benefit women.[16] If the secretaries at state universities and the clerks in departments of motor vehicles, social services, and human resources were eligible for flex time, mothers might choose to arrive at work earlier and leave earlier to be home when their children get out of school, while women without children might come in later and stay later. Longer hours would fit the needs of both providers and consumers of state services since many people cannot leave work before 5:00 P.M. to conduct business.

Local Policies

The same flex time policies proposed for the state level could be adopted at the local level. County government offices, for example, are staffed predominantly by women. Staggered hours would allow employees greater flexibility in meeting family needs and would allow citizens time to purchase parking decals or dog licenses after they get off work.

Two other local policies that might reduce the time burden on families have been tried in the past but have been virtually abandoned. One is the practice of sending bookmobiles into the community instead of requiring patrons to come to the library. Budget cuts and suburban sprawl have reduced the ability of libraries to provide such services, but they are needed today even more than they were twenty years ago, when fewer mothers worked. The contemporary version might include videos and computer games in addition to books that appeal to children, but the principle is the same: taking services to the neighborhood reduces the travel (and thus time) demands for parents.

Along the same lines, localities might consider encouraging street vendors. People selling produce, milk, and bread throughout suburban neighborhoods would save travel and shopping time for countless families. Vendors could be issued business licenses after passing appropriate health inspection guidelines, generating additional local tax revenues and opening doors to microenterprise efforts. According to historian Ruth Schwartz Cowan, the demise of home delivery services during the 1930s contributed to a significant growth in the amount of time that women spent behind the wheel. Once grocery stores and butcher shops eliminated deliveries in order to compete with supermarket chains, the burden of providing transportation shifted from sellers to consumers—typically women. Cowan notes that "by midcentury the time that housewives had once spent in preserving strawberries and stitching petticoats was being spent in driving to stores, shopping, and waiting in lines."[17] Bringing delivery services back to the home is thus another way to reduce the time demands on families.

Finally, modifying zoning laws to permit mixed-use development could introduce a commercial and residential combination that would reduce travel time and encourage pedestrian activity. This idea has been proposed by numerous others but needs to be repeated often.

Life is typically a trade-off between time and money. In the traditional family, men had the money and women had the time; a sufficiency of both is what many baby boomers remember about their childhoods. But the decline in the proportion of all families maintained by married couples, the increase in mothers' labor force participation, and the persistently gendered nature of domestic work has created historically new demands on women that affect the entire family's disposable time as certainly as their disposable income. "If you've got the money, honey, I've got the time" is a refrain that only Willie Nelson now has the luxury of singing. Many parents now have the money provided by their jobs, but few have as much time as they would like.

Public policy can address the time shortage in American family life in several ways. At the federal level, proactive family leave and child care policies coupled with a shorter work week could facilitate the combination of family life and paid employment. States could implement school calendar changes, transit-based day care, and flex time employment options as corollary contributions to the reduction of time demands. Localities could use flex time, delivery of services to the neighborhood, and mixed-use zoning to compensate for the family time that most mothers now lose to the labor force and to travel demands. And lest we forget the individual household level, husbands or children could do more of the domestic work that women traditionally have performed.

I began this chapter by asking why women are still blamed somehow for raising children outside marriage while men seem to escape comparable social and economic stigma. Part of the answer, of course, is that women still bear the physical responsibility of pregnancy and that men still are employed for more hours and earn more money. But as women adopt more of men's social patterns by choosing to drive cars, finish college, work outside the home, smoke, and drink, they may also choose life without children. So I will end with a still more important question for the twenty-first century: what will American society do if both women *and* men decide they have no time for children? Before we reach that point, we must implement policies that will make it unnecessary to ask such a question.

Notes

1. Juliet Schor, *The Overworked American: The Unexpected Decline of Leisure* (New York: Basic Books, 1992); Steven Covey, *Seven Habits of Highly Effective People* (New York: Simon and Schuster, 1989).
2. Talcott Parsons and R. F. Bales, *Family: Socialization and Interaction Process* (New York: Free Press, 1955).
3. U.S. Bureau of the Census, "Household and Family Characteristics: March 1994," *Current Population Reports* P20–483, (February 1996): tab. F; Population Reference Bureau analysis of the March 1996 *Current Population Survey,* 1996.
4. David Popenoe, *Life Without Father* (New York: Free Press, 1996).
5. U.S. Bureau of the Census, *Statistical Abstract of the United States, 1996* (Washington, D.C.: U.S. Government Printing Office, 1996).
6. Paul W. Kingston and Steven L. Nock, "Time Together among Dual-Earner Couples," *American Sociological Review* 52 (June 1987): 391–400; Steven L. Nock and Paul W. Kingston, "Time with Children: The Impact of Couples' Work-Time Commitments," *Social Forces* 67 (September 1988): 59–85.
7. Sandra Rosenbloom, "Travel by Women," in *Demographic Special Reports from the 1990 NPTS Report Series* (Washington, D.C.: U.S. Department of Transportation, 1995), 2–9.
8. Dolores Hayden, *Redesigning the American Dream: The Future of Housing, Work, and Family Life* (New York: Norton, 1984); Marsha Ritzdorf, "Women and the City: Land Use and Zoning Issues," *Journal of Urban Resources* 3 (May 1988): 23–27.
9. Daphne Spain, "Run, Don't Walk: How Transportation Complicates Women's Balancing Act," paper presented at the Second Annual Conference on Women's Travel Issues, Baltimore, October 24–26, 1996.
10. Daphne Spain and Suzanne M. Bianchi, *Balancing Act: Motherhood, Marriage, and Employment among American Women* (New York: Russell Sage Foundation, 1996).
11. Catherine Bateson, *Composing a Life* (New York: Dutton, 1990).
12. Hayden, *Redesigning the American Dream,* 3, 4.
13. Suzanne M. Bianchi and Daphne Spain, "Women, Work, and Family in America," *Population Bulletin* 51, no. 3 (1996): 42.

14. Cindy Aron, *Ladies and Gentlemen of the Civil Service* (New York: Oxford University Press, 1987).

15. Alex Daniels, "Making a Connection Between Day Care and Commuting," *Governing* 8, no. 11 (1995): 60.

16. Bianchi and Spain, "Women, Work, and Family in America."

17. Ruth Schwartz Cowan, *More Work for Mother: The Ironies of Household Technology from the Open Hearth to the Microwave* (New York: Basic Books, 1983), 85.

Chapter 10

David Popenoe

American Family Decline
Public Policy Considerations

It is surprising that a debate still ensues within the academic world over the issue of family decline. While virtually all Americans believe that the family as a social institution has weakened in recent decades, many voices in academia, especially within the social sciences and humanities, stubbornly cling to the belief that the family has not declined or weakened but has merely changed and that the many new alternative family forms we see around us have surprising strengths. Indeed, some see marked improvements as a result of recent family trends. Yet if virtually all empirical trend indicators provide the basis for judgment, the family declinists have the case sewn up. And if child outcomes provide a good measure of family progress or decline, the case for decline is even more certain.

The Evidence
Let us consider the evidence.[1] Between 1960 and the present, the divorce rate has increased between two and three times. The chances of a marriage ending in divorce in 1960 were below 20 percent; today they are between 40 and 50 percent. The out-of-wedlock birth rate has increased from 5 percent in 1960 to 32 percent today. In other words, nearly one-third of all American children are born outside of marriage. In the great majority of cases, this means without the father living with the mother, whether married or not. Mainly because of these two factors, divorce and nonmarital births, the percentage of children living apart from their biological fathers increased from 17 percent in 1960 to nearly 40 percent today.

Have these family changes helped children? Hardly. By some measures—such as more years of education and better medical care—American children have continued the gains of recent centuries. But the American public is correct in its belief (documented by numerous public opinion polls) that, in fact, child well-being in recent decades has deteriorated markedly. As Senator Daniel Patrick Moynihan has observed, "the United States . . . may be the first society in history in which children are distinctly worse off than adults."[2]

Juvenile violent crime has increased sixfold, from 16,000 arrests in 1960 to 96,000 in 1992, a period in which the total number of juveniles in the population remained relatively stable. Since 1976, when the data were first collected, reports of child abuse and neglect have quintupled. Eating disorders and rates of unipolar depression have soared among adolescent girls. Teen suicide has tripled.[3]

Since 1970, despite widespread economic growth, the percentage of children who are poor has increased; poverty has shifted from the elderly to the young. Substantial agreement now exists that the growth of child poverty is in large part due the retreat of fathers from the lives of their children: in other words, the rapid growth of single-parent, mother-headed families.[4] The chances of being poor when growing up in a single-parent family are five to six times stronger than they are when growing up in an intact family (that is, a married couple family).

Beyond poverty, however, the academic world has been surprisingly reticent to link other negative child outcomes to family change. Certainly many other factors have adversely affected children in recent decades, including television and the mass media, commercialism and consumerism, the decline of neighborhoods, and the widespread availability of guns and addictive drugs. Yet a myriad of studies now firmly links family decline to poor child outcomes, a conclusion that anyone could have predicted based on one simple fact—that a child's family is by far the most important influence in his or her life. For many serious outcomes, including becoming a delinquent, dropping out of high school, having an out-of-wedlock teen birth, and having a failed marriage, young people from non-intact families have two to three times the likelihood of occurrence compared to young people from intact families.[5]

Surprisingly, it is not simply having two parents that makes the difference. Stepfamilies have about the same negative child outcomes as single-parent families. Indeed, for child abuse the statistics on stepfamilies look exceedingly gloomy. According to several studies, a child in a stepfamily, compared to a child in an intact family with two natural parents, is seven times more likely to suffer sexual abuse, forty times more likely to suffer physical abuse, and a staggering one hundred times more likely to be killed when under the age of 3.[6]

As sociologists Sara McLanahan and Gary Sandefur concluded after an exhaustive study:

> If we were asked to design a system for making sure that children's basic needs were met, we would probably come up with something quite similar to the two-parent family idea. Such a design, in theory, would not only ensure that children had access to the time and money of two adults, it also would provide a system of checks and balances that promoted quality parenting. The fact that both adults have a biological connection to the child would increase the likelihood that the parents would identify with the child and be willing to sacrifice for that child. . . . While we recognize that two-parent families frequently do not live up to this ideal in all respects, nevertheless we would expect children who grow up in two-parent families to be doing better, on average, than children who grow up with only one parent.[7]

Why Is There Still a Debate about Family Decline?

In view of this overwhelming evidence, on what possible basis can it be held that the family has "just changed" and, it is said, often for the better? The possible basis is certainly not evidential; rather, it appears to be mostly ideological. There are strong ideological bases for maintaining the belief that families today are well and fine.[8]

First, radical feminists have long held the view that the traditional nuclear family made up of breadwinning patriarch husband and homemaking wife was the root of much evil in the world. They manifest a generalized anxiety that anyone who shows concern about family change is really seeking to return to the past, to return to the patriarchal family in which women were kept at home. To suggest that the demise of this family form should be thought of as decline is simply out of the question. What it really represents, in their view, is progress.

Second, alternative family forms now encompass a large number of people—so many, in fact, that it is tempting to normalize the situation. Why should people in single-parent families and stepfamilies be singled out as in some way deviant or as inhabiting weaker family forms? Indeed, many such families are highly successful; and if society would just accept and help them, they could be even more successful. Moreover, if successful child outcomes are desired, to stigmatize these families is about the worst thing society could do. So let's stop all this decline talk and just get used to it: get used to all the bright, new family forms we see around us. This line of thinking is especially strong among front-line social workers, who are closely involved with alternative families, and among many leaders and advocates of minority communities, especially blacks, where alternative family forms are now in the statistical majority.

Third, the gay and lesbian communities have achieved enormous cultural clout in recent years. Gays and lesbians do not live in nuclear families, and they therefore have a large stake in maintaining the proposition that nuclear families should not be the norm. Why should their family (and nonfamily) forms be thought of as weak or deviant?

Fourth, some observers are incorrigible optimists and believe that feeding the public a steady supply of pessimism only makes things worse. Let's look on the bright side, they say, and emphasize the positive in recent trends.

Fifth, the family outlook of some appears to be based mainly on their personal biographies. They may have gone through a divorce or a family breakup, for example, and firmly believe that the decision they made was best for all concerned. The idea that family breakup is, in general, a negative does not sit easily with them, and they do not feel comfortable with the thought that they may in some way be implicated in the decline of an institution.

None of these arguments is inherently unreasonable. A strong case can be made showing that women were not well served by the traditional nuclear family; it is manifestly not helpful to existing single-parent and stepfamilies to stigmatize their members; gays and lesbians, who are not permitted to marry, should not unfairly be penalized on that account; too much pessimism in the public debate can be unhelpful; and the private decisions many have made surely were the right ones. But we must always keep in mind the larger picture: in general, most of the family changes of recent decades have not been in the national interest. They certainly have not helped children; and if we continue on the present path of family development, children will be even more seriously affected. It is arguable whether or not these changes have even helped most adults. Adults in general have been made no happier, it seems. The percentage of American adults who say they are very happy remains virtually unchanged since the 1950s. Meanwhile, the happiness level of youth has dropped, which is not surprising given the fact that the main source of happiness is having close, warm, enduring relationships.[9]

If we are concerned about our future as a nation, therefore, it would be wise to discontinue the now-unconstructive debate about whether or not the family has declined and focus instead on the national policies that are needed to shore up the family. Surely as a nation we can find ways to lower the divorce rate and the out-of-wedlock birth rate and thus increase the percentage of children being raised by two parents without making life worse for those who find themselves in alternative family forms or insulting those who have made bad marriage choices. Indeed, if we act decisively now, many things could help to regenerate family life in America and substantially improve the situation for children and probably for the overwhelming majority of adults.

Our national goal should be to restore the married, two-parent nuclear family for as many children as possible. No doubt child well-being would be further improved if the restored two-parent families were able to live among caring relatives and in supportive neighborhoods and communities. Yet the trends away from living with extended families and in cohesive, homogeneous neighborhoods are probably irreversible. The state has tried to fill the vacuum but typically without success. We should continue to do what we can to build a "village" around the family. But the two-parent family must stand today largely on its own; therefore, its condition is more important to children, and to society in general, than ever before in history. If it fails, children will have little else to fall back on.

The Changing Marital Relationship

Fundamental to restoring the two-parent family is the regeneration of the institution of marriage because the stability of the two-parent family is largely dependent upon the marital relationship of the parents.[10] Although there are many caring and responsible nonresident fathers, the alarmingly simple fact is that a man is unlikely to stay close to his children unless he is married to his children's mother. Men tend to view marriage and child rearing as a single package. If they are not married or are divorced, their interest in and sense of responsibility toward children diminish. Some studies have found that at least half of all divorced or unmarried fathers lose all regular contact with their children over time.[11]

Why is marriage so important to fatherhood? Because being a father is universally problematic for men. While mothers the world over bear and nurture their young with an intrinsic acknowledgment and acceptance of their role, fathers are often filled with conflict and doubt. Men are not biologically as attuned to being committed fathers as women are to being committed mothers, even though high paternal investments in children have been a source of enormous evolutionary advantage for human beings. The evolutionary logic is this: women, who can bear only a limited number of children, have a great incentive to invest their energy in rearing children, while men, who can father many offspring, do not.[12] Left culturally unregulated, men's sexual behavior can be promiscuous, their paternity casual, their commitment to families weak.

Marriage is society's way of engaging the basic problem of fatherhood: how to hold the father to the mother-child bond.[13] Simply defined, marriage is the social institution whereby society socially approves of and encourages sexual intercourse and the birth of children. It stresses a strong interpersonal bond that includes the long-run commitment of the male, the durability of the marital relationship, and the importance of the union for children. In addition, because marriage includes exclusive sexual obligations and rights, the institution helps to prevent men from openly pursuing other men's wives. This, in turn, increases what is called paternity confidence, which is critical to the involvement of fathers in child rearing.

The goal of restoring marriage is considerably complicated by the fact that a major reason explaining why the nuclear family has become so fragile in modern times is that the nature of the marital relationship has changed. Not so long ago the marital relationship consisted of three main elements: an economic bond of mutual dependency, a social bond heavily upheld by extended families, and a religious bond of great spiritual worth. Today, many marriages have none of these elements. The economic bond has become weakened and even displaced by material well-being, by the economic independence of wives, and (where necessary) by state economic support. Husbands and wives do not have the economic interdependence that they once did. The social bond has diminished as extended family and broader community pressures on marriage have all but vanished. Gone are the days when marriage was a bond between two families more than a bond between two individuals. Finally, as societies have grown increasingly secular, the religious component of the marital tie has weakened significantly.

The marital relationship has become a mostly individual endeavor, a link between two people designed to satisfy their needs for intimacy, emotional dependency, and sex. When these needs are not satisfied, when they change, or when a presumptively better partner is discovered, marriages are easily dissolved. Economic, extended family, and religious ties are seldom adequate to hold an otherwise unhappy relationship together. Moreover, many personal needs can now be satisfied apart from the marital relationship—through nonmarital cohabitation, for example, or through paid services in the marketplace.

Yet there is no going back. The best marriages today are probably much more rewarding than those of the past because they are less coercively maintained and involve more friendship, equality, communication, and intimacy between wife and husband. It is not the traditional marriage that needs to be reestablished but the new form of marriage that must be further developed and shored up. Public policies oriented to traditional marriages are not likely to have much success.[14]

Family Policies

What can possibly be accomplished through public policy to promote stable marriages and the two-parent family? Obviously, public policies are not particularly well suited to changing matters of the heart. Without significant cultural change (for example, a dampening of the sexual revolution, moral responsibility on the part of the organized entertainment industry, and a renewed cultural focus on children), the battle is probably lost. Nevertheless, there is a significant role at the margins for government to play.

Lying behind all government family policies should be two simple propositions: (1) children are our future, and (2) the family is the most important institution for child well-being. Senator Moynihan once said that "the principal social objective of American Government at every level should be to see that children are born to intact families and that they remain so."[15] This can be rephrased as follows: the goal of government should be to increase the proportion of children who are living with and cared for by their two natural, married parents and to decrease the proportion of children who are not.

What follow are some key pro-marriage and pro-family policies that the national government could institute. I shall limit this discussion to the national government; state governments have a different role—for example, in writing the laws of marriage and divorce. I shall also limit this discussion to initiatives that apply to all economic segments of the population, leaving for others the issue of how to deal specifically with welfare and other very low-income populations.

1. *Extend the terms of the current family and medical leave act to permit parents time off from work for a period of at least six months following the birth or adoption of a child, with partial pay for at least the first three months.* According to abundant empirical evidence, the months following the birth or adoption of a child form the most stressful period in the life course of the average marriage, often setting the stage for later divorce. Giving parents more time to be with their children, and with each other, would help to alleviate this stress as well as generate enormous direct benefits for children.

2. *Create a universal, refundable, fully indexed income tax credit of at least $1,000 per child.* Apart from more time, money is what child rearing couples say they are most in need of. This credit would leave with or transfer to every family with children greater income for discretionary use. For families of very low income it would represent the creation of an income floor. The amount of the credit could vary depending upon the age of the child.

   This credit is a modern substitute for what used to be called the "family wage system," which recognized that child rearing is a society-wide concern and that child rearing families have many necessary expenses not incurred by childless families.[16] It should be noted that the current income tax exemption for dependents ($2,550 in 1997) is worth only about a quarter of the value it had in 1945 as measured by the percentage of personal income shielded from taxation. This new credit, therefore, would merely help us to return to a level of government financial support of children that once prevailed.

3. *Remove the various marriage penalties in the federal income tax code.* With the same income, a person who is single often has a lower tax burden than a person who is married and filing a joint return. We should not be economically penalizing people who marry.

4. *For married couples with dependent children, increase their personal tax exemption for each year, after five years, that they remain married.* Not only should marriage be unpenalized by the tax system, it should be favored with a tax reward. This marriage bonus would not have to be great; it could be mostly symbolic. It could also be capped after a certain length of marriage. But it would be a stunning affirmation that longlasting marriages are in the national interest.

5. *Provide educational credits or vouchers to parents who leave the paid labor force for extended periods of time to care for their young children.* Along the lines of the G.I. Bill for World War II veterans, these credits or vouchers could be provided for high school, vocational, college, graduate, or postgraduate education. As developed by Richard T. Gill and T. Grandon Gill, the premise of this "parental bill of rights" is that parents who raise their own children perform an important social service and that in doing so they may imperil their long-run career prospects. In return for this sacrifice, society should compensate their further education so that they can more effectively reenter the labor force or become reestablished in their careers.[17]

6. *Develop, test, and circulate widely, on an advisory basis, premarital education programs.* Such programs have been found to be effective both for strengthening future marriages and for alerting couples to factors associated with the risk of divorce (thus leading some badly suited couples to abandon their marriage plans).[18] We should strive nationally for every marriage to be preceded by thoughtful consideration. This effort might be thought of as akin to the federal government's cooperative extension programs in agriculture, which have been instrumental in promoting scientific agriculture and have led to the world's most productive agricultural economy.

7. *Develop and widely promulgate an annual measurement of our nation's marital and family health, much like the government today provides annual measurements of our economic health.* The importance of marriage and the family must be publicized more widely; this would be an effective way to

start. In addition to divorce and out-of-wedlock birth rates, it should include indicators such as the percent of children living apart from their two married parents and the percent of children living apart from their biological fathers.

8. *Provide a parental dividend through Social Security whereby the Social Security taxes of children in their working years are invested in a trust fund to benefit their parents in retirement.* We should launch a society-wide discussion of what would be the most far-reaching family policy of all: restructuring the national Social Security system. This proposal has recently been put forward by economist Shirley P. Burggraf.[19] She builds on the assumption that just as the traditional economic tie of marriage has been weakened, so has the economic tie that once bound the generations together. In short, the economic rug has been pulled out from under the family. Whereas children once were an economic asset to their parents, thus providing a strong economic motivation for good parenting, children today are quite the opposite. People raising children can expect to get back far less in economic rewards than they actually pay out in expenses, which typically amount to hundreds of thousands of dollars per child. "Our economic systems tells parents," she notes, "that children are a very expensive proposition but parental investment in children has no economic value."[20] This has led to a growing underinvestment in the task of child rearing.

Because high parental investments benefit us all, we have to find a new way to reward parents for economically, socially, and psychologically investing in their children. Burggraf suggests a major shift in old-age insurance whereby children's Social Security taxes are transferred to their parents. Under the current system of collectivized Social Security, young people pay into a system that provides generous retirement benefits for all older persons, irrespective of whether they have been good parents. As she notes, "people who never have children, parents who abuse or neglect or abandon their children, deadbeat dads who don't pay child support—all have as much claim (in many cases more) on the earnings of the next generation via the Social Security system as the most dutiful parent."[21] Under Burggraf's proposal, parents who do the best job of child rearing would reap the most economic benefits in the long run. This system would not discriminate against the childless. Adults without children would be expected to set up their own retirement trust funds; they could, in effect, invest in the stock market instead of in children, using the considerable disposable income advantage that they hold over child rearing adults.

There obviously would be enormous problems in shifting from our current Social Security system to a parental dividend system. And many serious issues remain to be resolved in this new system, such as how to handle the Social Security consequences of divorce. Yet at the very least, it is reasonable to think that parents should have some increased preferential claim in any insurance scheme that is based solely on the next generation of children.

As the quintessential seat of the private sphere, marriage and family life are rightly thought to lie beyond the reach of the federal government for most purposes. Yet the family is so important for the life of the nation, not to mention the nation's future through successive generations, that national governments everywhere must more assiduously address one of the major trends of modernity: the decline of the married, two-parent family. The evidence is now strong that, no matter how wealthy advanced nations become, life will be unsatisfying at best—especially for children—if the social capital of families and the moral infrastructure generated by family relationships are allowed to deteriorate further.

There are a number of policies that national governments could take that have the potential to shore up family life and restabilize the institution of marriage. Some of these policies are already in place in many European nations. Rather than continuing our silly and unproductive debate about whether or not the family is declining, let us get on with the task of assuring a better future for our children and our nation.

Notes

1. The evidence is reviewed in David Popenoe, *Life Without Father: Compelling New Evidence that Fatherhood and Marriage Are Indispensable for the Good of Children and Society* (New York: Free Press, 1996), and David Popenoe, "American Family Decline, 1960–1990: A Review and Appraisal," *Journal of Marriage and the Family* 55, no. 3 (1993): 525–42.
2. *New York Times,* September 25, 1986, p. C7.
3. Data sources can be found in William J. Bennett, *The Index of Leading Cultural Indicators* (New York: Simon and Schuster, 1994), and *The Social Report* (Tarrytown, N.Y.: Fordham Institute for Innovation in Social Policy, annual).
4. David J. Eggebeen and Daniel T. Lichter, "Race, Family Structure, and Changing Poverty Among American Children," *American Sociological Review* 56, no. 6 (1991): 801–17.
5. For a full review of the impact of divorce, see Barbara Dafoe Whitehead, *The Divorce Culture* (New York: Knopf, 1997), and David B. Larson, James P. Swyers, and Susan S. Larson, *The Costly Consequences of Divorce: Assessing the Clinical, Economic,*

and Public Health Impact of Marital Disruption in the United States (Rockville, Md.: National Institute for Healthcare Research, 1995).

6. The stepfamily data are reviewed in Popenoe, *Life Without Father,* chap. 2.

7. Sara S. McLanahan and Gary Sandefur, *Growing Up With a Single Parent: What Hurts, What Helps* (Cambridge, Mass.: Harvard University Press, 1994), 38

8. See, for example, Judith Stacey, *In the Name of the Family* (Boston: Beacon, 1997), and Stephanie Coontz, *The Way We Really Are* (New York: Basic Books, 1997).

9. David G. Myers, *The Pursuit of Happiness* (New York: Morrow, 1992); Angus Campbell, *The Sense of Well-Being in America* (New York: McGraw-Hill, 1981).

10. See David Popenoe, J. B. Elshtain, and D. Blankenhorn, eds., *Promises to Keep: Decline and Renewal of Marriage in America* (Lanham, Md.: Rowman and Littlefield, 1996).

11. Judith A. Seltzer, "Relationships Between Fathers and Children Who Live Apart: The Father's Role After Separation," *Journal of Marriage and the Family* 53, no. 1 (1991): 79–101.

12. See Robert Wright, *The Moral Animal: Why We Are the Way We Are* (New York: Vintage, 1994).

13. This is fully explored in Popenoe, *Life Without Father,* chap. 6.

14. For more on marriage, see Popenoe, Elshtain, and Blankenhorn, *Promises to Keep.*

15. Interview on "Meet the Press," September 19, 1993.

16. Allan C. Carlson, "Gender, Children, and Social Labor: Transcending the 'Family Wage' Dilemma," *Journal of Social Issues* 53, no. 3 (1996): 137–61.

17. This proposal is fully explored in Richard T. Gill, *Posterity Lost: Progress, Ideology, and the Decline of the American Family* (Lanham, Md.: Madison, 1997).

18. A national clearinghouse for such programs is the Coalition for Marriage, Family, and Couples Education, directed by Diane Sollee, 5310 Belt Road, N.W., Washington, D.C. 20015–1961.

19. This proposal is fully developed in Shirley P. Burggraf, *The Feminine Economy and Economic Man* (Reading, Mass.: Addison-Wesley, 1997).

20. Shirley P. Burggraf, "The Feminine Economy," paper presented at the Bunting Institute, Radcliffe College, January 11, 1995, p. 13.

21. Ibid., 12.

Part VI
America in Transition

Chapter 11

Edward Blakely

Separate and Not Equal

America's Diversity Crisis

It has been more than three decades since the United States outlawed all forms of racial discrimination. Yet today the challenge for the nation to integrate people of all races and sexes socially, spatially, and economically remains an even more daunting task than it was at the time of the passage of the civil rights legislation. Americans are increasingly segregated by race and ethnicity, while white women's economic progress seems to have been permanently arrested at the lower-middle-class level.

The socialscape of discrimination has changed dramatically. It is no longer a matter of legal right to officially discriminate, nor are discriminatory ideas uttered in public or even many private conversations. Instead, new code words and actions have taken the place of the old forms of publicly accepted exclusion. In economic terms the distance between the rich and the poor has grown to the point that 20 percent of the nation's population controls more than 58 percent of all the wealth. Black female-headed households form the largest segment of African American families, with lower incomes and greater poverty than those found in any major industrialized nation. In terms of diversity, these data are symptomatic of a weak social system with low commitments to social justice. The real story in America, however, remains not income or gender equality but the accommodation of racial and ethnic change. The issues of racial and ethnic diversity are the bedrock and linchpin to all other forms of participation in American society.

The Diversity Crisis

The Census Bureau has sharply upgraded its population forecast for the midcentury population in the next millennium. At the conclusion of the last census in 1990, the bureau's demographers were talking about a slowing population growth, with the nation reaching some 300 million by 2050. Only five years later the census was recalculating the nation's population to accommodate a surging 7.8 percent annual population increase, recognizing the higher fertility rates of native-born minorities (primarily Hispanics and Asians), immigration policies, as well as the longevity of the nation's rising numbers of black, Hispanic, and Asian families. According to the Census Bureau's new projection, the nation will grow to 383 million by the middle of the next century.

This percentage increase is not unprecedented in the nation's history. America grew even faster during the first industrial revolution, from the end of the nineteenth century to the middle of the twentieth. Nevertheless, the dimensions of these new population dynamics are the focus of intense public policy attention. The reason for alarm is that the earlier wave of immigration was European and was swiftly assimilated into the national value structure. Whites represented 84 percent of the population base in 1970; however, by 2050, in a more urban and possibly more economically challenging environment, whites will comprise barely 50 percent of the demographic base of the nation. Herein lies the rub. Can a nation that was primarily western European become a nation that has its base stock from all over the world? Can the national search for social and economic parity that is the bedrock of the social philosophy of the nation survive in a changed context in which the old majority may well be, in many urban areas of the country, a new minority? What will be the nature of public policy when race matters in a far different way than it did in the past? Who will govern America as the voting population structure shifts from whites and blacks to Hispanics and Asians?

Clearly these questions are already part of the subscript of public debates. There are few radio talk shows that do not feature issues of race in one manner or another. Sometimes the debate takes the form of English-only language laws. In other instances, it takes the form of laws eliminating affirmative action and other set-asides for nonwhite males. In still other forms the debate is carried on in terms of land use policies that aim to restrict access, such as gated communities, single-family–only areas, and no-growth initiatives. Race shapes the American social life more than any other issue. It will dominate public concern and policy formation in arenas from criminal law to international trade. Let's take a look at the dimensions that form the core of this debate.

The Black Problem

African Americans form a unique subgroup within the nation's population base—the only group brought to the United States as slaves. Although some attempts were made to enslave Native Americans, and there was some indenture of Irish immigrants and penal colonists, the onerous burden of slavery remains an identifiable color barrier for blacks. We must remember that until 1967 it was illegal for blacks to marry whites in most southern states, and many forms of racial exclusion still remain for blacks, from country club memberships to social ostracism. Blacks, by any scale, are the least well integrated group in American society.

The black issue has been the focus of national policy in one way or another since the advent of the nation. Nevertheless, for nearly two hundred years after the writing of the Constitution, blacks did not compete with any other groups for center-stage minority status. Black colleges and universities were formed as conscious national and state policy acts, a compensatory means of addressing socially recognized disadvantages.

Blacks fall into two categories: southern low income and urban ghettoized. Between the 1920s and the 1960s, they formed a comfortable minority of 10 to 12 percent of the nation's population. Given these factors of geography and economics, national policymakers found social remedies to be fairly obvious. But when the Watts riots erupted in Los Angeles in 1965, conventional assessments regarding the black problem were blown asunder. Blacks in Watts were scarcely imprisoned in a typical high-density dark ghetto. Watts had no tenements, no absence of essential public services, no rundown neighborhoods—only a modest but growing crime problem. What became clear was that Watts was in transition from in-migration, economic restructuring, and changing patterns of access to jobs and social opportunity. It was becoming a new form of black ghetto, close to but not part of the dominant culture. As a ghetto, it was developing its own value sets separate from those of the dominant culture and was less willing to accept the traditional set of national aspirations. In this way the black problem has become difficult and dangerous for policymakers to understand and deal with effectively. According to the Kerner report, the problem involves deeply segregated housing, poverty life-styles, and crime along with uneven employment opportunities and educational achievement.[1] The black issue must be examined through the lens of geo-psychology and economic distance, not only through legally imposed discrimination.

Separate Space

Black Americans remain deeply spatially segregated in spite of suburbanization trends for all groups. Blacks are not randomly distributed across the United States. They have systematically migrated to the northeast and the midwest or have remained in or migrated to the south. In each of these areas, however, they form a core of city dwellers. Blacks are primarily concentrated in fewer than fifteen metropolitan areas, which are accommodating more than 60 percent of the black population.

Black migration has reinforced this pattern. Successive generations of black migrants move to these venues in part for economic reasons but more importantly for networks. This observation is borne out by recent carefully controlled analyses of the census data examining black migration streams to urban areas. Black migrants move to places that improve their economic opportunity and their kinship links. Issues such as welfare or other public service amenities play no important role in this migratory movement, despite popular views.[2] Thus, blacks are electing seemingly safe harbors, places of acceptance, and at least low resistance to relocation. They will move for work within this system but seldom outside of it. As a result, the acknowledged black social separation is reinforced by both black perception of limited choices and white actions to reinforce this behavior. According to Barry Bluestone and Bennett Harrison, "the pattern suggests . . . each group has found, in the geography of economic and population growth, a 'niche' destination where it is already concentrated."[3] The black niche is the inner city. As a result, *inner city* has become a code phrase for "black," "poor," and "crime." At the current levels of black segregation from whites and other groups, black migration would have to be adjusted for more than fifty years to achieve even the same level of racial integration as Hispanics in 1990.[4] This seems a very unlikely outcome.

If we were dealing only with metropolitan locations, the issue would be difficult enough to solve. Within metro segregation, however, we have high concentrations of blacks in or near the poorest census tracts. Blacks live in tracts that have incomes almost $5,000 per year lower per household than the incomes in white neighborhoods. Even when black incomes improve, blacks are less likely to live in a community composed of whites of similar incomes. Moreover, in some black neighborhoods poverty is so deep and persistent that the majority of residents live well below the poverty line on some form of public assistance, with chronic unemployment and out-of-wedlock births.

Dissimilarity indices that measure degrees of spatial separation show that in 1990 the black poor were the most socially isolated group in the nation (79 percent), while white poor were the least isolated (34 percent). In these underclass zones, "social isolation, defined as 'lack of contact or sustained interaction with individuals and institutions that represent the mainstream society[,] . . . makes it more difficult for those who are looking for jobs to be tied into the job network."[5] Television news graphically portrays these areas as the major habitat for black Americans, even though only about 4 or 5 percent of blacks fit this profile. The black middle class is residentially segregated from poor whites and all other groups. As a consequence, we must view the black problem within a geography of isolation, crime, economic underachievement, and social dysfunctionality. Public policy must address all of these dimensions to be successful.

Family Value: Isolation, Criminality, and Poverty

Black isolation is more than a pattern of housing discrimination. It is a pattern of "residential segregation [that] underscores the distinctive castelike social distance that separates black from white in our society."[6] Distance among blacks, whites, and all other minorities can be identified very quickly by language and life-styles. Black language is essentially a different dialect and, as rap music shows, has a recognizable form and expression. This speech has a communication value to its user but also restricts the user, who has not mastered standard English, to lower-level economic opportunities unless he or she is an athlete.

Isolation has many other attendant effects. For example, black communities have social structures that differ from the dominant models. As Daniel Patrick Moynihan has pointed out, "three centuries of injustice have brought about a deep-seated structural distortion in the life of the Negro American. At this point, the present tangle of pathology is capable of perpetuating itself without assistance from the outside world. The cycle can be broken only if these distortions are set right."[7]

What are these distortions? The greatest distortion for blacks is the apparent weak attachment to family formation. William Julius Wilson ascribes the dire situation of black males as one of low-paying and poor jobs that do not allow them to support a family.[8] This argument, however, fails to explain the high levels of family disruption among middle-class blacks. Black couples with their own children were a minority of all such married-couple families in 1990 (46.8 percent). Black men are not only less likely to stay in a marriage and raise their children through schooling years but are also less likely to provide economically for their children.[9] As a result, black men force more black women into poverty or low-income status. Black female-headed households account for 47.8 percent of all black families, while there are only 13.6 percent of similarly situated white female-headed families.[10] Even if the black male provides economic support, the absence from the family structure is destructive for the entire social-family network, including grandparents and other relatives. Moreover, this familial system prevents wealth accumulation within the family unit. Black males who dissolve their families cannot provide a comfortable inheritance for any portion of the family system. Black middle-class males supporting their families fell from 59 percent in 1970 to only 38 percent in 1990. If black males remarry, they seldom accumulate sufficient wealth to provide for both the old and the new families. If they do not remarry, they consume most of their income, invest little, and maintain a relatively high-consumption lifestyle.

Additionally, many black males never attempt to provide for their offspring. Among this group we have teenagers who father the children of teenage and subteenage women. But this is a small group compared to the larger group of older adult black males who father children in the black community with no intention of providing for them. This pathology may go back to the time of slavery and forced copulation. It fails, however, to explain the fact that in the early 1960s black family structures did not differ too dramatically from those of whites. Divorce among blacks was similar to that of whites until the mid-1960s. On the other hand, out-of-wedlock births were more prevalent in black than in white communities.

This pattern of household and social structure reinforces family disruption, meaning that almost 54 percent of all black children were living in poverty in 1990.[11] This pattern gives males fewer reasons to enter wedlock or provide lifetime support for their children. It is difficult to single out the female as the problem as too many pundits do. Since black females are isolated, their choices of males are equally limited. Black women were four times as likely to be single mothers as were their white peers. Importantly, black middle-class men contribute to this high abandonment rate. To make matters worse, it is more difficult for a black woman with children to marry than for a white woman. This pattern must change—not according to a social or religious prescription that has the intention of reinstituting socially restrictive behaviors but to provide some stability for the future and an entry point for black Americans into the national economy.

Marriage is an issue precisely because more women are going into the labor market. As white women enter the labor market, the competition for scarce commodities such as housing and good education increases. As a result, anyone outside of this competitive sphere, black or white, cannot compete. Further, education levels of disrupted families are lower than that for intact families. Finally, the network options of a two-parent system of workers is far superior to that of one person, no matter who they are. In the black community, since these networks are already slim, the absence of any component of the network has disastrous consequences. The restoration of family systems that contain two persons with incomes must be the focus of more direct public policy. A national family policy that rewards intact families through a more vigorous earned income tax credit program that would provide payment to working intact families below the poverty line should be explored. Without such change, unstable families will continue to produce unstable and, too frequently, criminal youth who destroy opportunity for all.

It's a Crime: The Process of Black Criminality

Criminality as an accepted way of life has become endemic in the black community. There is no doubt that there is a black criminal culture. Even though the use of drugs has recently made this problem far more lethal and noticeable, visitors to the colonies more than two hundred years ago noted the criminal activity in the ex-slave areas of colonial settlements. Crime rates have been higher among blacks since the Emancipation. It is hard to shrug this off as merely another manifestation of poverty. Other groups in America are poor and discriminated against, too. Hispanic crime has recently mushroomed to rival black criminality, but the data provide a clear message with respect to crime among black Americans. Compared to any other group in the nation, black Americans are far more likely to be both victims and perpetrators of crimes. A black teenager is more likely to die of a gunshot wound than go to college. Blacks are far more likely not only to commit crimes but to enter the penal system. The black prison population is growing at an alarming rate, which is taking a very large toll on the black working population in several ways.

Black undereducated males are viewed as criminally oriented or associated with criminals. As a result, even minority employers (including blacks) are reluctant to hire them. Black males are considered dangerous and untrustworthy.[12] As the nation's streets fill with a very high proportion of black homeless males, this perception increases. In addition, although crime rates may be falling nationally, the appearance of crime and criminality has not dropped, leading to irrational behavior from whites, such as excluding theaters and even transit stops from their neighborhoods on the grounds that outside criminal elements may penetrate these areas. Increasingly acrimonious arguments are going on in zoning hearings all over the country as both city dwellers and suburbanites object to housing, recreation, even parks on the grounds that these places are sanctuaries for what they consider to be the "wrong element"— meaning black or Hispanic teenagers. National paranoia on this score can scarcely be overstated, resulting in a continued reduction in black-white contact at every age and income level.

Criminality has also limited the availability of quality retail services in black neighborhoods, where the population base would ordinarily accommodate them. Because of criminal activities, black communities have fewer retail and service outlets and cultural, recreational, and other public venues than do other communities. In addition, black communities have low tolerance for police, causing many crimes to go unreported and known criminals undetected. In a sense, a very small segment of the community is destroying the options and opportunities for others. As long as this situation persists, black neighborhoods will continue to decline in service provision. As one federal official observed, "there are some of these [inner] cities so empty they look as though someone had dropped nerve gas."[13]

Deteriorating communities become more lawless and overwhelm federal and local urban development policies. In St. Ann's Precinct in the Bronx, a community of 48,000 residents (one-third black, two-thirds Hispanic), eighty-four people were murdered in 1991, half of whom were under age 21. Jonathan Kozol asks, "What is it like for children to grow up here?"[14] No matter how public policy is developed, it must address the pathology that allows such activity to persist. As Todd Clear says, "isn't it a bit much to believe that removing some men from their streets will change the factors that promote law-breaking among the many who remain?"[15]

As crime worsens, the job base deteriorates so that the underlying opportunity structure for black neighborhoods is worse today than it was twenty years ago. Unless crime and poverty are reduced, no community development strategies will ever work. Crime must be reduced through increased prevention strategies as well as improved community-based policing.

Persistent Black Poverty

The continuing high concentrations of poverty in many inner-city black communities has become the subject of much discussion. The issue is not only that these communities contain poor people; rather, the residents do not move out of poverty regardless of the numbers and types of publicly supported programs aimed at them. It is difficult for most Americans to accept the notion that a group of people, no matter whom it comprises, does not rise out of poverty when given aid and when discriminatory barriers are removed. Every other immigrant group in the nation, including those of other racial stocks, have made economic progress from their enclaves to the wider social system. It is even less likely for the average American to accept persistent black poverty when so many blacks occupy highly visible positions in mainstream society, from politicians to athletes and actors. What is the problem?

Black poverty is a peculiar mixture of social and economic problems that combine into an intractable mixture. The poverty rate for black children has remained at about 42 percent since 1970, while the overall poverty rate has risen from 15 to 19 percent for all children. During this period the size of the ghettos has also increased. In 1990 about 11.2 million people lived in ghettos, with *ghetto* defined as an area in which poverty rates are in excess of 40 percent of the census tract population. Between 1980 and 1990 the percentage of metropolitan blacks living in poverty increased from 20.2 percent to 23.7 percent, with the increase of the poor metropolitan black population skyrocketing to 45.2 percent of the urban population. Not only did the population grow in size, but it expanded geographically in many big cities. For example, between 1980 and 1990 the Chicago ghetto increased from 143 census tracts to 231, a 61.5 percent increase in a decade. As a result, more black children were trapped in areas where the only visible civic icon was that produced by the trash-strewn streets, abandoned autos, drug addicts, and the homeless.

The overall poverty rates rose for blacks in the cities; they fell for those who opted for suburban living. This change in black poverty rates for non-ghettoized blacks provides comfort for those who propose breaking up the ghettos. An even more powerful argument for this position can be found in the Chicago Gautreaux experiment that moved public housing welfare residents to nearby interracial suburbs. The experiment has had dramatic effects on those who have moved, with a vast majority changing their lives and the lives of their children. An assessment of this project indicated that suburban movers were far more likely to get jobs and their children to improve in school performance. As the evaluator points out, "Gautreaux adults reported that they, too, could have jobs [because they saw their neighbors work] and they wanted to try. In the city few adults saw neighbors working."[16] Seeing is believing. When ghetto dwellers see adults with low aspirations, poor services, criminality, and low performance, they become overwhelmed by this culture. Unfortunately, too many people give up and join, a behavioral model that is very different from that of the European migrants, who have used the enclave as a stepping-off point to economic and social integration. This is why it is so hard for the average American, black or white, to accept welfare as a continuing pattern of life.

There is no doubt that any public policy will have to transform these expanding islands of urban neglect, and there are ways to do this. One is to increase the ability of the ghetto residents to work by bringing more work and working people along with different value sets into the ghetto. It will do no good to merely bring the jobs to the area. Most experiments, such as enterprise zones and similar approaches, indicate that local labor is seldom absorbed by these programs in spite of training and other incentives. As Sidney Wong says, "programs specifically attempting to link employment . . . to distressed neighborhoods did not achieve their objectives." He goes on to surmise, "Even when economic development programs do succeed in inducing employment or business growth in a locality, the new opportunities may not necessarily benefit surrounding residents."[17] Only by mixing the residential base with workers will residents' work culture be transformed. In some ways this sounds like gentrification, but it is cultural and not necessarily racial gentrification. As anyone on the street knows, if you get a good job, you get out. We have to find ways to keep jobs, build jobs, and keep job holders in the community as well as bring job holders into these areas.

The old model of assimilation does not work for all of the new non-European groups in our diversifying nation. New Asian and Hispanic immigrants are beset by various forms of economic and social discrimination as well. On the other hand, they are moving up economically, competing for some forms of employment and capturing space in ways very different from the black population.

Cultural Competition

Interestingly almost no immigrant group has sued a school district for segregation from the mainstream population. In the Los Angeles School District, nearly half of the schools are 90 to 100 percent Hispanic, but there is little outcry. In some school districts, Asian families drive their children several miles each day to attend schools with more Asian students. Even in schools with 80 percent black or Hispanic students, where general test scores and achievements are low, Asian students are scoring well on SAT and similar standardized tests. In fact, the real issue for affirmative action is the high proportion of Asians with higher qualifications than native-born whites and other minorities opting for state universities. If education is a proxy for attainment in the United States, then all of the new immigrants with the exception of Hispanics from Mexico and Central America are doing very well.

Immigration in the United States has changed dramatically—from being primarily European as recently as 1970 to primarily Asian and Latin American in 1990. The immigration diversity issue is the result of volume and suddenness, not presence. As the world becomes increasingly unstable, the United States represents a safe economic and family environment. Not only has the nation attracted a large legal immigration flow in the past twenty years, but it also has become the home of a large segment of illegal immigrants. The legal issues are fine points in public discussion. The real issue remains the threat of the ethnic values of these new people to the dominant culture.

New immigration is not geographically uniform. Immigrants have always been clustered, but these particular clusters are far denser than any earlier pattern. First, the immigrants are overwhelmingly urban. Second, they have clustered in six states. An incredible one-third of the foreign-born immigrants live in California, and only 47 of the nation's 3,141 counties account for nearly 90 percent of all of the new migrants. Migrants are clustered, some might say huddled, in Los Angeles metro, Dade County (Miami), New York metro, San Francisco, Dallas, Houston, and Seattle.

Since immigrants are not dispersing, the full impact of immigration is not a shared national experience. It is fairly clear that some areas do not want the experience. Jingoism and anti-foreign sentiment are palpable in many mid-western and mid-south states, so the immigrant network avoids them. Other more clear signals are being sent out when local school boards and cities pass English-only ordinances. Immigrant politics is replacing immigration politics.

Immigrant Politics

As immigrants cluster, they form an important political block. Local and national politicians are increasingly conscious of the immigrant political dynamics because immigrants are clustered in the most industrial states. As a result, the combined immigrant and black vote can have a very direct impact on national and even statewide elections. Immigrant groups do not become citizens in the same numbers, nor do they seek voting rights equally. Asian immigrants have the highest naturalization rates, Mexican the lowest. In voter participation, European and Canadian immigrants have high rates, Asian and Mexican low rates. As a result, white voters have a disproportionate impact on political outcomes because of their higher participation rates, giving rise to a situation in which a minority has majority control by simply exercising the national right to vote. This is working for black politicians as well as white. Black politicians in California, Illinois, and New York have large numbers of foreign-born constituents but maintain control via larger black voter turnouts.

Voting and political rights are coterminous, so it is important for immigrants to participate in the political process. Moreover, these immigrants are sending their offspring the wrong signal by nonparticipation. Not surprisingly, voter turnout among American-born Asian immigrants is only 13 percent of eligible voters. Incorporation in political life is absolutely necessary for immigrants and their second-generation offspring to become full economic participants in the society. While the notion of compulsory voting has been rejected for a variety of reasons, it needs to be reconsidered at least at the state and local levels. The only way to secure our democracy is to increase the number of stakeholders in it. The vote, rather than riot, is the most powerful tool in this regard.

The Immigrant Jobs Puzzle

Are new immigrants taking away jobs for locals? Yes and no. Yes, new immigrants with skills compete well for available jobs. These immigration streams, however, are filtered into certain industries and, within these industries, into certain job categories. For example, the hotel industry has one of the largest immigrant pools in the work force. But hotel workers are highly stratified. Immigrants do the service jobs, such as laundry, room cleaning, and restaurant operations; but Europeans or white Americans do all of the managerial work. Some industries are almost completely composed of a single ethnic work force; for example, furniture manufacture is almost entirely Mexican. Filipinos have become administrative and financial officers in many organizations, while much computer production is dominated by Asians and software by Indians.

It is obvious that job networks are now international. As the jobs in a certain area, such as the garment industry, expand, the international network identifies near relatives outside the United States and pulls the work force from that system. As a result, many native-born Americans feel left out of the job competition in certain industries and subfields. The same process does not work in reverse: an American is not favored over a German or a Japanese worker. As a matter of fact, Americans have the lowest out-migration rate in the world. As a result, the American worker feels the pressure of immigration but does not know what to do about it.

Immigrants are a source of employment friction precisely because they are good labor. Asian and European immigrants come with high levels of education: a mean of 13.2 years of schooling for European men and 14.1 years for Canadian men (although this group also includes a substantial number of Canadian Asians). On the other hand, Mexican men have only 7.5 years of education. While Mexicans compete with undereducated blacks for lower-paid unskilled work, Asians compete with whites for highly skilled jobs. Asian immigrants have high self-employment levels and consequently own more of the stores and retail activities visible to and within the Hispanic and black communities. This is a source of serious friction, accentuated because these employers frequently employ their own family members. Moreover, Asian response to their black customer base has been a source of considerable cultural friction. Asians are frequently frightened by large groups of loud, young black males, who talk quickly and sometimes make menacing gestures. Newspaper stories about these misunderstandings and the consequent deaths of people on both sides provide graphic evidence of the problem. To ask an Asian to hire locals seems a strange and unworkable concept. Nevertheless, the absence of hired locals creates friction that leads to foreseeable problems.

As work becomes increasingly internationalized, new processes are going to have to be developed that diversify the work force across industrial sectors instead of just inside firms. The work force gap is widening in the same way that income and racial separation is growing. "A culture is," as Bluestone and Harrison assert, "more than a list of things we 'value': family, education, self-reliance, initiative. We cannot identify what is distinctive and what is common about our lives and problems, if our understanding of culture and social fabric are limited . . . and our comparison groups primarily serve to invidiously assert and affirm . . . the values that promote success and failure in the United States."[18]

Values are the center point of the debate. How can we share values and economic equality? We must make value sharing a more central task of national policy through the promotion of voting and local-level community building among merchants and residents. All of this will take conscious national policy. We cannot reuse old models and methods that do not serve these times.

Directions for National Diversity Policy

As diverse as this nation is, it has never had a national diversity policy. The Clinton administration has embarked on a dialogue on race that could create momentum for such policy. We have developed immigration laws and even championed something called Americanization. Some national policy on diversity has been in place in a de facto manner since the Emancipation and later industrial immigration. The philosophy that drove these policies was simple: make everyone a Euro-American so that the value structures of England modified by the colonial experience can be the national value structure. This simple assumption worked more or less for more than one hundred years. European immigrants were only mildly hostile, and no one else counted. An entire social framework was built around the Americanization model, with the YMCAs and YWCAs as fundamental blocks. In addition, the settlement house movement helped achieve social melding in the urban ghetto and low-income neighborhoods. A common feature of such efforts was to devise a youth program as a means of attracting parents. YMCAs and YWCAs continue to play this role as social gatekeeper. But as the template for inclusion widened, these institutions were not entirely prepared to meet the large new influxes. Nor have these organizations been able to cope with the rapid social dysfunctionality of the inner city.

It is important for the goals of a national diversity policy to be clear. Such goals might include the following:

1. *Reduce metropolitan sprawl.* The single most important national policy is not crime reduction but land use. Crime is an increasingly difficult problem precisely because of the economic and social distance that breeds crime centers. Cities and suburbs must face a common fate with respect to crime and economic disintegration. We need to develop a model of national growth management that would allocate resources more efficiently

and reduce racial and economic isolation.

Regional growth management is the only means of accomplishing this objective. Housing and Urban Development (HUD) and the major domestic policy agencies need to cooperate in establishing a joint set of guidelines for regional and local development plans. Federal grants should not be provided to local jurisdictions unless they have produced comprehensive regional plans. These plans should be far-reaching, converting all of the social and economic challenges of the region and detailing the scenarios for solution. Regional plans would aim at enhancing those communities that are heavily in poverty. Programs would be aimed at locked-in geo-ethnic nodes that are fragmented and isolated from the mainstream. Policy should aim at reseeding these areas with the latest information and economic development infrastructure, educational resources, and physical improvements.

2. *Improve ghetto and immigrant employment.* Policy geared at improving ghetto and immigrant employment would include a very substantial land-owner-occupier land tax savings. In these communities the home land taxes would be frozen or rolled back for owner-occupiers who work within the prescribed zones. Immigration employment programs must be devised to increase the opportunity structure for new immigrants. Moreover, firms hiring either immigrant or disadvantaged workers in these zones would be reimbursed for child care and social supports, education, and health benefits for five years or until the employee terminates from the firm. Each firm would have credits based on its size.

3. *Make geographic affirmative action.* Newcomers and low-income groups are isolated linguistically and socially from the mainstream. Targeting these areas for enriched problem solving is very important. On the other hand, they cannot become the locus for more individual welfare and failed economic development policies and programs. Since the locations themselves are valuable and the labor and social problems are the focus of concern, it might be wise to examine geographic affirmative action. That is, target the nation's affirmative action efforts on the people from certain locations rather than on race. In this manner, as the individuals gain skills and improve their circumstances, they remain in the zone. If on the other hand, they move out after they achieve economic improvement, the firm simply loses credit for them in the affirmative action plan. This type of affirmative action would be easier to verify than the current system since addresses are easier to ascertain than self-identified race. Finally, such a plan would have far more popular support than one designated by race.

It is important to add value to labor from such areas. This could be accomplished by providing educational vouchers for the residents of such communities that could be used anywhere in the metropolitan region at public or private schools. Finally, to encourage both work and home ownership, residents of these areas would be given a $25,000–per-year federal homeowner tax exemption for living in a home in the zone and an additional $10,000 exemption beyond the current exemption for children-under-18 dependents for joint income tax filers.

The issues described in this chapter will be the focus of community and national concern for the next decade and beyond. We cannot hope that nonaction is the best policy. We need to intervene in the system to obtain appropriate outcomes. We have always done so. Now is not the time to shrink from problems just because they are complicated. The proposals that I have discussed may or may not be the right ones, but they may be in the right direction. We can do worse by doing nothing at all.

Notes

1. *Kerner Commission on Urban Disturbances* (Washington, D.C.: U.S. Government Printing Office, 1968).
2. Seong Woo Lee and WooSuk Zhee, "Independent and Linked Migration: Individual Returns of Employment Opportunity and Household Returns of Poverty Status to African-American Inter-State Migration in 1975–78 and 1985–88," report from the University of Southern California, Lusk Center for Research Institute, December 1996.
3. Barry Bluestone and Bennett Harrison, *The Deindustrialization of America: Plant Closings, Community Abandonment, and the Dismantling of Basic Industry* (New York: Basic Books, 1982), 153.
4. Ibid.
5. William Julius Wilson, *The Truly Disadvantaged: The Inner City, the Underclass and Public Policy* (Chicago: University of Chicago Press, 1987).
6. Bluestone and Harrison, *Deindustrialization,* 167.
7. Ibid., 200.
8. Wilson, *The Truly Disadvantaged.*
9. William Goldsmith and Edward J. Blakely, *Separate Societies: Poverty and Inequality in U.S. Cities* (Philadelphia: Temple University Press, 1992).
10. U.S. Bureau of the Census, public microdata samples, 1990.
11. Ibid.
12. Jollen Kirschenman and Katryn M. Necekerman, "'We'd Love to Hire Them, But': The Meaning of Race for Employers," in *The Urban Underclass,* ed. Christopher Jencks and Paul E. Peterson (Washington, D.C.: Brookings Institution, 1991), 203–32.
13. Robert Wood, "Cities in Crisis," *Domestic Affairs* 1 (1991): 221.
14. Jonathan Kozol, *Amazing Grace: The Lives of Children and the Conscience of a Na-*

tion (New York: Harper and Row, 1995).

15. Henry Richmond, "Rationale and Program Design: National Land Use Policy Institute," working paper, *National Growth Management Leadership Project*, October 4, 1994, p. 16.

16. James Rosenbaum, "Lessons from the Gautreaux Program," *Housing Policy Debate* 6, no. 1 (1995): 239.

17. Sidney Wong, "Local Enterprise Zone Programs and Economic Development Planning: A Case Study of California and Four Mid-Atlantic States," Ph.D. diss., University of California at Berkeley, Department of City and Regional Planning, 1995.

18. Bluestone and Harrison, *Deindustrialization,* 206.

Chapter 12

Richard C. Leone

Baby Boom Retirement Crisis

Myth or Reality?

One of the lesser stops on Gulliver's travels is the strange land of Luggnagg, where he encounters the nearly immortal race of Struldbruggs. Unlike our own aging baby boomers, there are not all that many Struldbruggs; but they live so long that the majority of Luggnaggians have seen fit to take rather extreme steps to cope with their "problem of the elderly." At 80, Struldbruggs are looked upon as dead in law, and their property passes to their heirs. "Only a small pittance is reserved for their support. . . . After that period, they are held incapable of any employment of trust or profit." Clearly, if Swift were writing today, on the eve of the retirement of the baby boomers, we would be as familiar with Luggnagg as we are with Lilliput. Moreover, another of his famous "policy ideas," the notion that the potato famine in Ireland could be solved if the Irish consumed their young, might be dusted off as a solution to the task of supporting the nonworking elderly. Swift's fantasy is a powerful reminder that the rhetoric currently in use to describe the consequences of the aging of America's population is not the first case of senior phobia. Nor was his work the last example of fantasy on this subject.

Today, alarmists portray America's future as an older nation as bleak. They exaggerate to the point of obscuring realistic assessment of the implications of the aging of the immense generation known as the baby boomers. They have succeeded in one respect, however; both young and old often seem uniformly pessimistic about the next century. Those nearing retirement are concerned that they will live out their last years in a desperate struggle against poverty. They fret about the burdens that their longevity will impose on their own children. In addition, youthful Americans wonder just how much they will suffer because of the need to cope with the cost of supporting the elderly boomers.

The alternate answers to these speculations would come as a surprise to most citizens. Rather than suffering, the working population in the twenty-first century should have a remarkably rosy future. On very reasonable assumptions about the future, the likelihood is that both the boomers and our youngest adults will coexist quite nicely for the next fifty years or so. Nonetheless, those who are filled with foreboding about the task of housing, feeding, and replacing the hips of aging baby boomers are right about one thing: the last chapter of America's large postwar generation will mean, as it has at every other stage of their lives, many changes in many aspects of how all of us live.

Demographics

For most of history, mankind has struggled to extend life span; for most of the modern era, societies have worried about the political, economic, and environmental consequences of high birth rates. What has become commonly known as the crisis of aging is a direct consequence of the success that all modern nations and, increasingly, even third world countries have had in diminishing both of these problems. Rather than celebrating increased longevity and smaller families, however, the current popular wisdom is that these "achievements" are a good example of "be careful what you wish for."[1] In fact, for almost all nations, average age is on the rise. Most of the people in economically well-off countries are already older than those in the United States and, although we shall catch up, will remain older for the foreseeable future.

Obviously, the exact circumstances and economic and other consequences vary depending on conditions in individual nations. In developing countries, for example, improvements in public health and other factors are creating very different pressures from those felt in the advanced countries. With a few exceptions (Ireland, Australia, and New Zealand), rich nations are headed toward about the same place, with about a quarter of the population over age 65 in 2050. After that, it is guesswork. It has never been easy to predict either fertility or immigration. Indeed, as a rule of thumb, the uncertainties about future population patterns are likely to be much larger than expected. The various forecasts by the Census Bureau and the Social Security Administration offer a range of estimates, differing by more than 50 million from the high to the low for America's population in the middle of the next century. A note of caution about all these estimates, then, is in order. As economists James Poterba, Larry Summers, and their colleagues emphasize, "fertility forecasts are subject to large standard errors and are notoriously inaccurate. . . . The range of historical experience dwarfs the range between the Social Security Administration's optimistic and pessimistic projections. . . . Postwar fertility projections in the United States anticipated neither the beginning, nor the end, of the baby boom."[2]

Still, what we know about the aging of people already born is enough to justify the sharp focus of American concern about one large group: those born between 1946 and 1964. During that period about 17 million more babies were born than would have been the case if birth rates had remained at 1940 levels. The sheer size of this group, therefore, has been the major demographic reality of the last half century. The baby boomers are the catch-up generation: the product of an explosion in family creation that had been delayed by the combined effects of the Great Depression and the Second World War.

By the time the explosion in postwar birth rates began to recede in the mid-1960s, nearly 78 million American children were changing the face of the nation. At their peak, in 1964, boomer children under the age of 20 accounted for more than 40 percent of the population; today, the boomer share is 10 percentage points lower; in retirement, they will be a smaller share still. Despite occasional bursts in fertility during the past twenty years, there is general agreement that there is no prospect of regaining post–World War II levels. If the twentieth-century experience of other industrialized nations is any guide, in fact, it is reasonable to question even whether current birth rates are sustainable. Virtually all the "mature" nations of Europe, for example, have had stable or even declining populations in recent years.

In industrialized nations, aging is projected to level out late in the next century; unless there is a new burst of fertility or immigration, all these countries will have a more or less permanent percentage of seniors in the 25 to 30 percent range. Thus, while the shift in demographics now underway seems significant, the long-run pattern of population composition is likely to be more or less permanent. American public policy debates are often conducted as though the rest of the world were irrelevant; but, in fact, because the other industrialized countries are aging even faster than the United States, international comparisons about aging issues can be very instructive.

Dependency

The discussion about an older population would be quite different if seniors remained self-supporting or in the work force throughout their lifetimes—ignoring, of course, what this would mean for the job and promotion prospects of the generation that followed them into the workplace. But Americans are not only living longer; they are living most of those extra years as retirees, adding to the strain upon personal savings and private and public pensions. The real issue, then, is dependency, not age. In this sense, a boom in seniors has much in common with the dependency consequences of a boom in babies: another group that spends fifteen to twenty years living and consuming without working. Of course, this characterization of both young and old simplifies a much more complex picture of actual practice among both groups. Some of them earn income, are wealthy, or contribute productively through volunteer and family activity not normally counted in calculating national output. For the sake of simplicity if not accuracy, economists, demographers, and policymakers analyze the dependency ratio as though all young and all old were neither holding jobs nor producing in other ways.

The debate about America's aging boomers is built on one key set of statistics; the ratio is that of retirees to workers (the elderly dependency ratio). But the actual circumstances facing the United States and other nations involve a combination of factors, including more old people and fewer children. This more complex reality is clarified by a second set of statistics, the ratio of all dependents to workers (the total dependency ratio). While it is well known that the elderly dependency ratio is on the increase, the ratio of total old and young dependents per one hundred working-age individuals in the United States and Canada in 2030 will not be much different from 1960 levels.

Oddly, most of the debate about the projected burden on workers in the next century is conducted as though the only relevant measure is the aged to worker ratio. Of course, the total dependent calculation, since it reflects the relative number of *all* potential workers to *all* those not working, is where the focus should be. Today, 46 percent of Americans are in the work force; when the boomers are all retired in about 2030, that share will decline slightly to 44 percent. In 1964, when the baby boomer population was at its height, however, there were only 37 percent of Americans in the labor force, a ratio considerably "worse" than we can expect in the twenty-first century.

When the International Monetary Fund estimates twenty-first century economic growth rates for the G-7 countries, the United States, because of relatively greater anticipated labor force increases, is expected to outstrip Germany, Japan, and the others. Whether this actually proves to be the case, of course, is, like all long-term predictions, problematic. Among other things, a certain amount of future growth could depend upon whether we continue current immigration polices; new immigrants compensate for the decline in birth rates in terms of their effect on labor force.

Here, of course, our politics is hopelessly confused. Often we hear the same people conduct public campaigns of alarmism about both the aging of the population and the dangers of continuing immigration at present levels. There has been, in fact, a large surge in the number of foreign-born residents in the

United States in the past fifteen years—more than 15 million. Today about 8.7 percent of our population is of foreign origin—22.6 million people.

Economics

In 1996, the first boomers began to hit 50 years of age at the rate of 10,000 people a day; for the first time, the generation is within sight of retirement. One of the practical issues posed by the aging of the boomers is that in the United States today seniors are 12 percent of total population and receive, from all sources, about 13 percent of income (9.7 percent of gross domestic product [GDP] in 1993). At the peak of boomer retirement, their share of income, other things being equal, will continue to approximate their share of the total population. Thus, in 2030 seniors will constitute about 20 percent of the population and probably will receive a proportional share of income. Not all groups of Americans, of course, receive a proportionate share. Between 1970 and 1995, for example, the share of income for the richest 20 percent of American families increased from 41 percent to 47 percent.

A second important perspective on the economics of the aging of the boomers requires us to escape from the common analysis of future disaster that is based, almost exclusively, on straight-line projections of current statistics. Instead, consider how, at any given point in time, the *real* economy actually is divided up. After all, we all consume out of the real economic pie that exists while we are alive. Total output, of course, is a product of many inputs: the labor of those working, the use of resources (some of them irreplaceable), and the exploitation of the capacity created by past generations. Much of the capital stock used in creating today's economic output, for example, was built up over many years.

The way in which the real economy's goods and services are allocated among people of every age is the result of a combination of factors. In our society, in addition to the accident of birth and inheritance, what one gets depends on how he or she fares according to the complex mix of outcomes produced by the interaction of capitalism and democracy. If people do well in American capitalism, they can take care of themselves when they are old. If they do not do well, the American political system has produced a limited safety net, composed largely of Social Security, Medicare, and Medicaid, that covers minimal needs. These bedrock programs of senior support are not large by the standards of rich nations. However, in the United States they are often compared to the very limited transfers available for our youngest citizens. When measured against the lamentable support provided for children, it somehow looks as though we have been especially generous to seniors. But, of course, for a wealthy country like America, this is a false choice premised, apparently, on the notion that each grouping of citizens can only be raised above the poverty line at the expense of others who remain in poverty.

Still, the real basis for the attack on current policy is this very argument: we are too generous to the elderly, and their growing numbers make current generosity unsustainable. In the future, it is asserted, there simply will be too few workers to produce enough to support the social safety net. The coming shift in the composition of the population, however, is not even the biggest shift in living memory; that occurred when the baby boomers were kids. There were even more of them then, and for fifteen or twenty years they produced very little. They had rather complicated demands, and the society had to respond to those demands out of the much smaller real economy that existed at that time. Yet no one, including the boomers' parents, recalls the 1960s as an era of economic deprivation.

Moreover, since the sixties, the size of the economic pie available, in constant dollars per capita, has been growing and, even given modest assumptions about the future, will continue to grow. Economist Robert Eisner and others point out that, compared to 1964, we shall have triple the resources available in the next century. The boomers' parents shared a GDP that, per capita, was $12,195 (inflation adjusted). We now produce $20,469 per capita, and in 2030 we will have an estimated $35,659 per capita—at the height of the boomer retirement years. These numbers accept conservative (less than 2 percent) growth projections for the next seventy-five years. Indeed, if growth rates instead simply matched the average of the past, not very sensational twenty years, the projected deficit for Social Security, for example, would disappear.

We can bring much needed perspective to present concerns about the future by keeping in mind how we solved yesterday's problems. How, then, did the boomers' parents cope with their own extraordinary fertility? As kids, boomers formed more than 40 percent of the population; today, they are 30 percent; in retirement, they'll drop below 25 percent. The cost of raising the boomers was high; very conservative estimates of the average cost of raising a child are about $300,000, in current dollars. (Coincidentally, this number is almost identical to the insurance value to a family of Social Security coverage.) But there was no free lunch: boomers, as children, consumed goods and services from the real economy, just as they will as seniors.

In the postwar era, school systems routinely were overloaded. The consumer goods market was transformed by the special demands of millions of children and teenagers. Boomers started changing American culture during the 1940s, and they are still at it. Rock and roll, increasing crime rates, and suburbanization are all related to the youth and numbers of the boomers. Subsequent revolutions in the labor market, family and marriage, the status of women, and the civil rights movement are all, to varying degrees, connected to the sea changes brought about by the boomer generation.

From the beginning, the Americans who had lived through the Great Depression and World War II expected the public sector to play an immense role in the adjustments caused by the arrival of 78 million boomer children. And the government did produce vast programs to build schools, train teachers, and, later, to provide college loans and grants. Between 1952 and 1970, elementary-secondary school expenditures increased more than 275 percent in inflation-adjusted dollars. Between 1964 and 1980, the number of college and university students increased more than 125 percent, and the number of college instructors more than doubled. America also housed and fed the nearly 30 percent of boomers who lived some part of their childhood in poverty. In fact, the shift in GDP required to pay for school expansion for boomer kids—from 1.4 percent to 4.1 percent—is larger than that required to keep Social Security at current levels during the next century: 0.8 percent.

With fewer resources and with higher marginal tax rates, the boomers were fed, clothed, and educated; they got their polio shots and spent money to create rock and roll, all at a time when we had a higher national savings rate—in other words, a considerable amount of foregone consumption. The boomers' parents also shared (not only with their own children but with other people's children) through the public sector, especially through taxes to build schools and colleges. Theda Skocpol emphasizes that the society invested much in upgrading the boomers' parents through programs such as the G.I. Bill. Eight million veterans sought higher education, more than doubling the percentage of Americans who went to college. The cost was about $100 billion in 1996 dollars. But the real purchasing power was even greater: one could go to Princeton on the G.I. Bill's $500 stipend. Veteran's Administration housing subsidized about a quarter of all the new residences in the nation. In fact, public investment in people and infrastructure was very high during the entire postwar period.

Today, the success of the adjustment to the baby boomers is explained largely in terms of the extraordinary economic growth for twenty years after World War II. To be sure, the psychological effect of being part of a rapidly rising tide of income was an important factor. Similarly, the sense of the nation's ability to deal with big problems through the public sphere was another unprecedented characteristic of the era. The boomers' parents, after all, had lived through the Great Depression and World War II. These back-to-back events created an overwhelming sense of America's ability, with people pulling together, to overcome obstacles. Families having more children could hardly have seemed like a catastrophe.

The optimistic view of America's future does not depend solely on the empirical evidence of economic success during the boomers' youth. There are several scholarly analyses of the consequences of aging that provide a strong rebuttal to the alarmists. Economists James Poterba et al. note, "Our general conclusion is that demographic changes will improve American standards of living in the near future, but lower them slightly in the long-term. Other things being equal, the optimal policy response to recent and anticipated demographic changes is almost certainly reduction rather than an increase in the national savings rate. Slowing population growth will reduce the investment that must be devoted to equipping new workers and housing new families." Even more striking is their conclusion that "the decline in living standards caused by the increase in dependence would be fully reversed by 0.15 percent increase in productivity growth." In other words, the real key to our future prospects remains, as in the past, how successful we are at growing the American economy. On that score as well these scholars conclude that "a more definitive finding is the absence of *any empirical support for the pessimistic view that aging societies suffer reduced productivity growth*" (my emphasis).[3]

Inequality

What, then, is the crisis that America faces as its population ages? The question can be answered definitively with a simple statement: income and wealth inequality. Although, thanks in large part to Social Security, poverty rates among the elderly have declined from about 40 percent during the 1940s to about 11 percent today, a majority of retired workers could not maintain a reasonable standard of living if current support programs (Social Security, Medicare, and Medicaid) were cut back. Seniors reflect the overall historically high rate of inequality in the nation.

A few familiar facts about the nation's families are a good place to start. According to the Concord Coalition, the leading lobby *against* the current system of social insurance, half of American families have financial assets of less than one thousand dollars. Half of those families headed by someone 50 years old and over have financial assets of less than ten thousand dollars, reflecting the fact that 85 percent of all financial assets are in the hands of the richest 10 percent of Americans. The numbers for minorities are even more striking. Future Social Security benefits, for example, represent 70 percent of the wealth of black and Hispanic families. Even for white households, with twice as much average wealth, the value of Social Security is a hefty 40 percent of wealth.[4] Finally, only 7 percent of the elderly have incomes of more than $75,000 per year.

It will come as a surprise to those blanketed by rhetoric about greedy geezers that senior families are, on average, not as well off as are working American families. In 1995, according to the Census Bureau, the median family income for those over 65 was $28,301; for those under 65, it was $43,635. Female personal income is especially striking (and relevant, given the fact that women live so much longer): for those under 65, it was $13,484; for females over 65, it was only $9,355. Moreover, the impression that a huge number of undeserving elderly are already wealthy and getting more than their fair share is not supported by the facts. The median income for the elderly is slightly under $11,000 per year, down rather sharply from 1989, according to the latest figures from Employee Benefit Research Institute. Social Security is currently providing a larger share of that income than it was in 1979. Interestingly, income from assets fell from a peak of 28 percent in 1984 all the way back to its 1974 level of 18 percent in 1994.

In the United States, for more than 60 percent of the elderly, Social Security provides 50 percent or more of total income. Too much of the debate is conducted as though the top 20 percent (in terms of income) of the elderly were representative of the group as a whole. Even for this group, of course, Social Security provides a quarter of its income; only near the very top of the income and wealth pyramid do we find those who truly can and should go it alone.

Still, in the face of this information, some conclude that it would be desirable to phase out Social Security and replace it with a fully privatized system of individual savings for old age. The notion that this large number of American families could somehow stay out of poverty without the government's social insurance program and that all of these families could accumulate enough assets to take care of their own retirement is based on idealized views of potential investment success. Indeed, it seems more motivated by the potential for big fees for money managers than by any serious assessment of the circumstances of most families let alone the intense financial pressures on growing numbers of elderly women living alone.

The continuing importance of Social Security, then, is undeniable: even small reductions in the program would make a significant difference in the poverty rate among the elderly. The much ballyhooed idea of politically altering the annual cost of living increase for retirees—and thus the consumer price index (CPI)—has been studied by Barry Bosworth of the Brookings Institution. He found that a 1 percent change in the CPI, if it had been in place over the past twenty years, would have increased the percentage of elderly over age 80 living in poverty from 18 percent to 30 percent.

Despite Medicare and Medicaid, American seniors also spend an exceptional proportion, by international standards, on health care. Americans, for example, who are not poor enough to qualify for Medicaid must pay for the one-third of acute health care expenses not covered by Medicare from their own resources.

Growth

Whatever the reality, some alarmists about aging apparently lie awake nights worrying about the destructive potential of our limited social insurance programs—programs that provide lower support levels than those in almost any other industrialized nation. During daylight hours, they generate gloomy news stories, eliciting praise for their candor, political courage, foresight, and realism. While trying to do justice to the substance behind their arguments, I think that it is fair to say that the central alarmist assertion is quite simple: many boomers are likely to live to a ripe old age, and that will make the country a poorer, less desirable place for everyone, especially those still in the work force.

The remedy that the alarmists offer to head off this end-of-the-world-as-we-know-it crisis is to end Social Security, Medicaid, and Medicare as we know them. Otherwise, in the most extreme formulation, they project that, in the next century, we will have a tax of more than 80 percent on wages to pay for entitlements. (I leave it to others to explain how, in this era of strong anti-tax sentiment, such statements get someone labeled as refreshingly realistic whereas proposals to refinance Social Security with a 1 or 2 percent increase in the payroll tax are considered politically crazy.)

For cultural and political reasons, the European nations and Japan have much stronger social safety nets in place. They already devote more resources, particularly in Europe, to providing a floor of support for citizens, so the crisis will not be quite the same. The United States, for example, provides, through Social Security, about one-third of median income; the other industrialized countries average one-half. Obviously this fact is related to the larger context: the United States has about the lowest tax burden of any of the industrialized countries.

In other words, by the standards of Europe, we could simply pay more for these things and be more like they already are. In addition, we continue to have higher birth rates and larger immigration of new workers than do most other industrialized countries. Thus, our situation probably will be further eased because our population will continue to grow faster than theirs. Indeed, a recent International Monetary Fund (IMF) study, assuming that future growth would be almost exclusively based on population growth, projected very low rates of economic growth for most industrialized nations.[5]

The signal importance of future economic growth rates in assessing the consequences of an aging population are easily expressed: increased productivity growth, for example, of 0.1 percent per worker in the United States would completely offset the additional burden of an increased elderly population. Perhaps, then, we would do better to focus more attention on public strategies that have the potential to increase our prospects for even moderate growth, similar to what we have had for the past twenty years. If, in fact, we grow above the projected levels of less than 2 percent per year, the Social Security "crisis" simply vanishes. As Robert Eisner notes, the low-cost projections from the Social Security trust fund trustees for the next century (2.2 percent average growth) would result in the fund's building to more than four times annual expenditures by 2018 and never falling below three times the expenditures for the balance of the next century![6]

In any event, the IMF study, after focusing on the relative cost of adjusting current pay-as-you-go systems versus moving to fully funded systems, concludes that the U.S. Social Security system could stay solvent with a modest increase in contribution rates. The IMF calculated that we would have adequate funding through 2050 if we raised contribution rates by less than 1 percent of GDP. A shift of this magnitude is hardly unprecedented; as I have noted, it occurred when the boomers were schoolchildren. More recently, the so-called Reagan defense buildup involved a large spike in GDP for a particular public purpose.[7]

Policy

One of the arguments for a pay-as-you-go system, such as Social Security, is that it reflects the reality that each generation lives out of the real economic pie that exists at that time. No matter how desirable savings are—and they are very desirable—it is still true that when it is time for people to consume real resources, what they buy and what they use up comes out of the real economy that exists at that time. Savings and investment can make the pie larger, but it is still true that how much the elderly, or any other age group, gets depends upon the claims that they are in a position to make on the society as a whole.

Advocates of privatizing social insurance programs often justify their views by arguing that this approach will increase savings. Ignoring for a moment that the level of prefunding in a pension program is a separate issue from whether or not it is public, the political sales pitch for their proposals depends upon both wishful thinking about markets and disguising the need for coerced savings (higher taxes). Nonetheless, a minority of the members of the 1997 Advisory Council on Social Security recommended full funding and privatization of Social Security. Implementing this idea would not be cheap: the proposal involved increasing taxes by $6.5 trillion over the next seventy-two years.

Another way of measuring the cost is to ask what would happen if the United States made a gradual transition to such a system. The IMF compared this approach with repair of our existing pay-as-you-go system, calculating that to switch we would need to increase our cyclically adjusted deficit, excluding net interest, to 3.4 percent of GDP. To continue current policies, on the other hand, only 1.5 percent of GDP is required to modify the Social Security system. Overall, the IMF finds that, over the next fifty years, changing to fully funded pension systems inevitably would involve very large transition costs.

America will do better to consider whether we have a crisis at all and what are the real challenges of an aging population. Why, in fact, are the elderly such a special burden? It is not because they are not working; neither are most people. It is not because they are the poorest or because they force general health costs to go up; 85 percent of health care cost increases are not related to the aged. Indeed, there is even a legitimate question about whether people need to retire at age 70. We are less sure than ever when people are *too* old to be productive. In 1974, the average educational attainment of the elderly was eighth grade; now the average is twelfth grade and going up.

Indeed, when one considers the alleged concerns of, say, Generation X, which will inherit the largest economy in the history of the world, contemporary fears of the future seem somewhat out of proportion. As far as we know, we face nothing like the Great Depression or international threats of the scale of Hitler, imperial Japan, or the Soviet empire. The fact that there will be a larger number of older people would seem, by twentieth-century standards, a reasonably modest challenge. It is not given, after all, to any generation to have completely smooth sailing. Americans have been fortunate in that each generation has had greater resources than existed in the past to cope with whatever troubles come their way. This is certainly the case for those who will live well into the next century. A realistic assessment of the balance between the challenges that Generation X is likely to meet and the resources available to meet them should be a source of optimism rather than of apprehension.

For a nation, it may well be that demography is destiny, meaning that we are sentenced to a particular fate. That means that we must adjust to the realities of our circumstances. Relatively low birth rates and a fairly steady advance in life span are already well-established trends in the countries of Scandinavia, western Europe, and Japan. Yet no one would say that the last half-century has been, by historical standards, a particularly bad era for any of those societies. Indeed, quite the contrary is true. They have reached unparalleled levels of prosperity, they have enjoyed an era of unusual peace and disarmament, and, while they are not without problems, they are scarcely among the globe's great trouble spots.

In this comparative perspective, the demographic changes in the United States are something well short of a catastrophe, perhaps more accurately described as a mild challenge. More to the point of this chapter, the sharp differences between rich and poor are misfortunes that can be corrected. We are not, like some third world nations, destined to be dominated by an elite that accumulates vast percentages of the country's wealth. We have plenty to go around, if only we can reintroduce the concept of fairness to public policy, industrial relations, and personal ethics. A new nation of older Americans will put us, whether we like it or not, in a position to test our capacity for that sort of change.

Realism about the size of the overall economic pie and guidance derived from the lessons of the past should shape the necessary future adjustments in entitlements for seniors. But our approach also should conform to basic values shared by most Americans. Let us avoid solutions such as privatization of Social Security that are sure to increase the already serious levels of inequality. Let us insist that, if you work hard and play by the rules, you can count on a social safety net in old age. Let us reject plans that are likely to increase poverty among any age group, and we can stay true to tested principles simply by fighting harder for policies that are already part of mainstream politics: controlling the budget deficit while protecting Social Security and Medicare, increasing the minimum wage and expanding employment to bolster savings and growth, and directly addressing the corrosive effects of the growing income and wealth inequality.

Finally, there are those who insist that in the pinched, slow-growth economy of the future, it would be unjust for seniors to have so much of the pie. This argument, usually couched in terms of "generational justice," implies that we cannot afford the consumption of those who have contributed so much to building the economy. Remember that the boomers represent the largest work force we have ever had—a work force that expanded the economy more than any previous group. The boomers' children will inherit a vastly expanded economy with enough resources for all. Every generation, for that matter, depends on others: parents who raise children as well as strangers who build bridges, plants, schools, office buildings, and industrial equipment. Even the debt a new generation must pay off is accompanied by the government bonds and other assets that it inherits. Should boomers charge rent for the portion of the nation's capital stock, including knowledge and inventions, built or dreamed up by their generation?

While boomers came into the world with nothing, on their way out they will have a few trillion in pension funds—more than any previous generation—and substantial real estate to help pay the freight. But they are not all likely to get lucky and fully fund their own retirement with no help from Uncle Sam at all; capitalism just does not work that way. Of course, if somehow all the elderly did turn out to be like Bill Gates, they would be able to command all the goods and services they wanted. Then they would get more of the pie, and other younger people would get less.

More specifically, consider the preferences of rich seniors as consumers: it is a good bet that they buy as much or more medical care than those completely dependent on Medicare. Since most aging Americans are not wealthy, however, the question of how to finance their growing need for health care will be resolved not in the marketplace but in the public sector. The current infatuation with a bipartisan commission to study Medicare is only a first step. The coming struggle is sure to be politically brutal, with no winners and lots of painful choices. The issues in health care are simply much harder to deal with than are the rather modest adjustments necessary to sustain Social Security. For years to come, the politics of Medicare will be incendiary, involving daunting questions about tax increases and health care rationing. The debates will be emotional, so it is especially important to keep in mind that what is occurring is essentially a shift in consumer and voter preferences. Indeed, from a purely economic standpoint, such a shift is not, in itself, bad for the nation. Health care, after all, is a pretty high-tech domestic industry, with a growing base of jobs that pay reasonably well. Thus, a population that spends even more on health care will not necessarily be worse off than we are today. In any event, the realities of politics, along with other factors, will moderate the growth of health care spending.

The boomers' children, like the boomers' parents, will adjust. In the real economy, resources will get shifted; but as with the young boomers, there will be shortages—remember double sessions in schools all over the country, and the crisis over the need for more college spaces and faculty. The boomers will get less than they want but more than the alarmists think is possible, and politics will continue to play the most significant role in how this shift takes place. In the final analysis, then, both the values of a democracy and the realities of capitalism support the basic soundness of the framework for policy, albeit with changes that strike a balance among the competing demands of Americans of all ages.

Notes

Portions of this chapter have been adapted from other publications by Richard C. Leone: "Why Boomers Don't Spell Bust," *American Prospect* 30 (January–February 1997): 68–72; "Stick with Public Pensions," *Foreign Affairs,* May 9, 1997, pp. 33–

53; and "America Can Afford to Grow Old," *Public Policy and Aging Report* 7 (Fall 1996): 1, 15, 16.

1. The one pocket of contrarians about these matters belong to the ecological and environmental movement. Concerned about the pace of global population growth (28 billion in 2150 at a constant birth rate of only 2.5 children per female), activists sensibly see a silver lining in stable, albeit more silver-haired, populations.

2. D. M. Cutler, J. M. Poterba, L. M. Sheiner, and L. H. Summers, "An Aging Society: Opportunity or Challenge?" *Brookings Papers on Economic Activity* 1 (1990): 6, 7.

3. Ibid.

4. James P. Smith, "Unequal Wealth and Incentives to Save," documented briefing DB-145–RC (Santa Monica, Calif.: RAND Corporation, 1995), ii, 37.

5. Sheetal K. Chand and Albert Jaeger, "Aging Populations and Public Pension Schemes," IMF occasional paper, no. 147 (Washington, D.C.: International Monetary Fund, December 1996), 11.

6. Robert Eisner, *The Misunderstood Economy: What Counts and How to Count* (Boston: Harvard Business School Press, 1994), 282.

7. Chand and Jaeger, "Aging Populations," 11.

About the Contributors

Edward Blakely is former dean of the School of Urban Planning and Development and Lusk Professor of Planning and Development at the University of Southern California. He also serves as a consultant and advisor for several California cities and government agencies in the United States, Europe, and Australia. He is active in Asian development, serving in 1993 as president of the Pacific Rim Council on Urban Development, where he remains on the board of directors.

Jane S. De Lung is president of the Population Resource Center in Washington, D.C., and Princeton, New Jersey. She brings to the center twenty years of experience in family planning, demographic research in health and human services, and public policy.

Thomas J. Espenshade is professor of sociology and a faculty associate of the Office of Population Research at Princeton University. His research interests include patterns of undocumented migration to the United States, the fiscal impact of new immigrants, and attitudes toward U.S. immigration. He is presently directing a study on the contributions of immigrants to the science and engineering work force in the United States.

William H. Frey is senior fellow of demographic studies at the Milken Institute in Santa Monica, California, and research scientist at the University of Michigan's Population Studies Center. He has written widely on issues related to migration, immigration, and the demography of metropolitan areas and is directing a research project on the impacts of immigration on race and socio-economic population shifts in the United States.

James W. Hughes is the dean of the Edward J. Bloustein School of Planning and Public Policy at Rutgers, the State University of New Jersey. A member of the faculty since 1971, he has also been the director of the *Rutgers Regional Report*, along with Joseph J. Seneca, since 1988.

Richard C. Leone is president of the Century Foundation, a public policy research institution. From 1990 to 1994, he served as chairman of the Port Authority of New York and New Jersey.

Frank Levy is the Daniel Rose Professor of Urban Economics in the Department of Urban Studies and Planning at the Massachusetts Institute of Technology. He is associated with the Brookings Institution and is a research advisor for Public/Private Ventures, Manpower Demonstration Research Corporation, and the Committee on Economic Development.

Peter A. Morrison is an applied demographer whose research has had a variety of domestic and international applications. Since 1969, he has been a senior staff demographer and resident consultant for the RAND Corporation.

Dowell Myers is a professor in the School of Policy, Planning, and Development at the University of Southern California. A specialist in demography and urban development, he also directs the Southern California Immigration Project and serves on the Professional Advisory Committee of the U.S. Bureau of the Census.

David Popenoe is a professor of sociology at Rutgers University, where he also serves as co-director of the National Marriage Project. He specializes in the study of family and community life in modern societies and is the author or editor of nine books.

Martha Farnsworth Riche served as director of the U.S. Bureau of the Census from 1994 through 1998. Previously she served as a founding editor of *American Demographics* and as the director of policy studies for the Population Reference Bureau, a nonprofit organization devoted to disseminating demographic information and educating the public about the demographic component of policy issues.

Joseph J. Seneca is university vice president for academic affairs at Rutgers, the State University of New Jersey. Since 1994, he has served as the chairman of the New Jersey Council of Economic Advisors.

Daphne Spain is a professor of urban and environmental planning in the School of Architecture at the University of Virginia. Previously she worked for several years as a statistician at the U.S. Bureau of the Census and as a freelance writer. She is currently conducting research on the historic role of voluntary women's associations in shaping the city.

Judith Waldrop is currently working in the Census 2000 Publicity Office on a communications plan for the year 2000 census. From 1995 to 1998, she was a special assistant to the director of the U.S. Bureau of the Census, Martha Farnsworth Riche.

Charles F. Westoff is a professor of demographic studies and sociology and a faculty associate at the Office of Population Research at Princeton University. His professional specialties include population policy as well fertility and family planning research in developing countries.

Index